This Monastic Moment

This Monastic Moment

The War of the Spirit and the Rule of Love

John W. de Gruchy

The Lutterworth Press

The Lutterworth Press
P.O. Box 60
Cambridge
CB1 2NT
United Kingdom

www.lutterworth.com
publishing@lutterworth.com

Paperback ISBN: 978 0 7188 9682 9
PDF ISBN: 978 0 7188 9683 6

British Library Cataloguing in Publication Data
A record is available from the British Library

First published by Cascade Books, 2021

This edition published by The Lutterworth Press, 2023,
by arrangement with Wipf and Stock Publishers

Copyright © John W. de Gruchy, 2023

All rights reserved. No part of this edition may be reproduced, stored electronically or in any retrieval system, or transmitted in any form or by any means, electronic, mechanical, photocopying, recording, or otherwise, without prior written permission from the Publisher (permissions@lutterworth.co).

CONTENTS

Acknowledgments | vii
Abbreviations | ix

Prologue: Listen to the Spirit | 1

1   Into the African Desert | 27

2   Into Europe's Dark Age | 60

3   In a Reforming World | 98

4   In This Time & Place | 137

Epilogue: On Writing a *Rule* | 175

Bibliography | 185
Index of Names | 195
Index of Subjects | 199
Index of Scripture | 214

To Isobel
Scientist, poet, artist & master chef
Mother, grandmother, sister, aunt, friend
Celebrating sixty years of life together

ACKNOWLEDGMENTS

After a lifetime of writing, the list of those I should acknowledge as mentors, inspirers, and companions along the way, is far too long to mention here, but they have all contributed to the process even if I get the credit. For this volume I especially thank:

The members of the Volmoed Community, our home for the past eighteen years, and without whom the book would not have been written.

Rondebosch United Church (Congregational & Presbyterian), Cape Town, our spiritual home and a covenant community of love and justice.

The monks of St Benedict's Priory at Volmoed, who live what I have written about.

My colleagues in the Faculty of Theology at Stellenbosch University, where I am honored to be an extraordinary professor.

My Dutch Reformed friends at the Andrew Murray Center in Wellington, who share the monastic vision.

My friend of many years, Keith Clements of Bristol, eminent Baptist and Bonhoeffer scholar, for his helpful comments.

Fr Mark, monk of Ambleforth Abbey in Yorkshire, whose knowledge of the tradition helped correct my monastic errors.

John Morris, owner of the Book Cottage, Hermanus, and conversationalist extraordinaire, for finding obscure books at a moment's notice.

Cascade Books, whose editorial staff make publishing a pleasure.

And, to Isobel, to whom the book is dedicated, who read the text several times with a critical eye, made sure Julian of Norwich was duly acknowledged, and who, for sixty years, has spent many hours as a writer's widow.

Volmoed
Easter 2021

Notes

*I have used the designation "St" (saint) when referring to those traditionally regarded as such, but only on first mention.

*I refer to the church in general, whether universal or local, using a lowercase c, but I use an uppercase C when referring to a denomination.

*"Eumenical church" either refers to the universal or catholic church, or more specifically to churches associated with the World Council of Churches, or regional councils such as the South African Council of Churches. The context will clarify which is meant.

ABBREVIATIONS

DBWE	Dietrich Bonhoeffer Works in English
LCC	Library of Christian Classics
LW	Luther's Works
RB 1980	Benedict, St. *RB 1980: The Rule of St. Benedict in Latin and English with Notes.* Edited by Timothy Fry, OSB et al. Collegeville, MN: Liturgical, 1981

PROLOGUE
Listen to the Spirit

Listen to what the Spirit is saying to the churches.
—REVELATION 2:7

Much of what we call Christian is purely and simply monastic.
—E. R. CURTIUS[1]

Those who question the structures of contemporary society at least look to monks for a certain distance and critical structure, which, alas, is seldom found. The vocation of the monk in the modern world . . . is not survival but prophecy.
—THOMAS MERTON[2]

Cheap grace is the mortal enemy of our church. Our struggle today is for costly grace.

Cheap grace means grace as bargain-basement goods, cut-rate forgiveness, cut-rate comfort, cut-rate sacrament; grace as the church's inexhaustible pantry, from which it is doled out by careless hands without hesitation or limit. It is grace without a price, without costs.
—DIETRICH BONHOEFFER[3]

---

1. Curtius, *European Literature and the Latin Middle Ages*, 515; quoted in Leclercq, *The Love of Learning and the Desire for God*, 256.
2. Merton, "Letter to Jean Leclercq, July 23, 1968," in *Survival or Prophecy?*, 129.
3. Bonhoeffer, *Discipleship*, 43.

Perhaps it was a moment of inspiration, a whispering of the Spirit that prompted me to ask: "Is this a monastic moment?" during a trustees' meeting of the Volmoed Community in February 2020. We were discussing the way forward as South Africa was about to go into its first lockdown due to the COVID-19 pandemic. Increasingly isolated from the world, we were unable to receive guests and provide the hospitality for which our community primarily exists. As a result, our revenue was rapidly dwindling, and the threat of staff retrenchment loomed. The normal was coming to an end and we were seeking to find our way into the future. Central to our discussion, apart from emergency fundraising, was whether we should become more intentional in character. If so, we were uncertain what this meant or how we should proceed. This book arose out of the ensuing conversation. I suspect it will strike a chord with others elsewhere who are engaged in a similar discussion.

Since its modest beginnings thirty-five years ago, the Volmoed Community today comprises a growing resident community, a relatively large staff, and many associates. Isobel and I became resident members in May 2003 after my retirement from the University of Cape Town.[4] Week by week, Volmoed welcomes guests and groups, young and old, from across South Africa and the world, people of different denominations, some of other faiths, and many who are searching for faith and renewal. We pray together; host retreats, workshops, and seminars; and run art and youth leadership programs. But the COVID pandemic halted us in our tracks. We were forced to face an uncertain future. Was this, then, a "monastic moment" for us, as the Spirit seemed to be saying?

There were tentative nods of agreement among the trustees, though uncertainty as to its meaning. The fact that a few months previously a small group of Anglican Benedictine monks had come to live among us, and that the prior of the Taizé Community in France, Br. Alois, had recently visited, undoubtedly triggered off something in our collective subconscious. For soon we were engaged in an intense discussion about becoming a more intentional community in partnership with our monastic brothers as they daily live among us according to the *Rule of St Benedict*. But this required that we should know more about that *Rule* and where the brothers were coming from. So, let me take you back to where it all began.

---

4. See de Gruchy, *I Have Come a Long Way*, 237–43.

Where Heaven and Earth Meet

The beginnings of Christianity in Africa can be traced back to first-century Egypt. According to tradition, the Coptic church was established in Alexandria by St Mark the Evangelist around 66 CE. Scholars may debate that claim, but there can be no doubt that Christian monasticism began in Egypt in the fourth century, making Africa its birthplace. Today, there are many monasteries spread across the continent, from Cairo to Cape Town. Volmoed lies 120 kilometers to the east of Cape Town en route to Cape Aghulas, the southern-most tip of Africa. Close to Cape Aghulas is the Blombos Cave, a site of Middle Stone Age human habitation and, more significantly, of human creativity. Some even claim that this is where human civilization as we now know it began. It is likely that the caves along the coast between Blombos and Volmoed, and even those along the Onrus River, which runs through Volmoed itself, were paleolithic dwelling places.

By any account, Volmoed is a remarkable location in which to live and write, beautiful and bountiful, and famous for its indigenous flowers and adjacent vineyards. This explains why the valley in which it is situated is named Hemel en Aarde, a mystical place where "heaven meets earth." People who come to Volmoed keep telling us that God meets them in this place. But earthly paradises are not exempt from sin and injustice, any more than monasteries, nor can beauty be fully appreciated unless coexisting ugliness is also recognized. In the early nineteenth century Volmoed was home to a leper colony, and the lepers lived at Volmoed because they were outcasts who were prohibited from living nearer to the fishing village of Hermanus eleven kilometers to the east. But around the year 1800, the British colonial government in Cape Town asked German Moravian missionaries from Genadendal, a mission station a day's horse ride away, to serve the needs of the lepers, and it was these missionaries who named the place Volmoed—meaning "full of courage and hope"—and gave the valley its name.

Eventually the valley was proclaimed farmland and the lepers were taken and confined to the notorious Robben Island in Table Bay where, a century later, Nelson Mandela would be incarcerated. We at Volmoed cannot ignore that underside of Volmoed's history as the graves of lepers on our property continue to remind us. And, today, for all its quietness and beauty, Volmoed is but a few kilometers from noisy and crowded townships where many live in shacks and are unemployed, some of them refugees from elsewhere in Africa, but most migrants from rural areas. We are daily aware of this enormous social and economic gap and the urgent need for a more just society.

The Volmoed Community was born during the state of emergency in South Africa in 1986 when many people were traumatized during the final days of the struggle to end apartheid.[5] Those who founded the community, Bernhard Turkstra, a hotelier by trade and a recent convert to evangelical Christianity, and Barry Woods, an Anglican parish priest, shared a vision of a place set apart for God's ministry of hospitality, healing, reconciliation, and hope. With few resources, but with the confidence of youthful faith, they managed to buy Volmoed, a defunct flower farm which boasted an old run-down farmhouse, a broken shed, and very few modern amenities. But it had a mystical aura and was surrounded by hills and caves where hermits would feel at home in "entertaining angels unaware," as some visitors to Volmoed claim to have done.

To make the vision he shared with Barry a reality, Bernhard and his wife, Jane, soon took up residency on the farm and pioneered the way. Within a short time, others, drawn from various churches and parishes, as well as from the local community and even from as far afield as England and Russia, shared in the venture, clearing alien vegetation, building accommodation, providing financial help, and participating in events. Legal documents were drafted to form a trust that could own property and open a bank account, and trustees were duly appointed. Soon others took up residency. Eventually Volmoed could accommodate sixty guests, and in 2002 its Chapel of Thanksgiving was completed and dedicated. But there was no handbook or *Rule* to guide the community. Everything depended on a shared commitment to Christ and the gospel, the wisdom of experience, and a desire to achieve its founding vision.

Isobel and I first visited the community the year it was founded at the suggestion of our son Anton, who was part of a youth group clearing the land of alien vegetation. We were accompanied by the distinguished American theologian Martin Marty and his wife, Harriet, who were our guests at the University of Cape Town. Not long after that visit, Marty contributed an article to the *Christian Century* in which he said:

> Thomas Merton once wrote of his monastery in Kentucky: "This is the center of America . . . an axle around which the whole country turns." I have also thought of Koinonia Farm in

---

5. See de Gruchy and de Gruchy, *The Volmoed Journey*.

Georgia, Ghost Ranch in New Mexico, and Holden Village in Washington. One afternoon . . . I stumbled on such a potential center for South Africa . . . Volmoed they call it.[6]

Among other early visitors to the community were nuns from the Evangelical Sisterhood of Mary, a Lutheran religious order founded by Basilea Schlink in Darmstadt, Germany in 1947, at a traumatic time in a postwar Europe. It was also a time in which monasteries around the world enjoyed a revival. During their brief visit to Volmoed, the Darmstadt sisters also prophesied that Volmoed would one day become a community as well-known as the Iona Community in Scotland and the Taizé Community in France, confirming what Marty had written. But in those early days such prophecies, while encouraging, seemed far from reality as the struggle against apartheid intensified in what turned out to be its final phase, and as Volmoed struggled to find its feet and survive.

Yet, providentially as it now appears, it was during those traumatic times of transition from apartheid to the "new" South Africa that Desmond Tutu (now the Patron of Volmoed) invited the Order of the Holy Cross, with its mother house in West Park, New York, to send monks to South Africa. He believed that the building of a just society was contingent on spiritual renewal, and that a monastery could play an important role in the process. Indeed, Tutu's own spiritual formation was profoundly influenced by the monastic tradition, as we shall later note.[7] As it happened, on the very day that Nelson Mandela was released from prison in February 1990, Isobel and a group of other South Africans were on a Benedictine retreat led by Esther de Waal, the internationally known Benedictine associate (or oblate), along with Br. Timothy, one of the monks who had been sent to establish the monastery. When it was eventually established in rugged hill country outside Grahamstown (now known as Makhanda) in the Eastern Cape, the monastery was named Mariya uMama weThemba (Mary the Mother of Hope).

In August 2013, ten years after we moved to Volmoed, Isobel and I went at the invitation of the monks to their monastery to lead workshops on Julian of Norwich (1342–1413), about whom Isobel has written and taught me much,[8] and on Dietrich Bonhoeffer (1906–1945). Little did we know that six years later, the monastery would relocate from Makhanda

---

6. Marty, "Hope and Courage in Volmoed."
7. See Battle, *Reconciliation*, 128–33.
8. de Gruchy, *Making All Things Well*.

to Volmoed in 2019 and take the name St Benedict's Priory. And to my delight, one of their gifts on arrival was a little book written by a member of their order, titled *Bonhoeffer: Prophet for Our Time*.[9] Another gift is the priory library, now housed beneath the chapel in their scriptorium, a treasure chest of monastic literature. And, of course, their gift of conversation—when silence permits—has added depth to my reflections.

The presence of St Benedict's Priory on Volmoed also brings stability in times such as these. Benedictines generally stay put. That is a remarkable gift in a global culture where people are always on the move and members of congregations continually go in search of a better preacher or choir. The gift of stability was especially welcome because the arrival of the priory coincided with the retirement of Bernhard and Jane Turkstra and their decision to leave Volmoed at the end of 2020. Quite apart from the impact of the COVID-19 pandemic, our new normal would certainly not be the same as the old, even though the vision of Volmoed as God's place of healing, reconciliation and hope remained its lodestar. But where was the Spirit taking us?

As the process of discernment began in earnest, following the meeting of the trustees, a group of pilgrims arrived at Volmoed. They were doing the Pilgrimage of Hope, our regional answer to the Camino de Santiago di Compostela. Volmoed is one stop on that lengthy trek from various points of departure to Cape Agulhas. At their request, I spent some time sharing with them our thoughts about this monastic moment. There was immediate resonance. As we journey through life, they said, we need places that provide space to catch our breath, unpack our backpacks, drop our burdens, and open our hearts. We need time to reflect, pray, and gather strength for the journey ahead. We need to regain hope. We need the rhythm of monastic *chronos* to cope with the *kairos* times in which we live.

Kairos: A Critical Time

This Monastic Moment might have been triggered off by the Volmoed Community's need to discern the way into the future, but it is also a response to what the New Testament calls a *kairos* moment in history, that is, a critical time of judgment and opportunity.[10] Unlike *chronos,* marked

---

9. Spencer, *Dietrich Bonhoeffer*.
10. For a more detailed discussion of the use of *kairos* in the New Testament, see

by the daily rhythm of life or the regular sound of monastery bells calling us to prayer, k*airos* refers to moments in chronological time when all hell is breaking loose and we are called to change our ways before we are dragged into the abyss. *Kairos* is apocalyptic time, and it is here and now.

Today, the environmental crisis is the cosmic framework of this *kairos* moment, and the COVID pandemic its wake-up call, dramatically revealing the fault lines of injustice that define global society. Such is the time in which we need to listen again to biblical texts such as those that St Benedict of Nursia (ca. 480—ca. 547) used in the Prologue to his *Rule*:

> Let us get up then, at long last, for the Scriptures rouse us when they say: *It is high time for us to arise from sleep* (Rom 13:11). Let us open our eyes to the light that comes from God, and our ears to the voice from heaven that every day calls out this charge: *If you hear his voice today, do not harden your hearts* (Ps. 94[95]:8). And again: *You that have ears to hear, listen to what the Spirit says to the churches* (Rev. 2:7).[11]

South Africa faced a *kairos* moment in 1986, the year the Volmoed Community was born, when the country was plunging ever deeper into civil war. In response, the apartheid government twice introduced states of emergency. This gave the security forces unlimited power to try and stop the inevitable. Many opponents of apartheid were arrested, imprisoned, or murdered. It was then that a group of theologians published *The Kairos Document* calling on Christians and churches to resist the state and support the liberation struggle.[12] They distinguished between state theology, which sanctions the state; church theology, which sits uncomfortably on the fence; and prophetic theology, which supports the liberation struggle. This typology recurs throughout church history and is part of the narrative that follows. It is appropriate, for as Thomas Merton (1915–1968) believed, the future of monasticism lies in its being prophetic, not captured by the state or comfortable in the world—which is equally true for the church itself.

Jesus of Nazareth arrived on the scene of history at a *kairos* moment. Palestine, an outpost of the Roman Empire, was restless as heavily burdened peasants were reduced to poverty, priests did their devotions but passed by on the other side, zealots plotted rebellion, and some of the

Barr, *The Semantics of Biblical Language*.
    11. Benedict, prologue, verses 8–11 (*RB 1980*, 159; italics original).
    12. Kairos Theologians, *The Kairos Document*.

more pious fled into the desert to live in caves near the Dead Sea. Those were apocalyptic times awaiting a messiah, times of fear tinged with hope for the dawning of a new age. Jesus proclaimed that this new age was at hand, and called followers to become part of it; it was a kingdom unlike any other, for it did not derive its authority from worldly powers. So Jesus's disciples had to choose between obeying God or Caesar, for they could not serve two masters. But if they followed Jesus, they would have to deny themselves and take up their cross. Persecution would be their lot, and martyrdom their badge of honor.

Christians were regularly persecuted in the Roman Empire during the first two centuries after Christ. Then, in the fourth century, when the empire in the West began to decline and power shifted to Byzantium in the East, an apparent miracle occurred. In 312, after he had defeated his rival Maxentius at the Battle of the Milvian Bridge, Constantine became emperor, converted to Christianity, and unbanned the church. Following a brief hiccup during the reign of Julian the Apostate, who had little time for either Christian superstition or indolent aspiring monastics, Christianity finally became the established imperial religion, giving birth to Christendom. This happened during the reign of Theodosius (r. 379–395), when paganism was outlawed and heresy became illegal.

The future of the church, previously a marginalized and persecuted sect, now seemed assured. Christians were in a privileged position, but the church was also co-opted to serve the empire. This had enormous consequences for the future of Christianity, establishing a principle and a process that would enable Christianity to spread far and wide, but always living between compromise and conviction. With the dawning of the Constantinian era, it became increasingly the case that if emperor, king, prince, or chief (they were invariably male) converted to Christianity, the population followed suit. But what did this mean for Christian discipleship, and how could this new alliance be justified?

Prior to his victory, Constantine had received a vision in which he was told that he would conquer "in the sign of the cross," which was then explained to him by Christ in a dream. At any rate, that was the story as told by Eusebius of Caesarea (c. 260–c. 340), the first church historian and apologist for state theology. Constantine's heavenly vision of the cross at the Milvian Bridge, said Eusebius, was a sign of God's favor. God gave him the victory and, from then on, he would reign under that sign.[13]

---

13. Robin Lane Fox, *Pagans and Christians*, 611–16.

But this effectively removed the "scandal of the cross."[14] It was now costly *not* to be a Christian. Prophetic witness gave way to fence-sitting. But Eusebius's state theology—the first of many variants in church history to justify imperial, colonial, or state power—gave birth to what I call the *triumphalist heresy*, one of several perennial heresies that have plagued Christian faith, though not one condemned by any council of synod. We shall meet it frequently in what follows.

Heresies: Gnostic & Triumphal

Heresy (*haeresis*) literally means choosing the wrong direction at a crossroad. I am fully aware of the dangers in identifying heresies, not least of which is the persecution of those found guilty, and the self-righteousness of those who represent "the truth." After all, who is to say whether the road on which we choose to travel is the wrong one or not? Simply to accept what others claim to be the truth without questioning it is seldom a good idea. Doubt is the handmaiden of faith, and dogmatic certainty without love and humility is but a clanging cymbal. As the sociologist Peter Berger once said, the heretical imperative is both inevitable and necessary.[15] Heresy in science can lead to new discoveries, just as heresy in religion can uncover truth. But heresy, like fake news and alternative truth, can also have destructive consequences if not checked.

Not so long ago I was engaged with others in a heated debate about whether the Christian justification of apartheid was a heresy.[16] It was as intense as any debate about heresy has been since the first Christian centuries. But it was necessary to pull the rug from under the feet of those who claimed that the policy of apartheid was Christian. Apartheid was no more Christian than is racism or sexual discrimination, or the justification of Nazism by German Christians. Opposing and rejecting heresy does not mean that heretics should not be heard, nor does it give anyone license to persecute them. But neither should it prevent us from trying to distinguish Christian truth from error, especially when error leads to injustice in the name of Christ. The Christian justification of war, crusades, pogroms, and the like, are nothing but heresies to be rejected. But

---

14. See 1 Corinthians 1:23.
15. Berger, *The Heretical Imperative*.
16. de Gruchy and Villa-Vicencio, eds., *Apartheid Is a Heresy*.

equally, if the truth is not expressed in love, justice, and mercy, then it is equally heretical, for only such truth is, Christianly speaking, credible.

Many Christian heresies dot the landscape of the monastic story. They are invariably christological or anthropological in character, that is, inadequate or misleading answers to the questions, Who is Jesus Christ, and who are we humans? Heresies generally distort the truth by overemphasizing some aspect. Such deviations may happen with the best of intentions, but eventually there is consensus within the ecumenical church—which I will later define—about what is right belief or orthodoxy, and, we must add, orthopraxis, that is acting rightly.[17] Of course, some heresies are more serious than others, and some might simply be splitting hairs motivated by political, personal, or ecclesiastical interests.

Two heresies that had serious consequences for the future of Christianity accompanied the emergence of monasticism. They were Gnosticism, a religious philosophy that predated Christianity, and triumphalism, which accompanied its birth. Gnosticism comes from the Greek word *gnosis*, which means "knowledge." The word was coined by its first Christian critics because gnostics claimed to possess secret divine wisdom. The true God, gnostics insisted, did not create the material world as claimed by the Old Testament, nor did God love or want to save it. The material world was evil; so too was the human body within which our immortal souls are trapped. But, gnostics claimed, through initiation into *gnosis* or "true knowledge," the soul could escape bondage to the material world and enter the heavenly realm of the spirit.[18]

This dualistic understanding of reality, radically separating the material from the spiritual, appealed to many Hellenistic Christians, as it still does to many Christians today. After all, the world is so full of evil and tragedy that it is difficult to believe that a loving God created it. In any case, is not Christianity about nurturing and saving the soul, and is not salvation about leaving all worldly cares and troubles behind? This kind of spirituality certainly attracts those who are pessimistic about the future of the world, as it does those who say that we should forget about the Old Testament and its God of vengeance along with the legalistic Jewish roots of Christianity, and concentrate on the New—a view propagated in the early second century by Marcion (85–160), the son of a bishop, but a heretic nonetheless.

---

17. Bauer, *Orthodoxy and Heresy in Earliest Christianity*.
18. See Pearson, *Ancient Gnosticism*.

Contrary to what scholars previously believed, the origins of Gnosticism in its varied forms can be traced back, not to the Orient but to an amalgam of Jewish and Hellenistic sources predating the rise of Christianity. And, as the Nag Hammadi Coptic manuscripts discovered in the twentieth century tell us, Gnosticism was rife in Egypt long before the emergence of monasticism in that region.[19] And because it bore a superficial resemblance to Christian monasticism it was a particular threat. After all, did not monastics flee the world, and did they not have a superior knowledge of divine wisdom?

Until recent times, much of what we know about the Gnostics came from their Christian opponents, the so-called apologists, or defenders of the faith. The best known of these was Irenaeus (130–220), the martyr-bishop of Lyons in Gaul, who was originally from Asia Minor. Anyone familiar with his writings on the various forms of Gnosticism that were often prevalent in church circles will know how difficult they are to codify and assess. But he and other apologists identified two main dangers.[20] The first of these was its undermining of the biblical understanding of the world as created good by God. As Dietrich Bonhoeffer would say centuries later:

> The earth remains our mother just as God remains our father, and only those who remain true to the mother are placed by her into the father's arms. Earth and its distress—that is the Christian's Song of Songs.[21]

If we regard the material world and the material order as evil, we will not treat the world, our bodies, or those of others responsibly.

The second danger, which followed from the first, was Gnosticism's denial of the incarnation. Gnostics rejected the belief that in Jesus Christ God entered history as a human being or, as John's Gospel states, "the Word became flesh and lived among us."[22] Gnosticism therefore undermined the central tenet of the Christian faith, reducing Christianity to a religious philosophy for the spiritual enlightenment of a few rather than good news for the transformation of the world. It was also a denial that all our bodily senses—sight, touch, smell, taste, and our ability to hear—are involved in our knowledge of God. As John the Elder, the author of 1

---

19. Pearson, *Ancient Gnosticism*, 7–24.
20. See Oulton and Chadwick, eds., *Alexandrian Christianity*, 39.
21. Bonhoeffer, *Barcelona, Berlin, New York*, 378.
22. John 1:14.

John in the New Testament makes explicit: "We declare to you what was from the beginning, what we have heard, what we have seen with our eyes, what we have looked at and touched with our hands, concerning the word of life" is what we witness to in Christ.[23]

If Gnosticism threatened Christianity by its disregard for the world and the body, the triumphalist heresy threatened to make the church captive to the values of the empire and the dominant culture. The crossroads facing Christians in the fourth century, then, was whether the church could better fulfill its role as witness to Christ under the auspices of the state and in its service or by remaining critically independent. Given the circumstances, and Eusebius's interpretation of the situation, the die was soon cast. Caesar, it was said, would enable the church to fulfill its mission better. A benign state with plentiful resources was surely better than the reverse. I have a sense of what that temptation was like for those early church leaders. For, after the ending of apartheid, the ecumenical church, that is, those churches associated with the South African Council of Churches,[24] assumed that its prophetic work had been accomplished, that the demons of racism and injustice had been overcome, and therefore we could now move on in solidarity with a state committed to justice in building a new nation. But we were wrong. The prophetic role of the church on behalf of the powerless and poor should have continued irrespective of who is in power.

If heresy is a false choice, triumphalism conjures up an image of those famous triumphal arches in ancient Rome through which victorious armies marched to the acclaim of the people, the equivalent of a tickertape parade in more recent times. Before Constantine, Christians—along with slaves and other victims of conquest—were forced to march behind their conquerors; after Constantine, the church sometimes led the way, and its leaders were in the grandstands cheering them on. Such is the character of the triumphalist heresy—the justification of a reversal of roles as the church becomes part of the ruling class. A stark contrast to the triumphal entry of Jesus into Jerusalem riding on a donkey on the way to the cross![25] But despite this obvious irony, Christian triumphalism has recurred throughout the history of the church to our own day. It lies behind Christian nationalism and exceptionalism, the Christian

---

23. 1 John 1:1.
24. See de Gruchy and de Gruchy, *The Church Struggle in South Africa*.
25. See Matthew 21:1–2.

justification of crusades, pogroms, slavery, apartheid, and wars of aggression. A welcome mat at the White House is always more attractive to church leaders than the rebuff of a closed door.

Christian heresies are invariably christological in character, usually denying either the divinity or the humanity of Christ. If Gnosticism rejects the incarnation, the triumphalist heresy undermines the lordship of Christ. It has to do with the spurious claim that God is on the side of the empire or state irrespective of what they do, that princes rule by divine right and can do as they please, that being a Christian means uncritical and enthusiastic patriotism, and that the cross is a symbol of political power rather than of God's solidarity with the poor and downtrodden.

There were undoubted advantages for the church when Christianity became the imperial religion, but they were ambiguous at best.[26] The church now had some influence in shaping imperial public policy and mobilizing opinion according to Christian principles,[27] but the emperor also had a defining say in church affairs. Maintaining church unity was considered necessary for keeping the empire intact. Heretics needed to be rooted out not just to keep the church pure, but also to maintain social cohesion. Even the cross itself, the sign of God's suffering and redemptive love, was appropriated as a sign of divine blessing on imperial might and conquest. A golden cross was deemed better than a rugged wooden one.

The relationship of the church to the state, and more broadly to the world and culture, has become more complex over time than this either/or position suggests. In his classic study *Christ and Culture*, H. Richard Niebuhr provides a typology of the five alternatives that have emerged in dealing with the problem: First, the rejection of culture in the name of Christ; second, the accommodation of Christ to culture; third, giving Christ a transcendent place above culture; fourth, maintaining a paradoxical tension between Christ and culture; and fifth, regarding Christ as the transformer of culture.[28] The story of monasticism can be told largely in terms of the first and fifth of these types: rejecting the world and transforming the world, or maintaining a critical distance from the state but seeking to ensure that the state exercises its power in the service of justice.

---

26. See Cochrane, *Christianity and Classical Culture*, 213–60.
27. See Cochrane, *Christianity and Classical Culture*, 190.
28. Niebuhr, *Christ and Culture*.

Following the conversion of Constantine, thousands of citizens followed him into the fold. Becoming a Christian was the new normal. Baptism became a rite of passage into social privilege rather than a commitment to costly discipleship and possible martyrdom. So grace became a cheap commodity, to use Bonhoeffer's phrase, and church discipline grew lax. Bonhoeffer, of course, had the German church in the Third Reich in mind when he wrote those words, but the rot had begun with the birth of Christendom. In both instances, the world found "in this church a cheap cover-up for its sins, for which it shows no remorse and from which it has even less desire to be set free." But this, says Bonhoeffer, was a "denial of God's living word, denial of the incarnation of the word of God."[29]

The troubling question for many committed Christians was how they could remain Christian in a world that had become nominally Christian at the stroke of a pen, and therefore how they could remain in a church that was becoming too attached to worldly values. How could they obey Christ's call to a simple lifestyle when the church was embarking on "one of the greatest and most costly building programmes in European history."[30] As someone who appreciates the architectural beauty and significance of many of those buildings that still stand, among them Hagia Sophia in Istanbul (then Constantinople) and San Vitale in Ravenna, I do not raise this issue without some reluctance. But it must be raised nonetheless.

The growing wealth and worldliness of the church was, however, the major reason for the rise of Christian monasticism. For Christians should neither obey both Christ and Caesar as lord, nor worship God and mammon. Previously, if Christians disobeyed Caesar in following Christ, they faced the death penalty. The only alternative now was a life of self-denial in which they left wealth and marriage behind and, like the first disciples, took up their cross. In that way, Christians could resist the values of the empire and express their disapproval of the state capture of the church and a decadent culture. Monasticism thus began as a protest movement against the social norms and practices that had seeped into the life of the church.

As would later happen in Nazi Germany and apartheid South Africa, the struggle of the church to be a prophetic servant of the world

---

29. Bonhoeffer, *Discipleship*, 43.
30. Freeman, *The Closing of the Western Mind*, 238.

invariably begins with an inner church struggle over the claims of the gospel. For judgment, so the New Testament tells us, begins in the household of faith.[31] We glimpse this happening in the opening chapters of the book of Revelation, written in apocalyptic times, when John the seer speaks a word of prophecy to the seven churches of Asia Minor and tells them to listen to what the Spirit is saying to them. Each is addressed specifically with words of judgment and encouragement. The most damning judgment is that one had grown lukewarm while another had lost its first love.[32] This is what the first monastics heard when they listened to what the Spirit was saying to the church of their day.

This present monastic moment is no different—far too many of us Christians have either been seduced by the false values of the age and the spirit of Christian triumphalism, or else have been attracted to gnostic forms of spirituality that provide a means of escape from reality and responsibility. Any delay in responding to this *kairos* moment increases the danger that we fail to change our ways and grasp the opportunity God gives us to receive the coming kingdom in greater fullness now. So, St Benedict, fifteen hundred years after he wrote his *Rule*, continues to tell us to "listen," "wake up," and "run" while there is still light, otherwise "the darkness of death" will overtake us. This is a time for both contemplation and action, prayer and doing justice, a time for mystics and prophets to join hands and hearts for the sake of the world, indeed, for the sake of the *oikumene* (that is, the whole inhabited universe)—the word from which we derive the word *ecumenical*.

An Ecumenical Gift

Monasticism evolved before major schisms divided the church. It was ecumenical before it became confessional. But the Council of Chalcedon, convened in 451 by Emperor Marcian to deal with a perceived heresy (Monophysitism), ended up with the withdrawal of what became known as the Oriental Orthodox Churches: the Coptic, Syrian, and Ethiopian. Over the following centuries, a growing alienation between the Eastern Orthodox and Roman Catholic Churches led to the Great Schism in 1054, forcing monasticism unhappily to follow suit. Then, following the Protestant Reformation in the sixteenth century, my Reformed ancestors

---

31. 1 Peter 4:17.
32. Revelation 2:4; 3:15.

followed Martin Luther (1483–1546) in rejecting monasticism altogether. For them, Luther the monk was right to leave the monastery to save his soul, for he could not do so within. He was also right to encourage Christians to pursue their vocation in the world rather than to hide behind a religious façade and the hypocritical claim to Christian perfection. For the past five centuries we Protestants have lived outside the cloister.

But there is another side to the story. If it were not for monasticism, there would have been no Protestant Reformation. For it was in the monasteries that the Scriptures were preserved and copied, along with writings of the early church fathers, on which the Reformers depended; it was there that many women and men renounced wealth to follow Christ, that preachers were nurtured who proclaimed the gospel across Europe, and prophets emerged to challenge poverty and injustice; and it was in the monasteries that the desire for God and the love of learning were encouraged and expressed.

Like the Reformation, every genuine reform, renewal, or restoration movement in the church begins by a return to the Scriptures and early Christian tradition. This return is not driven by antiquarian interests, but by a contemporary demand to discern what the Spirit is saying to the church today amid the present *kairos*. This is what the Protestant Reformers attempted in the sixteenth century, though it led them to leave the monastery and further divide the church. Nearer to our time, it was the First World War *kairos* that led to the renaissance of biblical theology associated both with the Swiss Reformed theologian Karl Barth (1886–1968) and to monastic scholars such as the Benedictines at the Abbey of Saint-Pierre de Solesmes in France.

These initiatives helped foster the ecumenical movement around the same time as the rise of Nazism and the Second World War. They did so in tandem with an emerging ecumenical spirituality—an "invisible monastery," some called it—that found its focus in the annual Week of Prayer for Christian Unity initiated by Abbé Paul Couturier in 1936.[33] Without this it would have been impossible to engage in dialogue on the difficult issues that had long divided Christians or to respond together to the crises of the time.

Around the same time, Dietrich Bonhoeffer, who was then deeply involved in the ecumenical movement, began to speak of the need for "a

---

33. Villain, *Unity*, 213–37.

new kind monasticism."[34] In doing so, he was not rejecting the old but envisaging something that would develop out of it, much like the scribes of the kingdom of God Jesus spoke about who brought out of the treasury things that are both old and new.[35] In reflecting on Bonhoeffer's vision of a new monasticism, as we shall do later in the book, we must keep in mind that he primarily had the churches of the Reformation in focus. For it was they who either rejected the old without providing an alternative, or else recovered elements of the old but kept it peripheral to the life of the church rather than integrating it into the whole. But we also need to remember that monasticism, especially the Benedictine version had already left its imprint on the churches of the Reformation without them always being aware of, or acknowledging, the fact. It is these churches especially, Bonhoeffer believed, who need to listen to the Word and Spirit in company with monastics who share our concern for the church and the world today. This requires that we have some understanding of the history of monasticism, the experience of monastics, and the contemporary ferment in many cloisters since the Second World War and the Second Vatican Council.

Of course, Benedictine monastic spirituality left its imprint on the Anglican Church from the beginning and remains deeply embedded in its parish and liturgical life. There are also important elements in the Methodist Church that derive from the Benedictine tradition via its Anglican heritage. But the Methodist "class meeting," emphasis on Christian perfection, and evangelical piety also have monastic roots. More unexpectedly, there are some within the Dutch Reformed Church in South Africa today who acknowledge the biblical roots of Benedictine spirituality and connect them to the legacy of Andrew Murray Jr., the influential leader of that Church in the late nineteenth century, whose evangelical passion and mystical spirituality has left a lasting legacy. Significantly, Murray named his house, now restored at the Andrew Murray Center in Wellington, Clairvaux, after the famous Cistercian abbey.

In my own Congregational tradition, shared by Baptists, the Benedictine way of life resonates with the emphasis placed on a lifelong commitment to a particular congregation. In joining a local church, you become part of a family in a particular place, just as monastics do in joining a monastery. You are baptized into the church of Christ, but

---

34. Bonhoeffer, *London*, 284–85.
35. Matthew 13:52

confirmation requires taking vows of commitment to the local church as well as being embraced by its members. Members also share together in the process of discerning and choosing those called to hold office within the congregation. Just as the monastery is, as Merton says, a "covenant community," so too is the congregation.[36] In the same way, like monasteries, congregations are related to each other in a covenant relationship.

What might be more remarkable is the way Benedictine spirituality has influenced some churches that have a Pentecostal background. This is true of the Mosaic Community in Johannesburg, which is largely Afrikaans-speaking in ethos but inclusive of others across the racial and cultural divides. Deeply influenced by the Taizé Community and the Cistercian tradition, Mosaic not only has a rural retreat center where contemplative prayer is practiced, but it manages to blend its own heritage with the monastic in other ways, including icon writing and meditation, at its large urban campus.

The truth of the matter is that the Benedictine tradition has influenced all of us who are part of the Western Church, for we all drink from the same well, namely the early apostolic church. The monastic vision and vocation are gifts to the ecumenical church because they remind us of our roots, as well as embody a charism that exists for the sake of the renewal of the church in its service of the world. Merton preeminently among modern monastics placed great emphasis on the importance of this charism for the life of the church. What was important for him was not the preservation of monasticism as an institution (the old monasticism if you like) but the renewal of the life of the church today. As Patrick O'Connell puts it, Merton rejected "any perception of the vowed life that fails to situate monasticism in the heart of the church and the world loved by God and redeemed by Christ."[37] Monastic vows should, Merton believed, "open wide the life of faith and love, not to close it in upon itself."[38]

How, then, do we appropriate the monastic charism, especially as understood by Merton, in the life of the ecumenical church today? Like many others, I believe that Bonhoeffer provides the key for us to do so.

Even though I was interested in the new monastic movement inspired by Bonhoeffer when it first emerged in the United States earlier this century, I was cautious about trying to transplant an American

---

36. See Patrick F. O'Connell's introduction in Merton, *The Life of the Vows*, lxix.
37. O'Connell's introduction in Merton, *The Life of the Vows*, lxx.
38. Merton, *The Life of the Vows*, 194.

model in our South African context.³⁹ But this *kairos* moment is an appropriate moment to consider Bonhoeffer's challenge and continue my lifelong conversation with his legacy in my own context.⁴⁰ It also provides an opportunity to explore connections between him and Merton, whose thoughts and concerns resonate so much with those of Bonhoeffer.

According to a note I made at the time, I first finished reading Merton's autobiography *The Seven Story Mountain* on March 15, 1981.⁴¹ By then I was already deeply into Bonhoeffer studies and not surprised that some of my peers compared him to Merton. I am sure Bonhoeffer and Merton would have had much to talk about had they met. Merton's high regard for Bonhoeffer is evident in many passages of his later collection of reflections *Conjectures of a Guilty Bystander*, as it is in some of his letters. In one of them, to Rosemary Radford Ruether, the Catholic feminist theologian, in 1966, he mentions that while he had not yet read Bonhoeffer's *Act and Being*—which she had recommended—he had read *Ethics* and *Letters and Papers from Prison*.⁴² In another, earlier, letter to a friend, he said he found Bonhoeffer a good "counterbalance" to St John of the Cross.⁴³

Merton also had great respect for the Reformed theologian Karl Barth, Bonhoeffer's famed mentor, who will likewise feature a great deal in the pages that follow. Indeed, Merton begins *Conjectures of a Guilty Bystander* with a chapter titled "Barth's Dream," in which he expresses appreciation for Barth's childlike faith in Christ and his willingness to stand against the values of the world while always in compassionate solidarity with it. For Merton, Barth is a "Father of the Church," a theologian who has "entered quite naturally and easily into" his "personal and monastic reflections" and "Christian worldview." In fact, writes Merton, "a Catholic monk is able to read Barth and identify with him in much the same way as he would read a Catholic author like Maritain."⁴⁴ Having introduced you to some of the themes and people you will meet in the book, let me now provide an outline of its contents.

---

39. Brook, "Resonance at Rutba."
40. de Gruchy, *Bonhoeffer's Questions*.
41. Merton, *The Seven Story Mountain*; Forest, *Living with Wisdom*.
42. Merton, *The Hidden Ground of Love*, 498.
43. Merton, *The Hidden Ground of Love*, 108.
44. Merton, *Conjectures of a Guilty Bystander*, 6.

The Book in Outline

In the first chapter, I reflect on the origins of Christian monasticism in the Egyptian desert in the late third century. It is true that monasticism also emerged in Syria, Asia Minor, and Palestine during the same period, but my focus is specifically on its Coptic origins because monastic renewal always returns to this ancient, pioneering source in North Africa for inspiration and guidance. In saying this I must pause to acknowledge the fragility of monasticism in the Middle East as a whole, never more so than is the case today, for it is continually under threat. In his absorbing travelogue *From the Holy Mountain*, William Dalrymple recounts the amazing history yet precarious existence of monasticism in the region. Noting that it was only in Syria that he saw a "Christian population looking happy and confident," he adds ominously, "even their future looked decidedly uncertain."[45] Tragically, his fear has come true.

In Chapter 2, I provide an overview of the growth of monasticism in western Europe, from the Dark Ages that followed the fall of Rome in 410 until the Carolingian period, and then through the even darker times of the Viking invasions, until its remarkable flourishing in the Middle Ages. Central to the story is St Augustine (354–430), who provided the theological basis for the survival and expansion of Christianity led by monasticism, and St Benedict of Norcia, who provided the *Rule* that enabled the monasteries to do so. We will meet many other monastic luminaries, including St John Cassian (360–435), who bridges the East and the West, and Celtic monks from Ireland and Scotland, who spearhead the evangelization of Europe. Key aspects of the story are the Carolingian Reforms which gave Benedictine monasticism preeminence, the rise of Cluny, which led to its medieval flourishing, and finally the Cistercian reform of Benedictine monasticism under the influence of St Bernard of Clairvaux (1090–1153). But the story is about more than its famous abbots and abbesses, monks, and nuns, for there were thousands of monastics who lived the story. Most were laypeople. Yet without them, there would have been far fewer available to sing the psalms, harvest the vineyards, work in the kitchens, or copy manuscripts in the scriptorium.

Ironically, medieval monasticism also provided the base for its rejection by Martin Luther, himself a monk, who launched the Protestant Reformation in the sixteenth century. This is where Chapter 3 picks up the story. The reasons why Luther left the monastery still raise critical

---

45. Dalrymple, *From the Holy Mountain*, 448.

questions that cannot be ignored, as Merton acknowledged, if we are to retrieve the monastic vision today. But I also take note that later in his life Luther appears to have regretted leaving monasticism behind when he embarked on his movement of reform. Why that might have been so, and what it means for us today in the churches of the Reformation, is central to this chapter. I explore this by discussing various Protestant monastic-type trajectories and seminal figures, from the Anabaptists to John Bunyan, and from Søren Kierkegaard to Karl Barth and Bonhoeffer, who help us rethink the significance of monasticism for the churches of the Reformation today.

In Chapter 4, I reflect on the significance of monasticism for the life and witness of the ecumenical church today in our post-Christendom, secular age characterized by diversity and complexity. To do so I draw chiefly, but by no means solely, on Bonhoeffer's legacy, exploring what he meant by "a new kind of monasticism" in relation to the old.[46] Central to this discussion is the spiritual hunger that has emerged in reaction to the rise of secularism, which, in traditional language, is the desire for God, and at the same time a concern for a world in which justice flourishes, and peace is achieved.

In the Epilogue, I conclude with some random reflections, on writing a monastic *Rule* and, more specifically, the *Covenant of Love* that we at Volmoed are seeking to write. Indeed, the weekend after I finished the penultimate draft of this book, I led a weekend seminar at Volmoed at which I shared an outline of what I had written. I was encouraged by the enthusiasm of the sixteen participants who attended, and learned much from their comments. Writing a monastic *Rule* is a process, sometimes undertaken by one person, sometimes by a small group. But it is always written first by lived experience, whether that of intentional communities, new monastic communities, or local congregations in specific times and places. Those who are inspired by the monastic story today are best equipped to discern where the Spirit is leading them, but we can help each other in doing so.

---

46. See Bonhoeffer, *London*, 284–85.

A Personal Journey

Without my planning it to be so, my three books *Being Human: Confessions of a Christian Humanist*,[47] *Led into Mystery*,[48] and *The End Is Not Yet*[49] turned out to be a trilogy. The first, a Christian anthropology; the second, a theology seeking to understand the mystery of God; and the third, *The End Is Not Yet*, an eschatology, that is, an exposition of the "last things," or the "end of history." *This Monastic Moment* turns that trilogy into a quartet, to use a musical metaphor; it is an ecclesiology, or an attempt to understand the church in relation to the story of monasticism. Ecclesiology has been my preoccupation since my student days, both in terms of my life's ministry and my more academic pursuits. My Bachelor of Divinity thesis was on Congregational ecclesiology, my Master of Theology thesis was on the local church and racism, and my doctoral dissertation was on the ecclesiology of Bonhoeffer and Karl Barth. Each of these endeavors has informed the others, as it has my ministry and teaching, and this book is no exception.

Like the others in the quartet, *This Monastic Moment* is also a mixture of theology, history, personal anecdote, politics, philosophy, spirituality, social commentary, and some practical suggestions. No wonder I could not give the publisher a satisfactory answer when he asked who I had in mind in writing—was it a book for academics, students, pastors or priests, informed laypeople, skeptics or seekers after God or truth, or maybe even a monk or nun? I hope it will be of interest to all. It could also be used by study groups comprised of people who are interested in the subject whatever their reasons, background, or academic track record.

But I am also writing the book for myself, for it is part of a personal pilgrimage. At every turn in the journey I have discovered new avenues waiting to be explored, and encountered remarkable people who became important conversation partners, many of whom I only vaguely knew before starting. The temptation to digress has been great, therefore, and sometimes too alluring to avoid. At the same time, the subject is too complex to cover everything, and beyond both my competence and the purpose of the book. I have therefore taken risks, made jumps, and done much which more careful scholarship seeks to avoid. As much as I respect intellectual inquiry, I did not intend that the project should be a purely

---

47. de Gruchy, *Confessions of a Christian Humanist*.
48. de Gruchy, *Led into Mystery*.
49. de Gruchy, *The End Is Not Yet*.

academic exercise any more than I wanted to romanticize monasticism by ignoring its faults, or by regarding all monastics as saints.

In engaging monasticism, I have no sense of being called to turn my back on the world, throw in the towel on the struggle for justice, or offer myself as a Benedictine novice in my eighties. Nor am I converting from being a Reformed theologian and Congregational pastor to becoming Catholic, Orthodox, or Anglican, the communions in which most traditional Christian monasteries exist and from which I have learned much. Nonetheless, the more I have explored the legacy of monasticism, the more I have come to sense a familiarity with traditions that have shaped my own Christian life and convictions. The reason for this has also become evident. I am tapping into something primordially Christian that ties together my life's experience, my theological quests, and the yearning of the world for love, beauty, justice, as well as authentic humanity and genuine community.

I have also discovered that there is no need for me to renege on my self-understanding as a Christian humanist.[50] Of course, some monastics may reject reason in pursuit of faith, but there is a broader love of learning among them as is evident in the writings of Jean Leclercq, a leading French Benedictine of the twentieth century.[51] Like many others, I have always experienced the tension between affirming my Christian faith at the same time as engaging in scholarly endeavor in a secular university. With Leclerq's help, I now appreciate better how much that tension runs throughout the history of Christianity as expressed in the tension between scholastic and monastic theology. For me, *this* monastic moment has become an opportunity to explore further my conviction that discovering our true humanity is rooted inseparably in the desire for God, the love of wisdom, and the struggle for justice. And this has never been more important than it is at this critical time in history.

Over the years, Isobel and I have had wonderful experiences of intentional and monastic communities. Let me mention some of them, not because it may be of interest as a monastic travelogue, but because as my writing unfolded—and being mindful that writing, as Cardinal John Henry Newman once said, can be a form of prayer—I discovered that my external journey to monastic places was also an inward journey of spiritual discovery. Monastics rightly tell us that we do not need to travel

50. See de Gruchy, *Confessions of a Christian Humanist*; Merton, *Conjectures of a Guilty Bystander*, 199–200; Zimmermann, *Incarnational Humanism*.

51. Leclercq, *The Love of Learning and the Desire for God*.

to distant places to find ourselves; we only need to travel deeper into ourselves. Yet travel abroad and visiting significant places often enables us to see the world and ourselves differently, and to change as a result.

Our first experience of an intentional Christian community was in 1964, during a year of graduate study at Chicago Theological Seminary, when we spent a weekend with the Reba Place Fellowship, largely Mennonite in background, north of the city. Some of the time was spent debating Bonhoeffer's role in the conspiracy against Hitler, but mostly we discussed Bonhoeffer's *Life Together* and the need to build intentional communities that serve the needs of society. Later that same year we passed through Washington, DC, for the first time, and visited the Church of the Savior, which impressed us as a model for reinventing the local church. From there, we went further south to Americus, Georgia, to spend a week on Koinonia Farm, led by a Baptist New Testament scholar and farmer, Clarence Jordan. A few weeks before we arrived, the Ku Klux Klan had burned a cross outside the gate of the farm, protesting its racially inclusive character. Each evening, as we sat in the kitchen and listened to Jordan read from his Cotton Patch Version of the Bible, we recognized the authentic voice of Christian witness in terrible, dark times.

Another experience, this time in 1983, was our visit to Holden Village, a Lutheran conference and retreat center in the Cascade Mountains of Washington. This was followed some years later by two enriching visits to the Sant'Egidio Community in Rome. This Catholic community, composed of laypeople—professionals, both men and women—combines a liturgical life based in a former Carmelite monastery with daily engagement in the service of the world, both near and far. Of great interest to us was that the community had helped broker peace in the Mozambican Civil War (1977–1992) a few years earlier.

My first experience of a living monastery came when I visited the Taizé Community for a weeklong retreat en route back from the US to South Africa in September 1964. How excited I was to discover that Taizé was an ecumenical community founded by a Swiss Reformed pastor. Closer to home, I have been a guest at Marianhill Monastery, near Durban, many times. Originally a Trappist monastery, it later became a center for missionary outreach in rural KwaZulu-Natal.[52] But, most remarkable of all was the visit that Isobel and I made as part of a South African ecumenical group to the Coptic monasteries in the Western Desert in 1997

---

52. See Green, *For the Sake of Silence*.

as guests of Pope Shenouda III. This took us to the roots of Christian monasticism, and now, as I reflect on that experience, it is not difficult to imagine what transpired there in the fourth century when it all began.

We have more briefly visited many other monasteries, including the Benedictine communities of Maria Laach near Bonn, and of Ettal in Bavaria, both of which Bonhoeffer knew well. We have also been enriched by a visit to the Iona Community in Scotland, with its Celtic roots and more recent Reformed connections;[53] the Holy Island of Lindisfarne, whose Benedictine monastery was the first to be sacked by the Vikings in the eighth century; the Jasna Góra Monastery in Częstochowa, Poland, celebrated as a place of healing and home to the Black Madonna; the magnificent monastery at Melk, along the Danube in Austria, mentioned in Umberto Eco's *The Name of the Rose*; the Monastery of Christ in the Desert in New Mexico, with its stunning chapel; St John's Benedictine Abbey in Minnesota, that has been a major center of monastic renewal and ecumenical engagement in recent times; and the monastery in Erfurt where Martin Luther was a monk. And then, after a visit to Flossenberg Concentration Camp, where Bonhoeffer was murdered and his body burned in a common grave, we visited the Cistercian Waldsassen Abbey in Bavaria, in which lie the relics of ten Roman martyrs, and which still attracts many devout pilgrims. The contrast between that Baroque abbey and the simple chapel at Flossenberg not too far away could not be greater, but the reality of martyrdom remains the same.

We have also visited the ruins of many other monasteries: among them Tintern Abbey in Wales, Glastonbury in Somerset, Riveaulx and Ripon in Yorkshire, Clonmacnoise in Ireland, and Cluny in France. Often well-preserved historic sites, many of these are still massive in size in stark contrast to the hermitages of the desert, but nonetheless reminding us of places of spiritual vitality and hospitality. They also remind us that monasteries come and go: they are built, they flourish, and they also die—too often destroyed by the power politics of the day. To keep that in mind is sobering, but it is also well understood by monastics, for that rhythm is true of all life, including our own. Yet new birth also takes place, just as spring follows winter, and often this happens in times which seem dark and foreboding, times in which we seek for some cracks through which the light might shine.

---

53. See Gardiner, *Melodies of a New Monasticism*.

In such *kairos* times, St Anthony (ca. 251–356), the first monastic, went into the desert, Benedict wrote his *Rule*, Bonhoeffer formed his community of brothers at Finkenwalde, Roger Shutz founded Taizé, and the Sisters of Darmstadt established their community. As I started writing with summer approaching in the southern hemisphere, dispelling the darkness even before the monks begin their early morning vigil in our chapel, I sensed something of significance was gestating at the southern tip of Africa. That is what I have set out to discover during a southern hemisphere winter of discontent in the hope that spring would soon come. Now, as I end writing, and fall has arrived heralding another winter of the pandemic, and the autumn of my life continues apace, I share what I have heard "the Spirit saying to the churches."

1

INTO THE AFRICAN DESERT

O that I had wings like a dove,
to fly away and be at rest.
So I would escape far away
and take refuge in the desert.
   (PSALM 54:7–8)[1]

Let us go outside the camp and bear the abuse Jesus endured. For here we have not a lasting city, but we are looking for the city that is to come.
   (HEBREWS 13:13–14)

Anthony persuaded many to take up the solitary life. And so, from then on, there were monasteries in the mountains and the desert was made a city by monks, who left their own people and registered themselves for the citizenship in the heavens.
   (ST ATHANASIUS)[2]

---

1. Gelineau, *The Psalms*.
2. Athanasius, *The Life of Antony*, 42–43.

> Here, on the boundary of the church, was the place where the awareness that grace is costly and that grace includes discipleship was preserved. People left everything they had for the sake of Christ and tried to follow Jesus' strict commandments through daily exercise. Monastic life thus became a living protest against the secularization of Christianity, against the cheapening of grace.
>
> (DIETRICH BONHOEFFER)[3]

DURING OUR VISIT TO Egypt in 1997, we attended a Sunday evening service in St Mark's Coptic Cathedral in Alexandria. The huge building was overflowing with some three thousand worshipers; the service was conducted by several bishops, all of them monks. Pope Shenouda III gave a lengthy homily on angels and answered questions from the congregation on being a faithful Christian in an alien world. As patriarch of Alexandria, Shenouda was a successor to St Mark, the companion of St Peter. According to tradition, Mark brought Christianity to Egypt, became the first bishop of Alexandria, and died there as a martyr. Before the service we were taken to the crypt where Mark's head is preserved; the rest of his relics, kept for centuries in Venice, are now beneath the Coptic Cathedral in Cairo. This is a potent reminder that the Coptic Church is built on its martyrs, the supreme model of discipleship.

Reflecting on that visit to Alexandria, and on how immediate the legacy of saints and martyrs remains for Coptic Christians, I imagine what it must have been like for Christians who lived there in the late third and early fourth centuries. By then, the Coptic (that is, Egyptian) church was strong, its patriarch occupied the second most important episcopal see in the catholic church after Rome, its "noble company of martyrs" were universally revered, and its theologians were becoming influential in the shaping of orthodoxy and combatting heresy.

But the Upper Nile region was also a place of intellectual ferment. Second only to Rome in the empire, Alexandria was famous as the "new Athens" because of its distinguished academy. This was the birthplace of Neoplatonism, a philosophy integrating Hellenistic and Oriental wisdom, sponsored by Emperor Julian in a "last great attempt of paganism to express itself in terms of a philosophical theology" that could

---

3. Bonhoeffer, *Discipleship*, 46–47.

counter Christian claims and promote both "science and life for the ancient mind."⁴ There was also a strong gnostic presence in the region, some of it predating Christianity, and some that arose within the church itself in an attempt to accommodate Christian faith to pagan ideas. Indeed, among the ancient Coptic texts found at the important archeological site of Nag Hammadi in Upper Egypt in 1945–1946 were some that were a mixture of gnostic and Christian ideas dating back to the fourth century, including the Gospel of Truth and the Gospel according to St. Thomas.

Alexandria was also home to the largest Jewish community outside Palestine. It was there that the Old Testament was translated into Greek (called the Septuagint, or abbreviated LXX), and there that Philo (20 BCE—50 CE), the Jewish philosopher, visionary, and mystic, brilliantly blended Neoplatonism with Judaism. But in Christian circles, Alexandria was best known for the Catechetical School, which was established in the second century and made famous by its founding theologians, St Clement (150–215) and Origen (185–254), who attempted to bridge the gap between the world of biblical faith and Hellenistic philosophy. Attempts to do so had already begun in Rome when Justin Martyr (100–165) followed Philo and adapted the Stoic understanding of the *logos*, the sustaining power of the universe, to the Word "made flesh" in Christ.⁵

It is also symbolic that we should begin our exploration of monasticism in Alexandria because there has always been a tension in its history between the city and the desert, as there has been between the academy and the monastery. When St Athanasius (296–373), patriarch of Alexandria, later wrote that the "desert was made a city by monks," he was being intentional, for the first monastics were engaged in building a new Jerusalem, firmly convinced that "here we have no lasting city, for we are looking for the city that is to come."⁶ Monasticism might have been conceived and gestated in the city or its surrounding villages, but it grew and developed in the deserts of Egypt, Syria, Palestine, and Asia Minor out of a burning desire of some earnest Christians to know God. To what extent this desire was influenced by Neoplatonism is not certain, but we do know that Neoplatonism, especially as interpreted by Origen, was an important source for the Christian mysticism that would eventually flourish within monasticism.

4. Tillich, *A History of Christian Thought*, 51.
5. Grant, *Greek Apologists of the Second Century*, 56–64.
6. Hebrews 13:14.

The Desire for God

Nancy Maguire devotes a chapter to desire in her remarkable book on Carthusian monasticism, which she describes as the "most austere monastic order." The desire for God, she says, is that which compels people to become monks, in the same way as mountaineers "feel a compelling attraction for the extremes of human experience. They want to push the limits in their search for God."[7] This desire can sometimes become unhealthy, even demonic, as Thomas Mann so powerfully explored in *Dr Faustus*, because the desire *for* God can become the desire to *be* God, a desire for power and control, not a desire for love.[8]

The desire for God is fundamental to human experience, whether expressed in those words, or as a striving for transcendence, a journey into mystery, or simply as mysticism. St Paul acknowledges this in his famous sermon on the Areopogus in Athens where, having debated with the Hellenistic philosophers of the day, he recognizes the "unknown God" described by one of their poets as the One "in whom we live, move, and have our being."[9] Among his handful of converts that day was Dionysius the Areopagite, someone who was later confused with another Dionysius, a sixth-century Syrian monk, who had a great influence on the development of Christian mysticism, as we shall soon see.

Paul's sermon in Athens gave Christians the go-ahead to engage non-Christian poets and philosophers in expressing their faith.[10] Both Clement and Origen at the Catechetical School in Alexandria grasped the opportunity.[11] Following Philo, they brought biblical faith into conversation with the Hellenistic mystical tradition exemplified in Neoplatonism. Philo's achievement was no mean feat. Neoplatonism spoke of the transcendent in impersonal terms, the ultimate or absolute One, whereas the Bible speaks of God as personal, the God of Abraham and Sarah. The Bible also understands the human person in terms of the image of this God and speaks of a relationship of trust in God as creator and redeemer. And salvation is not absorption of the soul into the absolute, but redemption from sin, human wholeness, the reconciliation of relationships, and the resurrection of the body. The Bible includes myth and saga, but it is

---

7. Maguire, *An Infinity of Little Hours*, 120.
8. Mann, *Doctor Faustus*.
9. Acts 17:22–31.
10. Grant, *Greek Apologists*, 24.
11. Grant, *Greek Apologists*, 175.

held together by a historical narrative made contemporary through the celebration of defining memories and the expectation of promises yet to be fulfilled. It is not a perennial philosophy, but a journey or pilgrimage of faith and hope. So, as Merton tells us, while much in Christian tradition about contemplation derives from Neoplatonism rather than the Gospels, we must always remember its Hellenistic roots "and take care not to lose sight of Christ himself."[12]

This comparison indicates that while all mystical *experiences* might have much in common, they are often *understood* and *described* in different terms in the history of religions. For Christian mystics the desire for God is not fulfilled in an ecstatic flight from reality, but in an experience of God that leads to a call to action in the world. Such was Moses's experience of Yahweh at "the burning bush,"[13] Isaiah's experience of God in the temple,[14] Elijah's experience of the "sound of silence,"[15] and St Paul's experience of being "caught up to the third heaven."[16]

Both Clement and Origen were aware of the danger involved in engaging Hellenistic philosophy while interpreting Christian faith and experience, so they did so in ways that remained rooted in biblical tradition. Nonetheless, their language often reflects that of Neoplatonism. It was Clement who first described the Christian life as a "ladder of ascent" on which the "soul progresses from faith to knowledge" by suppressing "unreasoning passions," and "by works of love (it) mounts to union with God and the beatific vision."[17] And Origen, whose father had suffered martyrdom, was one of the first great systematic theologians to demonstrate that it is possible to combine "intellectual passion with warm personal devotion to God in Christ and the practical virtues of being Christian."[18] He was the founder of what Andrew Louth calls "intellectual mysticism," that is mysticism centered in the mind or *nous*, not just ecstatic emotions.[19]

---

12. Merton, *Cassian and the Fathers*, 18.
13. Exodus 3.
14. Isaiah 6.
15. 1 Kings 19:9–13.
16. 2 Corinthians 12:2.
17. "On Christian Perfection," book 7, in Oulton and Chadwick, eds., *Alexandrian Christianity*, 93–101.
18. Oulton and Chadwick, eds., *Alexandrian Christianity*, 186–87.
19. Louth, *The Origins of the Christian Mystical Tradition*, 74.

Origen also developed the allegorical method of interpreting the Bible that subsequently had such an influence in the church and particularly on monasticism until the time of the Reformation. Indeed, writes Merton, "Origen is perhaps the one who remained the most influential in Western monasticism" even though Origenism, under questionable circumstances, was declared a heresy.[20] In fact, Origen is regularly associated with monastic revivals over the centuries, whether the Carolingian reforms of the ninth century or those associated with St Bernard of Clairvaux in the twelfth.[21]

Origen's theology was handed on especially by St Basil of Caesarea (330–379), the erudite monastic theologian from Cappadocia, whose *Philokalia* ("the love of the beautiful") is a well-known compendium of Origen's writings. Usually referred to as Basil the Great, he was one of the most remarkable and highly educated monastics of his day, and his *Rule* and influence remain fundamental to Eastern Orthodox monasticism to this day. Indeed, Basil along with St Gregory of Nazianzus (329–389) and St Gregory of Nyssa (330–395), the Cappadocian Fathers as they are generally called, are the theological fountainhead of Orthodoxy. But it was especially Basil's student Evagrius Pontus (346–399), an Egyptian monk, who spread Origen's teaching and influenced succeeding generations of monastic theologians. Evagrius wrote extensively on Christian spirituality and was widely regarded as the "greatest theologian of the desert."[22]

Origen's mystical theology, as passed on by Evagrius, was later referred to as *apophatic theology*, especially with reference to the writings of the anonymous sixth-century Syrian monk Dionysius, who adopted the name Areopagite after Paul's first convert in Athens (hence he is also called Pseudo-Dionysius). His *apophatic mysticism* is about experiencing God through a process of *unknowing* (that is, getting beyond conceptualizations of God) and remains at the heart of Orthodox spirituality. In his words:

> Unto this Darkness which is beyond Light,
> we pray that we may come, and
> may attain unto vision through
> the loss of sight and knowledge,
> and that in ceasing thus to see or to know,

20. Merton, "Cassian and the Fathers," 23.

21. Leclercq, *Love of Learning and the Desire for God*, 94.

22. Merton, "Cassian and the Fathers," 88; Louth, *Origins of the Christian Mystical Tradition*, 74.

we may learn to know that which
was beyond all perception and understanding,
for this emptying of our faculties
is true sight and knowledge.[23]

The root meaning of *mysticism*, which is a constant theme in what follows, is "full of mystery," which, as Karl Rahner says, connects the everyday "experience of transcendence" with the most profound or "strange experience" of the transcendence we name God.[24] Rahner also tells us that theology is all about "being led into mystery," something that I have discovered in my own life.[25] If God is "the One in whom we live, move, and have our being," as Paul says in apparent agreement with a pagan poet,[26] then a mystic is someone who lives with an intimate awareness of being embraced by the mystery of God. This is not a question of us finding God like we might "get religion," but of us discovering that God has all the time been drawing us towards himself as a magnet draws metal.

Dionysian apophatic mysticism is, as Vladimir Lossky tells us, "the fundamental characteristic of the whole theological tradition of the Eastern church";[27] but although regarded with some official reserve, it has also had its exponents in the West, notably Meister Eckhart (1260–1329), a Dominican who greatly influenced John Tauler (1300–1361), St John of the Cross (1542–1591), Julian of Norwich, and Martin Luther, as well as the Quaker George Fox (1624–1691). But in neither the East nor the West is Christian mysticism about the absorption of the soul into the divine. It is about the gracious restoration of the divine image in human beings, that is, "the divinization of the human." This does not happen in a moment of ecstasy but is a never-ending process of conversion in union with the love of the triune God. This mysticism of love, understood as both contemplation and conversation, is motivated by our desire both for God and for the fulfilment of God's purpose for the world. It is at the heart of prayer, that is, the conversation motivated by our desire for God and our desire that God's purpose for the world and our own lives be fulfilled.

---

23. Quoted in Housden, *For Lovers of God Everywhere*, 172.
24. Quoted in Kelly, ed., *Karl Rahner*, 227.
25. De Gruchy, *Led into Mystery*, 4.
26. Acts 17:22–28.
27. Lossky, *The Mystical Theology of the Eastern Church*, 26.

The attempt by Christian theologians to engage creatively with non-Christian philosophy has always been opposed by those who fear compromise with paganism. One of the first to reject the attempt was Tertullian (160–220), Origen's contemporary living near Carthage, a brilliant lawyer and theologian. With Clement and the Alexandrian school in his sights, Tertullian exclaimed, in words that have echoed across the centuries:

> What has Jerusalem to do with Athens, the church with the Academy, the Christian with the heretic? Our principles come from the porch of Solomon, who had himself taught that the Lord is to be sought in simplicity of heart. I have no use for a Stoic or a Platonic or a dialectic Christianity. After Jesus Christ we have no need of speculation, after the Gospel no need of research.[28]

Tertullian's counsel to Christian disciples was to resist the seductions of philosophy and follow Jesus "in simplicity of heart." For him, it was the "blood of the martyrs that is the seed of the church," not the wisdom of the theologians. Tertullian, in all probability, also coined the word *monasticism* to describe what he called a new form of martyrdom, and likened a hermit's cave to a prison cell in which so many persecuted Christians had languished.[29]

Tertullian eventually joined the Montanists, an apocalyptic and ascetic sect, which was declared heretical because it rejected the legitimacy of the institutionalized imperial church and its clergy. But his suspicion of academic theology has remained constant through the centuries among those for whom scholastic endeavors have little to do with the gospel. Tensions between the academy and the church, scholastic and monastic theology, philosophy and science, and Christ and culture, are perennial, whether in the history of monasticism or more generally in the history of the church.

Certainly, the first monastics were not intellectuals who felt at home in the academy, any more than they were priests comfortably at home in the church. They were lay men and women, mostly unschooled, and decidedly uncomfortable about the worldly condition of the church. Some were influenced by the teachings of Clement, Origen, Evagrius, and

---

28. Tertullian, "On Idolatry," in Greenslade, ed., *Early Latin Theology*, 36.

29. See the introduction in Oulton and Chadwick, eds., *Alexandrian* Christianity, 38.

Basil of Caesarea, but their thirst for the living God was awoken when they first listened to the gospel story read to them in the churches in Alexandria and its surrounding villages. They soon concluded that their desire for God could not be met in the city or the urban church any more than it could be explained in the academy. Instead, they decided to follow Jesus and, like the first disciples, left their nets, families, and friends, and journeyed with him into the wilderness in search both of their true selves and the living God.

Following Jesus

The Gospels, written several decades after Jesus's death, in the light of faith in his resurrection, are not biographies. They were written to proclaim the call to follow the crucified Jesus of Nazareth as the risen Christ. Coptic Christians would have had a special interest in the Gospel of Mark, their patron saint who, omitting the birth narratives found in Matthew and Luke, and offering no profound prologue as in John, gets straight to the point:

> Jesus came to Galilee, proclaiming the good news (*euanggelion*) of God, saying, "The time (*kairos*) is fulfilled, and the kingdom (*basilea*) of God has come near; repent (*metanoia*) and believe the good news."[30]

The coming of Jesus was a *kairos* moment—a moment in time when God judged the old world or passing age, and in which God's new age or reign of justice and peace was revealed. This is the good news Jesus proclaimed, and in which he invited his hearers to believe when he called them to follow him. But to do so required *metanoia*, a fundamental change of heart and mind. For those who followed Jesus, this became an ongoing process of conversion, described by the evangelists as they recount the journey of the disciples with Jesus from Galilee to Jerusalem.

The Gospels also told those early Coptic Christians that it was only after his baptism by the ascetic John the Baptist, followed by his forty-day-long struggle against temptation in the wilderness, that Jesus called men and women to follow him. Even Jesus, so they thereby learned, had to endure rigorous testing before he could begin his life's task. In addition, the Gospels told them that not everyone called by Jesus could literally leave

---

30. Mark 1:14–15.

everything behind; Mary and Martha could not, for they had to care for their brother Lazarus; nor could others who had to continue with their daily lives and work. But at least twelve young men and a few women did do so. They were mostly illiterate, had conflicting personalities and varied backgrounds, and were uncertain about who Jesus really was and where he was taking them. That would only be disclosed to them along the way as they listened to Jesus's teaching (often in parables designed to open their eyes to God's reign), or as they witnessed his dealings with people from priests to foreign women and Roman soldiers. Above all, they heard Jesus say: "If any want to become my followers, let them deny themselves, take up their cross daily and follow me."[31]

Although the canon of the New Testament only reached finality about the same time as the birth of monasticism, and its various texts had to be copied by hand and distributed on foot, the Gospels and Paul's Letters were generally widely known and available for use in catechesis and worship. So those early Coptic Christians would have heard them read Sunday after Sunday, and even if they were illiterate and could seldom possess them, they learned to memorize key portions. The extent to which they did so was remarkable but not unusual for those times, for the practice of memorizing texts was common among Jews and philosophers. So, likewise, most of those earnest Christians who went into the desert took memorized passages of Scripture with them. But there is the story of one later desert monastic, Abbot Serapion, who did have copies of the Gospels, which he treasured but gave away because he read in them that he should give away all his possessions.

In listening to the Gospels, those early monastics heard that Jesus healed the sick, showed compassion for the common people, embraced those excluded by the dominant society, and demonstrated what it meant to love God, their neighbor, and themselves. They probably puzzled over the parables Jesus told, but, like the first disciples, began to glimpse the world in a new way and therefore learned what it meant to live differently in God's kingdom. They learned that they had to obey God's rule of love above all else, for only then would they find true happiness, deep peace, and everlasting joy such as the present age could not give them. They also learned that God's new age of justice and peace would only come in its fullness at the end of the ages. In the meantime, they had to live in this moment in anticipation of its coming. But Jesus warned them that if they

---

31. Mark 8:34.

followed him, they would inevitably face opposition because those who benefitted from the way things were would always resist God's reign and persecute those who try to live by it.

Those early Coptic Christians also heard that Jesus did not tell his disciples to leave the world and live in sectarian exclusion in caves along the Dead Sea or to take up weapons against the empire and establish God's rule by force. Instead, Jesus offered an alternative way to work and pray in anticipation of the coming of God's new age, as those who were already living in it. This meant loving and forgiving others (even their enemies), providing hospitality to strangers, healing the sick, pursuing God's justice, and sharing God's peace. It also meant sharing their wealth and possessions, and if need be, forsaking their families and losing their lives, for they could not serve two masters at the same time.[32]

They also heard how Jesus took his disciples aside into the hills to pray together and rest a while, for they were on a difficult journey and no one can follow Jesus in their own strength. Nevertheless, they discovered that Jesus's rule for them was designed for each according to her or his personality and need, like the yoke of an ox, so that the discipline necessary to make discipleship possible, costly as it would always be, was not burdensome.[33] Jesus even promised never to leave them without the presence of his Spirit, for in that way he would journey with them into the future when God's reign would finally be established in its fullness. In the meantime, they had to learn how to love one another as his disciples and together witness to God's love for the world. And, even if only two or three of them were gathered to break bread in remembrance of him, he would be truly present.[34]

Throughout the history of monasticism, Jesus's call to men and women to follow him has remained fundamental. It is at the heart of the vows monastics make. Without a sense of that call and a willingness to obey, no novice will progress far. So, too, the call to follow Jesus and our willing response remains primary at *this* monastic moment. All else flows from that. And, if we reflect on the gospel narratives in doing so, then, like Bonhoeffer, we will soon discover that discipleship is not a program that can be set out in ten steps, nor a predetermined goal, nor even an

---

32. Luke 14:26.
33. Matthew 11:30.
34. Matthew 18:20.

ideal, but a bodily following. As Bonhoeffer tells us, it requires that we "step out" of our "previous existence" by giving up "former things."[35]

> An idea about Christ, a doctrinal system, a general religious recognition of grace or forgiveness of sins does not require discipleship ... Christianity without the living Jesus Christ remains necessarily a Christianity without discipleship; and a Christianity without discipleship is always a Christianity without Jesus Christ. It is an idea, a myth.[36]

To follow Jesus means that his "disciples had to give up everything" and "suffer and endure persecution." Yet, attached to the call to discipleship and the task of following Jesus bodily is a promised gift. For those who followed him "received back in visible form the very things they had lost—brothers and sisters, fields and houses."[37] And, ultimately, if they had a genuine desire for righteousness and achieved "purity of heart," they would "see God," the "pearl of great price."[38] In medieval monasticism this elusive quest would be described as the "beatific vision."

Those first Coptic hermits (from the Greek word *eremos* meaning "desert") would surely have been familiar with Jesus's parable of the sower as recorded in Mark's Gospel, and how the evangelist himself interpreted it.[39] Some seed was immediately devoured by Satan, and some took root until persecution came and then it fell away. And then there was the seed that fell among thorns, the "ones who hear the word, but the cares of the world, and the lure of wealth, and the desire for other things come in and choke the word, and it yields nothing." Worldly responsibilities, private possessions, and a desire to cling onto "other things" have to be shed, says Mark, if the followers of Jesus are to "bear fruit."

But how is this possible if we still live in the world? Indeed, how are we to understand "the world"? Is the world evil or good? Are material possessions and sensual pleasures sinful and therefore to be rejected, as the gnostics taught? How could this be if God created the world, declared everything good, and told humans to procreate and inhabit the earth? Indeed, how could Christians still regard the Jewish Scriptures—the Old

---

35. Bonhoeffer, *Discipleship*, 58.
36. Bonhoeffer, *Discipleship*, 59.
37. Bonhoeffer, *Discipleship*, 225–26.
38. Matthew 5:8; 13:46.
39. Mark 4:15–20.

Testament and the Bible of Jesus—as inspired? It certainly is a very earthy book.

Such questions deeply troubled the early Hellenistic Christians, not least because an ascetic life was characteristic of those who embodied the best in Greco-Roman society, just as hedonism characterized the worst.

The tension between asceticism and hedonism lay deep in Greco-Roman culture, often described as one between two conflicting worldviews: the Dionysian or Epicurean, with their emphasis on sensuous desire, artistic creativity, ecstasy, and notorious bacchanalian feasts, and the Stoic, or Apollonian, with their emphasis on rationality, discipline, and order. The latter was most notably taught by the Roman lawyer Seneca (4 BCE—65 CE), whose moral teaching approximated that of Christianity, and emperor Marcus Aurelius (121–180), the model good political leader. Discipline, or *ascesis,* including giving up whatever stood in the way, was necessary to achieve worthy goals whether in athletic competition, war, or philosophical inquiry.[40]

A Disciplined Life

When the first Christian monastics adopted an ascetic lifestyle, they were part of a broader cultural phenomenon not unlike the global movement of people today who opt for a simple, countercultural lifestyle, generally for ethical or health reasons. But those early monastics adopted a disciplined lifestyle to follow Jesus and come to know God. And some of them, there can be no denying, pushed asceticism to an extreme. For this reason, it is important to distinguish Christian asceticism from notions of spiritual heroics, as if Christian ascetics are the spiritual equivalents of Olympic medal-winners and therefore a superior breed of Christian. Christian asceticism properly understood is not a moral achievement but a means of grace that sets us free to love God and others rather than being controlled by self-centered desire. Indeed, one of the heresies we will encounter in the next chapter, Pelagianism, so moralized asceticism that it virtually replaced God's grace as the means of salvation. You saved your soul by mortifying your body. But certainly, those who take the call to discipleship seriously know that following Jesus is never a matter of cheap grace; denying oneself to follow Christ's way of love is always costly.

---

40. See Freeman, *The Closing of the Western Mind*, 238–40.

Indeed, for the first monastics, the ultimate ascetic act was martyrdom, which some ardent Christians desired so much that they had to be restrained from seeking it. But after 313, when martyrdom was no longer likely, becoming a monastic was the next best option. Instead of becoming a martyr you could "die daily," as exemplified both by St Paul and by St Anthony the first hermit and model monastic.[41]

Becoming a hermit or living the even more secluded life of prayer of an anchorite or anchoress totally withdrawn from society, was therefore the way that many earnest Christians sought perfection. If they could not be martyrs, they could at least become monks and nuns, and if they had difficulty living as virgins in society, then taking a vow of chastity and living in the desert was the way to go. But "living like angels" in a world regarded as decadent was challenging.[42] There were not only physical but spiritual dangers attached. Of the latter, pride was the most persistent. Just as gnostics considered themselves a spiritual elite with special insight into divine mysteries, so Christian ascetics had to combat the tendency to become self-righteous, to consider themselves a cut above other Christians.

As a young Christian growing up in fundamentalist circles, I knew that to be a "true" Christian I could not smoke, drink, dance, or have sex outside marriage. But I was not well instructed about all the deadly sins that Paul and Evagrius, among others, had identified centuries before, or about how to overcome them: gluttony, lust, avarice, melancholy, anger, boredom, vainglory, and pride. In fact, I do not remember any lectures on asceticism, at least under that rubric, during my theological training. We studied the fathers of the Eastern and Western Churches, but not the desert fathers, let alone the desert mothers. They were not on the curriculum. By contrast, if I had attended the Catechetical School in Alexandria, ascetic disciplines would have been at the center of the curriculum just as they are for monastic novitiates today.

Clement and Origen wrote a great deal about marriage, martyrdom, and Christian perfection, both to guide Christians in responding to the cultural crises of their times, and to counter the criticisms leveled against Christianity by its gnostic and Stoic opponents. For many cultured non-Christians also found Christian asceticism repugnant, even a threat to humanity. After all, if everyone practiced virginity humanity clearly had

---

41. 1 Corinthians 15:31; Athanasius, *Life of Antony*, 32 et al.

42. On the complexity of the issues, see Robin Lane Fox, *Pagans and Christians*, 336–74.

no future. Christians who lived ascetically were the ancestors of the later Puritans mocked by Shakespeare as well as by the Christian establishment and upper classes through the centuries. For such critics, asceticism was unnatural. It was taking discipleship too far.

Human sexuality, and especially the practice of chastity and virginity was, therefore, at the center of the debate, as it still often is. In his *Confessions*, St Augustine tells us that what prevented him from becoming a Christian, once he had overcome the intellectual difficulties, was having to adopt chastity. So he prayed that God would help him to do so, "but not yet," because he was afraid that God would answer his prayer and "cure him of his desire of lust," which he "desired to have satisfied rather than extinguished."[43] But the problem, as he came to see, was not the flesh, for had not God created the material world and pronounced it very good, and had not the eternal Word become flesh?[44] The problem was the sins of the flesh, that is, the misuse of the body, for the body itself, as Paul taught, was the temple of the Holy Spirit, and the marriage relationship was analogous the relationship between Christ and the church.[45]

The first Christians also believed that they were living in the "last days," between the *kairos* of the first and that of the second coming of Christ, and therefore, as St Paul had counseled, if it was possible, they should not marry.[46] Given the state of the world, and its pending apocalyptic demise, having children was not the most responsible thing to do. Many young people today have a similar concern given the state of the world. But back in the third century, Origen went even further and became a eunuch "for the sake of the kingdom of heaven."[47] Likewise the choice made by a woman to remain a virgin was considered a sign of holiness that mirrored that of the Virgin Mary. Significantly, it was in the fourth century, as monasticism took root, that the cult of the perpetual virginity of Mary also developed.

Virginity carried a different connotation back then than it does today in our largely sexually liberated Western world. Traditionally, whether then or now, the expected and only socially acceptable way for a woman to lose her virginity was through marriage, and that meant lifelong

---

43. Augustine, *Confessions*, book 8, chapter 7, 169.
44. Genesis 1:31; John 1:14.
45. 1 Corinthians 6:19.
46. 1 Corinthians 7:9.
47. See Matthew 19:12.

submission to a husband, usually not of her own choice. To choose to remain a virgin was countercultural, a rejection of convention, a refusal to become submissive and docile. This meant a radical equalization of sexual agency, and an opening up of possibilities for positions of greater power and influence for women, as happened in the course of monastic history. As Peter Brown puts it, for women to "make their bodies holy" meant that they were claiming "the right to dispose of their bodies as they pleased." In other words, the body, says Brown, "had become a tangible *locus* on which the freedom of the will could be exercised, in choices that intimately affected the conventional fabric of society."[48] In the beginning, women did not become monastics against their will or because they could not find a husband or afford a dowry; they chose the monastic life in order to follow their own calling, much as a modern woman might forgo marriage for the sake of her career.

Celibacy, was however, only one aspect of striving for Christian perfection. Those who went into the desert were not primarily opting for chastity but were prompted to heed Jesus's words to the rich young ruler that unless they gave away what they possessed they could not follow him.[49] But how austerely ascetic must ardent followers of Jesus be? Must they virtually starve themselves to death like Simeon Stylites, the Syrian monk who sat praying on the top of a pillar until he died? This question was not just about being a good monastic; for many, it was also about entering the kingdom of God, or "working out your own salvation in fear and trembling" even if, as St Paul said, it is God "at work within you."[50]

Clement of Alexandria was fully aware of the dangers of extreme asceticism. In writing about the story of Jesus and the rich young ruler, he tells us that that Jesus was "not forbidding us to be rich in the right way, but only a wrongful and insatiable grasping of money."[51] He then goes on to speak about the "human ideal of continence . . . set forth by Greek philosophers" and says that it is not wrong to have desires, only wrong to allow desire to get the better of us. "Our general argument concerning marriage, food, and other matters, may proceed to show that we should do nothing from desire," but "our will is to be directed only towards that which is necessary." And this is not just about "sexual relations," but

48. Brown, "The Notion of Virginity in the Early Church," 428.
49. Matthew 19:16–22.
50. Philippians 2:12.
51. "On Marriage," chapter 6, in Oulton and Chadwick, eds., *Alexandrian Christianity*, 66; see also Campenhausen, *Tradition and Life in the Church*, 90–122.

"money, softness, property . . . outward appearance," about controlling "one's tongue" and mastering "evil thoughts."[52] But, Clement concludes, "those who from a hatred of the flesh ungratefully long to have nothing to do with the marriage union and the eating of reasonable food, are both blockheads and atheists, and exercise an irrational chastity like other heathen."[53] This does not mean that the ascetic life is not to be commended; it is about the meaning and the spirit in which it is followed.[54] What is required of every Christian without exception is not "renunciation of possessions, but good works, almsgiving and compassion for the poor."[55]

There are several issues that I have raised that need to be taken further in later sections of the book. Let me mention three here in anticipations of that discussion. The first is the danger in monasticism of dividing Christians into those who are "true disciples" and those who are not, between the "perfect," as Jesus taught his disciples,[56] and the rest. The second follows from this and has to do with church discipline. If Benedictine monastics take lifelong vows of stability, obedience, and the conversion of lifestyle, what about other Christians, if costly discipleship applies to all followers of Jesus? The third issue has to do with self-knowledge, for we cannot know God unless we also learn to know ourselves; neither can we love "the other" if we do not learn to love ourselves. How, then, do we deny ourselves in order to love ourselves?

Retreating to the Desert

By the end of the third century and the beginning of the fourth, a handful of Christians who heard the call to follow Jesus turned their backs on the values of a corrupt world and a worldly church to seek God in the desert. To begin with, they followed him to the outskirts of the city or their home villages, but then they went deeper into the desert to Scetis or Wādi el-Natrūn, along the Nile and even farther into Upper Egypt and into Sinai. Each step towards that end widened the gap between them

---

52. Oulton and Chadwick, eds., *Alexandrian Christianity*, 67–68.
53. Oulton and Chadwick, eds., *Alexandrian Christianity*, 68.
54. See Campenhausen, *Tradition and Life in the Church*, 95.
55. Campenhausen, *Tradition and Life in the Church*, 96.
56. Matthew 5:48; and 19:21.

and the congregations to which they belonged.[57] They became hermits (*eremites*), or "people of the desert," living alone.

The desert is literally awesome, a place of absence and revelation, of death and rebirth, a place where we come face-to-face with ourselves and are surprised by God. It was out in the hill country of Samaria that Jacob experienced the mystery of God and in retrospect named the place Bethel—the "house of God"; it was at the burning bush in the Egyptian desert that Yahweh disclosed his name to Moses, and at Sinai that Yahweh gave him the Ten Commandments. It was as they journeyed through the wilderness that the Israelites were tempted to turn back and rely on false gods, but persevered and learned the hard lesson of what it means to live by faith and obedience. But, above all, it was in the desert that Jesus overcame the temptation to compromise with the kingdoms of this world, and it was to the desert that Jesus went to pray and find strength on his journey to the cross. So, it was into the desert that the first monastics went, and it was there that they engaged in their own ascetic struggles (often depicted as struggles with demons), and the deeper they went into the desert, the deeper they went into their own souls.

By the end of the fourth century, these hermits, collectively to be called the desert fathers and mothers, had attracted thousands of disciples who desired to follow Jesus and know God. Owen Chadwick describes the scene, which is still much the same today as I observed when visiting the Coptic monasteries in the Western Desert: "Monks living in isolated cells but joining together for worship, for buying and selling, for a rudimentary form of discipline; sightseers visiting the famous cells; enquirers travelling round the various societies, seeking instruction and edification."[58] It is remarkable to think that this has been so for sixteen centuries, but it is a major reason why the Coptic Church has survived, despite opposition and persecution for much of that time.[59]

Among the first hermits was an earnest young Christian named Anthony from a village near Alexandria. What we know about him is based on the *Life of Antony*, written later in life by his friend Athanasius, by then the bishop of Alexandria and a strong advocate of monasticism.[60] Athanasius's hagiography was written to portray the life and

57. See the Introduction by Owen Chadwick in Chadwick, ed. and trans., *Western Asceticism*, 15–16.

58. Chadwick, ed. and trans., *Western Asceticism*, 23.

59. See Meinardus, *Monks and Monasteries of the Egyptian Deserts*.

60. Athanasius, *Life of Antony*.

achievements—many of them miraculous—of a saint, to inspire others to follow his example. Some have called it romantic,[61] but there seems no reason to doubt its basic narrative, even if it is unlikely that Anthony was as familiar as Athanasius claims with Origen's Platonism or Christian philosophy more generally.[62] In any case, Athanasius's *Life* more than served its purpose, for as we shall see, it had a remarkable influence on monasticism, at least into the Middle Ages.

The story Athanasius tells starts one Sunday in 269 when Anthony, the educated son of prosperous parents who died when he was about nineteen, heard the words of Jesus in the gospel reading for the day: "If you want to be perfect, go, sell your possessions and give to the poor, and you will have treasure in heaven. Then, come, follow me."[63] In response, Anthony gave away his possessions and began to live in a tomb on the outskirts of his village before retreating more deeply into the desert.[64] There, like Jesus, he fought a constant battle against temptation, later depicted in iconography as a standoff against fantastic beasts, as in the famous sixteenth-century *Isenheim Altarpiece* painted by Matthias Grünewald (1470–1528). This celebrated work of Renaissance art also depicts Anthony alongside St Jerome (342–420) and Augustine, both of whom would later come under his influence. Indeed, Anthony came to be regarded as the "abba of all monks," and every monastic revival ever since, as Leclercq tells us, recalls "his example and his writings."[65] But more immediately, Anthony, like other celebrated desert fathers and mothers, attracted many disciples, some of whose stories soon circulated across the region, many of them later written down in hagiographical sketches by Jerome when he became a monk in Bethlehem.

The story of St. Hilarion of Palestine (291–371) is typical of the way in which early monasticism spread. He was sent by his parents to study in Alexandria where he was praised by his teachers for his rhetorical skills and seemed destined for public greatness. But, when he was still fifteen, he went into the Egyptian desert to find Anthony, and after two months with the celebrated hermit he returned home to Gaza where he lived as a hermit, performed many miracles, and attracted followers from across the region. Robin Lane Fox, who recounts the story, tells us that while

61. Goehring, *Ascetics, Society, and the Desert*, 13.
62. Williams, *Arius*, 89.
63. Matthew 19:21.
64. Athanasius, *Life of Antony*.
65. Leclercq, *The Love of Learning and the Desire for God*, 125.

Hilarion's conversion preceded Constantine's, his retreat into the desert "coincided with a time of rapid transition, when townsfolk and people of high position would venture out to the Christian perfectionists, now residing in the desert." They were attracted by "their poverty and charity, their awesome abstinence, their insight, their blessings and their way with demons and miracles."[66]

Towards the end of his long life, having lived in community among his followers in the area around Scetis, Anthony returned to live again as a hermit. This did not prevent him from supporting his friend Athanasius in defending Orthodoxy against Arianism, the heresy that was threatening to tear both the church and the empire apart at the time. Arianism, named after Arius (c. 256–336), an ascetic priest in Alexandria, questioned the full divinity of Christ, the idea that Jesus Christ shared the same nature as God. Arius, who was more at home in the world of the academy than the desert, was trying to make Christian dogma more intellectually acceptable, and his teaching won a great deal of support across the empire, even among some bishops, eventually becoming the creed of many Gothic Christians, some of whom brought about the fall of Rome in 410. But, for Athanasius and his followers, Arianism undermined the incarnation and therefore the very essence of Christian faith.

In the struggle against Arianism, the battle lines between what was becoming orthodoxy and what was deemed heresy were being drawn, and Anthony was willingly drawn into the struggle in support of Athanasius. Indeed, Anthony's support for Athanasius and other orthodox bishops enhanced their popular authority at a time when Arius had a considerable following.[67] In turn, this increased episcopal support for the desert fathers and mothers, just as it increased tension between monastics and the emperor, who several times forced Athanasius into exile. This, as we will see, helped the spread of monasticism to the West. What is noteworthy, however, is that even though Anthony and his fellow hermits had retreated into the desert, they could not escape from the struggles going on in the church and the empire, a story that would repeat itself over the centuries.[68]

Not long after Anthony became a hermit, a conscripted soldier named Pachomius (292–348) from Thebes was converted to Christ, and

---

66. Robin Lane Fox, *Pagans and Christians*, 19–20.
67. Williams, *Arius*, 89–90.
68. See Meinardus, *Monks and Monasteries in the Egyptian Deserts*, 6.

he too became a hermit under the instruction of an older anchorite. Pachomius was also influenced by monastic ideas germinating in Asia Minor associated with Basil, who had developed brotherhoods when he became the bishop of Caesarea. So, in 320, Pachomius founded a community of monastics at Tabennisi, near the Nile. In some records, for obscure reasons, Pachomius is also associated with the monastery of Debra Dano in Ethiopia. This is a good reminder of the spread of early Coptic monasticism throughout north Africa.

Pachomius's community was the first *cenobitic* (from *koinonia* and *bios*, "community" and "life") monastery, and it led to the formation of nine others, which included both men and women, with Pachomius as their abba. One description of this monastery tells that already back then the original monastery was a "fairly elaborate affair, capable of accommodating several hundred monks." Apart from its monastic cells and assembly room (called the *synaxis* because it was used for common prayer), it had a refectory, an infirmary, and various other facilities used for farming and handcraft. In other words, it was self-sufficient but also a center of hospitality. "In time of plague," we read, the monks "would care for the sick, feed the hungry and bury the dead."[69]

The life of this pioneering monastery was governed by a *Rule* drafted by Pachomius based on communal experience. "Rule," or *regula* in Latin, is a translation of the Greek *kanon* (or canon), used to indicate what is regarded as legal or binding, as in the canon of the New Testament. It is an important word in monasticism where the *canonical hours* determine the rhythm of the day, and canons are those who gather in *chapter* to advise the abbot in determining policy. Pachomius's *Rule* was the first of many monastic *Rules*, each of which usually had some influence on those that followed. But few, if any, were drafted in advance; they arose out of living in community and were guided by experience. And Pachomius certainly learned from experience that monastic and intentional communities invariably need to draft a *Rule*, however simple it may be, to guide their life together.

Another celebrated hermit was St Macarius (300–390), who as a young man of thirty, deeply influenced by Anthony, established a monastery at Scetis (Wadi el-Nátrūn), which would later become a major center of Coptic monasticism and, as we have seen, home for Anthony himself in later life. Macarius (to be distinguished from St Macarius of Alexandria)

---

69. Sheridan, "The Origins of Monasticism in the Eastern Church," 26–27.

was a scholar and student of Evagrius, who, so Merton tells us, was "the fountainhead of the desert school of mystical theology."[70] This reminds us that from the beginning, even in the desert, there were those hermits and monastics who were scholars whose love of wisdom was also expressed in reflection that drew on the patristic theology of that period.

In addition to many other male hermits, by this time there were almost three thousand female hermits or anchoresses living in the desert.[71] Among them was St Syncletica (d. 373), the first of the desert mothers, who, a century after Anthony, sold all her possessions, gave the proceeds to the poor and went into the desert.[72] The daughter of wealthy parents, Syncletica knew about the teaching of Clement and Origen[73] and even wrote a book on Evagrius. In it, she developed a balanced spirituality, distinguishing between divine asceticism and demonic tyranny, so, anticipating St. Benedict's *Rule*, she said that the former has the quality of balance. This balance is captured by Mary Earle when she writes that desert holy women like Syncletica, rediscovered a deep truth, a Christian humanist insight: "we are less than human without each other." And because these *ammas* were schooled in the love of God and love of neighbor, says Earle, they urge us to look beyond ourselves and practice an embodied spirituality that always questions whether my well-being comes at the cost of another's scarcity.[74]

As gender inclusivity is essential for us at *this* monastic moment, it is important to keep Syncletica in mind and consider the place of women hermits in that formative period for monasticism. John Chryssavgis speaks to this when in discussing the spirituality of the desert mothers he says that women were, in general, "welcomed in the desert for spiritual direction and instruction." For them, "moving into the desert meant taking a step into the realm of freedom: freedom from slavery, freedom from obligatory subjections, freedom from exploitation, and especially freedom from possession." Indeed, "by struggling to exclude and overcome the conventional forms, the desert mothers themselves became witnesses and martyrs of another reality." There was, it seems, mutual respect

---

70. Merton, *Cassian and the Fathers*, 81.

71. King, *The Desert Mothers*. Archived from the original on 24 August 2014. Retrieved 25 June 2018.

72. See Chryssavgis, *In the Heart of the Desert*; Earle, *The Desert Mothers*.

73. See the Introduction in Oulton and Chadwick, eds., *Alexandrian Christianity*, 38.

74. Earle, *The Desert Mothers*, 75.

deriving from their shared experience and commitment, and therefore the abbas also turned to the ammas for counsel.

> A monk ran into a party of handmaids of the Lord on a certain journey. Seeing them, he left the road and gave them a wide berth. But the Abbess said to him: If you were a perfect monk, you would not even have looked close enough to see that we were women![75]

This is the wisdom of lived experienced, not just the knowledge that comes from scholarly reflection.

The Wisdom of Experience

The wisdom of the desert fathers and desert mothers was communicated with few words and always to the point. Indeed, when people went to consult them, their constant refrain was simply: "give me a word." A word to live by, one that addresses my present plight, a word that brings reassurance, but above all, a word from God. And that is what they usually received, a few words that somehow hit the mark, as if the abba or amma knew them inside out. But sometimes that word was uttered in silence.

A certain brother came to Abbot Theodore of Pherme and "spent three days without hearing a word and went off sad."

> So, a disciple said to Abbot Theodore: Father, why did you not speak to him? Now he has gone off sad! The elder replied: Believe me, I spoke no word to him because he is a trader in words and seeks to glory in the words of another.[76]

For anyone who trades in words, as I do, that is a stern warning, as is the response of Anthony to a visiting philosopher who asked him how he could be happy without the consolation of books. "My book," Anthony replied, "is the nature of created things, and any time I want to read the words of God, the book is before me."[77] The desert fathers and mothers did not write treatises, homilies, or letters. Their words were few, pithy and concrete, addressed to seekers after God on the path to salvation. Yet, removed as their world is from ours, we recognize a common humanity

---

75. Saying no. 21 in Merton, trans., *The Wisdom of the Desert*, 32.
76. Saying no. 29 in Merton, trans., *The Wisdom of the Desert*, 34.
77. Saying no. 103 in Merton, trans., *The Wisdom of the Desert*, 62.

and a desire to discover the deep meaning of life. And that is why their wisdom remains pertinent, for it is the wisdom of the Spirit.[78]

Merton tells us that these strange somewhat unkempt hermits "steered clear of everything lofty, everything esoteric, everything theoretical, or difficult to understand."[79] They simply refused to discuss such things, nor were they keen to discuss matters of dogma. If they had not lived it, they would not say it. They had retreated to the desert to find themselves, knowing that only by doing so would they find God, not the God of orthodox dogma, which they in any case affirmed, but the God they experienced in the silence, the God who had become one with them in their humanity. This would be true of the generations of monastics who followed them through the centuries, as the famous anchoress Julian of Norwich so eloquently stated.[80] The "proximate end of all their striving," says Merton was "purity of heart—a clear and unobstructed grasp of one's own inner reality as anchored, or rather lost, in God through Christ."[81]

Several themes continually appear in the sayings from the desert, among them stability, hospitality, and humility. Here is an example of each, to illustrate their style and the content of their counsel. On stability, an anonymous hermit advises:

> If some temptation arises in the place where you dwell in the desert, do not leave that place . . . for if you leave it then, no matter where you go, you will find the same temptation waiting for you.

The same counsel is more graphically offered by Syncletica: "Just as the bird who abandons the eggs she was sitting on prevents them from hatching, so the monk [and] the nun [grow] cold and their faith dies, when they go from one place to another."[82]

On hospitality consider what another abba had to say:

> A brother came and stayed with a certain solitary and when he was leaving he said: Forgive me, Father, for I have broken in

---

78. See Cowan, *Desert Father*; Chryssavgis, *In the Heart of the Desert*; Byassee, *An Introduction to the Desert Fathers*; Earle, *The Desert Mothers*.

79. Merton, trans., *The Wisdom of the Desert*, 9.

80. Julian of Norwich, *Showings*, chapter 46.

81. Merton, trans., *The Wisdom of the Desert*, 8.

82. Norris, *Acedia & Me*, 88.

upon your Rule. But the hermit replied, saying: My Rule is to receive you with hospitality, and to let you go in peace.[83]

And on humility:

> A brother asks one of the elders: what is humility? The elder answered him: To do good to those who do evil to you. The brother asks: Supposing a man cannot go that far, what should he do? The elder replied: Let him go away from them and keep his mouth shut.[84]

Humility, a cardinal virtue in the New Testament and monastic spirituality, we should keep in mind, is rooted in the humiliation of Christ on the cross. In the wisdom of the desert it is not pathological self-abasement, but a recognition that we humans are "of the earth" (*humus*). To accept our humanness and live accordingly, not pretending to be who we are not, is the essence of humility.

While we might expect people who live austere lives to give us burdensome advice, they make few demands and simply advise us to follow Scripture and not move around too much. As Jason Byassee points out, "we are not told to memorize the creed, avoid all sin, exercise heroic virtue—just to meditate on God and stay put."[85] Indeed, writes Merton, "there was more real love and kindliness in the desert than in the cities where, then as now, it was every man for himself."[86] "Love ruled over everything, and everything, from self-denying asceticism to prayer, was guided by it, difficult as that was, for such love demands a complete inner transformation."[87]

Indeed, for monastics contemplative prayer was at the heart of daily life, and the source of their wisdom. The well-known Jesus prayer was probably first practiced in the desert: "Lord Jesus Christ, son of God, have mercy on me a sinner!" This prayer has been handed down from one generation of monastics to the next. Theophan the Recluse (1815–1894), a nineteenth-century Russian saint who probably resembles the desert fathers more than most since then, tells us that this prayer is not a technique any more than it is a talisman or simply a habit; it is a gift of grace that is received in a daily turning to God. Consider this story:

83. Saying no. 75 in Merton, trans., *The Wisdom of the Desert*, 51.
84. Saying no. 86 in Merton, trans., *The Wisdom of the Desert*, 53–54.
85. Byassee *An Introduction to the Desert Fathers*, 15.
86. Merton, trans., *The Wisdom of the Desert*, 17.
87. Merton, trans., *The Wisdom of the Desert*, 18.

> Once Abbot Anthony was conversing with some brethren, and a hunter who was after game in the wilderness came upon them. He saw Abbot Anthony and the brothers enjoying themselves and disapproved. Abbot Anthony said: "Put an arrow in your bow and shoot it." This he did. "Now shoot another," said the elder. "And another and another." The hunter said: "If I bend my bow all the time it will break." Abbot Anthony replied: "So it is also in the work of God. If we push ourselves beyond measure, the brethren will soon collapse."[88]

There is, then, a great deal for us to learn from the teaching of these desert fathers and mothers that is relevant to *this* monastic moment. But you only have to read Helen Waddell's marvelous but somewhat bizarre collection of stories about them, not least the harlots St Pelagia and St Mary, to recognize that they lived in a different universe from our own, one more akin to biblical times than the modern world.[89] They may be "models for imitation," but, as Merton says, not in all respects.

> *Not* in all their exterior actions—impossible to us—not at all suited to our situation; not in all their attitudes—they were extremists—they were often wrong. They are to be followed in their *faith*, their love of Christ, their zeal for the monastic state and their spirit of prayer and sacrifice.[90]

Yet, as he says elsewhere, "we must be as thorough and as ruthless in our determination to break all spiritual chains, and cast off the domination of alien compulsions, to find our true selves, to discover and develop our inalienable spiritual liberty and use it to build, on earth, the kingdom of God."[91] If we learn nothing else from these desert dwellers, let us learn that the love of wisdom that accompanies the desire for God is more than the love of knowledge. Wisdom is the outcome of prayerful, lived experience.

All Things in Common

Most desert monastics who lived a solitary life eventually came to accept that their desire for God could be helped rather than hindered by

---

88. Saying no. 106 in Merton, trans., *The Wisdom of the Desert*, 63.
89. Waddell, trans., *The Desert Fathers*.
90. Merton, *Cassian and the Fathers*, 100–101 (italics original).
91. Merton, trans., *The Wisdom of the Desert*, 24.

being associated with the life of a monastic community, as Pachomius taught. After all, this was the pattern in the Gospels. Jesus called each of his disciples in person, but he also called them into a community. So, being alone in a desert cave and being together in community are complementary. That is why it soon became canonical that all hermits should be connected to a community of monastics, even if they did not always live in the monastery, and no monastic should become a hermit unless the abbot or abbess and community chapter agreed that this was appropriate.

Certainly, those earnest Alexandrian Christians who responded to Jesus's call and went into the desert were familiar with St Luke's account of the birth of the church as described in his Acts of the Apostles. Cassian had this in mind when he wrote that the "cenobitic life came into being at the time of the apostolic preaching. It was all there," he continues, "in that crowd of believers at Jerusalem."[92] What Jesus began to do "in the flesh,"[93] Luke tells us in the prologue to his Acts of the Apostles (1:1), he continued to do through his Spirit at work in the Christian community or *ecclesia*.

Although we normally translate *ecclesia* as "church," it originally referred to an assembly of citizens called together, as in Athens, to discuss the affairs of the *polis* or city. In the New Testament, however, it refers to the *ecclesia* or assembly of God, literally those "called" together *out of* the world to be the people of God *in* the world. Apart from Luke's use of *ecclesia* in Acts, the word occurs almost exclusively in the letters of Paul, or with reference to the seven churches in the opening chapters of the Revelation of John. It also refers both to the church in each place, that is, to the local church or congregation, and to the church in every place—the ecumenical church—that is, throughout the whole inhabited universe or *oikumene*. Some later monastics would also refer to the monastery as an *ecclesiola in ecclesia*, that is a "little assembly" or "covenant community" existing *within* the church, an idea that would later resurface in Augustine, medieval monasticism, and the writings of Martin Luther.[94]

The first Christian *ecclesia* in Jerusalem, Luke tells us, embodied a common life (*koinonia*, which was translated *cenobitic* in Latin) of prayer and worship: they "broke bread together" (an early description of the Eucharist), they shared their possessions, and they daily learned from the

---

92. Cassian, *Conferences*, 186.
93. See John 1:14; 1 John 4:2.
94. See Introduction in Eberle, trans., *The Rule of the Master*, 61.

teaching of the apostles.[95] And again, in words that Benedict, Augustine, and many others in monastic history would frequently quote: "the whole group of those who believed were of one heart and soul, . . . but everything they owned was held in common."[96]

By the time Luke painted this model portrait of the original *ecclesia*, it was more an ideal than a reality in most congregations across the empire. This much we know from Paul's letters to the churches he founded and from the letters to the seven churches in the book of Revelation. The Christians in Alexandria also knew that their own church was not as much like the *ecclesia* Luke described in Acts as it should have been. It was too worldly, having lost much of its character as a community of committed disciples. It was no longer a church of martyrs faithfully witnessing to the gospel but too conformed to the values of the world.

Paul's letters provide ample evidence of the attempt to form *ecclesiae* or local churches that were united "in Christ" even though they embodied a diversity of ethnicity, gender, culture, class, intellect, and ability that was unique in the ancient world. In contrast to the Greek civic *ecclesia*, which was the domain of male, property-owning citizens, the *ecclesia* of God was in principle inclusive, attempting to become a new humanity composed of disparate parts. It is not surprising, then, that Paul had to deal with serious problems in planting the church across the Mediterranean world, as in Corinth where the members of the church almost drove him to despair.[97] Why could they not act as disciples of Jesus! For, as Paul insisted, every member was equally important; none should be excluded: and using the analogy of the body, every member had a role to fulfill, for they were all baptized into Christ. Members of the *ecclesia* may have different gifts, but this did not mean that some were more spiritual or perfect than others. All were equally called to follow Jesus, and leadership was not dependent on worldly knowledge or strong personality but on the wisdom of the cross, which was expressed in humility and service.

If Luke's portrait of the primitive *ecclesia* was an ideal, and Paul's letters depict congregations that are more inclusive and open to the world, a third ecclesial model presented in the New Testament is John's "beloved

---

95. Acts 2:42–45. This passage is referred to by both Augustine and Pachomius with reference to the monastic church. See also Eberle, trans., *The Rule of the Master*, 7 n120.

96. Acts 4:32–35.

97. 1 Corinthians 1:10–17; 3:1–23; 2 Corinthians 4:7.

community."[98] The Johannine *ecclesia*, the community beloved of God, rejected both the sinful values of the age and the prevailing gnostic docetism and Platonic dualism of the worldly wise who regarded matter or the material world (the *kosmos*) as evil.

Kosmos occurs far more often in the Johannine writings than elsewhere in the New Testament and is understood in both a positive and negative sense. In John's Gospel we read about God's love for the world and are told that God does not condemn the world, yet we also read that the world does not "know God," and that God judges the world.[99] This, in sum, lies at the center of Jesus's "high priestly" prayer in John 17 where he prays, on the one hand, "I am not asking you to take them [his disciples] out of the world, but I ask you to protect them from the evil one," but also declares that "they do not belong to the world, just as I do not belong to the world."[100]

The latter, more negative understanding of *kosmos* prevails in the Johannine letters, especially 1 John, which were probably written at the end of the first or beginning of the second century. In 1 John, which largely echoes the theology of John's Gospel, we are told "not to love the world," and that former members of the beloved community have broken ranks and returned "to the world."[101] The problem is not the *kosmos* as such, for that is, as Raymond Brown tells us, "the sphere of human beings and human experience" that is "related to the salvific action of God and Christ."[102] What is rejected as sinful are the values and ideologies that control the world, lead to the persecution of Christians and the denial of the incarnation. As Brown translates 2 John 7 and 9: "For many deceivers have gone out into the world, men who do not confess Jesus Christ coming in the flesh." Indeed, "anyone who is so 'progressive' that he does not remain rooted in the teaching of Christ does not possess God."[103] The penalty for not remaining so rooted was excommunication, literally, exclusion from fellowship. The beloved community could survive only if all its members lived in love and showed hospitality to one another. For

---

98. Brown, *The Epistles of John*.
99. John 3:16–21.
100. John 17:15–16.
101. 1 John 2:7–28.
102. Brown, *Epistles of John*, 222.
103. Brown, *Epistles of John*, 645.

"God is love" writes John, "and those who abide in love, abide in God."[104] The call to "live in love" defined "the beloved community," and 1 John was its *Rule*. It described the difference between the true *ecclesia* and the false, between the assembly of God and that of the world.

By the middle of the second century, as the catholic church began to take more definite shape, the *ecclesia* both local and ecumenical was increasingly modeled not on the ancient Greek assembly of citizens, but on Roman imperial organizational structures and hierarchical leadership. This might have been necessary to enable the church to function as the imperial religion and more easily proclaim the gospel to all nations throughout the empire, but the danger was that it then began to do so in the same way as the world.

Clearly the church faced a serious dilemma. Jesus had sent his followers into the world "to make disciples of all nations," but he had also called them to deny themselves and take up their cross to do so.[105] And that cross was not the cross of imperial triumph, the "iron cross" of military valor, but the suffering, redemptive wooden cross of prophetic-servanthood. The struggle was about the true cross, not about relics of the original cross that pilgrims tried to find in Jerusalem, but about the true meaning of the cross. And that struggle was also about the true church, for already by the time the first hermits were living in the desert, there were congregations around the empire claiming to be the true church as distinct from the false church of the establishment.

But where is the true church? That question was continually raised in those early centuries. Is it where the bishop rules with the emperor's approval, or where the risen Christ reigns from the cross? Are the true apostles those who stand in the correct line of succession, no matter what they say or do, or charismatic preachers and evangelists who practice what they preach? Such questions have reverberated throughout subsequent history. But, even back then, Bishop Cyril of Jerusalem (313–386) had to tell his catechumens:

> Since the word *ecclesia* has different applications ... should you ever be staying in some strange town, do not just ask, "Where is the church [*kyriakon*, i.e. the Lord's House, or church-building] ... but where is the Catholic congregation?"[106]

---

104. 1 John 4:16.

105. Matthew 28:19; and 16:24.

106. Cyril of Jerusalem, *The Catechetical Lectures* 18:26, in *Cyril of Jerusalem and Nemesius of Emesa*, 187–88.

For, as Cyril tells them, there were many congregations claiming to be the true *ecclesia*, but they were often "heretical gatherings," "churches of evildoers." But these schismatics were not only posing a threat to the established church; they were, like the desert hermits, also raising serious questions about the nature of the church, and what constituted the true church, and central to the debate was the relationship of the church to the world and the empire.

Whether Jesus intended to establish the church as we now know it has long been debated, but that he intended to form a community of followers is clear. It is also clear, as Hans Küng says, that Jesus did not want his disciples to live in isolation from the world, nor did he have a dualistic understanding of reality, condone legalism, austere asceticism, or hierarchical order.[107] For Küng, Jesus was not an ascetic monk striving for perfection, something implied in the Gospels' contrast between his lifestyle and that of John the Baptist. But I am not convinced that Küng, who expresses high regard for "religious communities and the great achievements of monasticism,"[108] is right in saying that "there was nothing eremitical or monastic about Jesus' community of disciples."[109] The Gospels suggest otherwise.

The first monastics might have been dismayed by the worldly way in which the church was developing, but while their asceticism might have been different in degree from one to another, they did not leave the church, nor was their flight from the world motivated by a gnostic disdain for the world as evil. They were not schismatics. They were usually strictly orthodox and accepted the authority of the local bishops, even if critical about some of them. Indeed, early monasticism, as Rowan Williams notes, fulfilled "the important job of restoring the charismatic spiritual authority of bishops" and provided "an interior foundation for the courageous resistance to imperial pressure."[110] But their retreat into the desert certainly raised some awkward questions about the *character* of the church, namely its worldliness, that is, its adoption of worldly values. In this respect monasticism was a prophetic presence *in* the church, not an Essene-like absence, and over time it became an agent of reform,

---

107. Küng, *On Being a Christian*, 195–200.
108. Küng, *On Being a Christian*, 175.
109. Küng, *On Being a Christian*, 193, 195, 196.
110. Williams, *Arius*, 89–90.

calling the church to recover its apostolic character as the *ecclesia* of God in the world.

We should also keep in mind that there was a difference between these desert monastic communities and others that would soon grow up in towns and cities alongside existing church communities. For the hermits, asceticism, not liturgy, was at the center of their life, and when they came together in community, it was to sing psalms and read Scripture before returning into the silence of their hermitage or their cell. By contrast, those monasteries that grew up in the towns and cities did so within the liturgical and sacramental framework of the local church within which the psalms were sung and the Scriptures read. This liturgical life or the *opus Dei*, the "work of God," became the heart of monasticism, and the lonely nightly vigil of the hermits became a regular public office to which others were gradually added, though, as yet there was no uniformity from one monastery to the next.[111]

But whatever else the *ecclesia* was, it was not an invisible community existing within the visible church known only to God. It was a community of real people living *bodily* according to the gospel, both in and for the world, even though they claimed not to belong to this present age.

This leads us to the recognition, important for *this* monastic moment, that the more the church opens itself to the world, as it must in existing *for* the world, the more committed it must be to its calling as the *ecclesia* of God. Otherwise, in gaining the whole world it will lose its soul. That is the lasting testimony of the desert monastics. Hence Jürgen Moltmann's observation that "asceticism and the eremitical life grew up side-by-side with the decision to be open to the world." Ever since, Christianity "has always existed in both forms of life: as a world-wide church, and in the consistent discipleship of Jesus."[112] Maintaining this necessary tension is fundamental to the ongoing reformation of the church if it is going to be the prophetic-servant of the world at this monastic moment.

In responding to Jesus's call to deny themselves and follow him into the silence and solitude of the desert, the first monastics were not only intent on saving themselves from a corrupt world but could not think of any better way to save the world. As Merton writes:

> The Coptic monks who left the world as though escaping from a wreck, did not merely intend to save themselves. They knew

---

111. Rees et al., *Consider Your Call*, 244.
112. Moltmann, *The Church in the Power of the Spirit*, 322.

that they were helpless to do any good for others as long as they floundered about in the wreckage. But once they got a foothold on solid ground, things were different, then they not only had the power but even the obligation to pull the whole world to safety after them.[113]

That is why through succeeding centuries monastics and reformers have returned to the desert fathers and mothers, as they have to the gospel that motivated them, to find inspiration and wisdom for the task.

---

113. Merton, *The Wisdom of the Desert*, 23.

2

INTO EUROPE'S DARK AGE

In the spirit he carried me away to a great, high mountain, and showed me the holy city Jerusalem coming down out of heaven from God . . . the nations will walk by its light . . . and there will be no night there.

—THE APOCALYPSE OF ST. JOHN[1]

However alien and eccentric Eastern asceticism sometimes seems, it had an extraordinary influence on the medieval West; indeed, the European monks of the Middle Ages were merely provincial imitators of the Eastern desert fathers.

—WILLIAM DALRYMPLE[2]

We intend to establish a school for the Lord's service. In drawing up its regulations, we hope to set down nothing harsh, nothing burdensome . . . But as we progress in this way of life and in faith, we shall run on the path of God's commandments, our hearts overflowing with the inexpressible delight of love.

—THE *RULE* OF ST. BENEDICT[3]

---

1. Revelation 21:10, 24.
2. Dalrymple, *From the Holy Mountain*, 106.
3. Benedict, prologue, verses 45–47 (*RB 1980*, 165).

But when I had passed my first youth and attained the age of perfect strength, I heard a voice from heaven saying . . . write what you see and hear.

—HILDEGARD OF BINGEN[4]

Rome fell on August 28, 410, when Alaric led his Gothic army into the imperial capital. Subsequent reports tell us it was evening, autumnal darkness was descending on the burning city, resistance had ceased, dead bodies littered the streets, and for the next three days there was pillaging and raping. Many citizens were dragged off into slavery, and others fled as refugees across the Mediterranean as far as Asia Minor and the Holy Land. It was much like what is happening in the Middle East today, only in the opposite direction, redefining the destiny of Europe, then as now.

The fall of Rome did not immediately usher in the Dark Ages, even though it did bring about a chaotic transfer of power. What was left of the imperial bureaucracy remained in place, as happened in Nazi Germany after its defeat in 1945, and after the demise of the apartheid regime in South Africa in 1994. Some optimists in Rome even thought that the new normal would be a reinstatement of the old order under new management, as theaters and circuses revived to keep such hopes alive. But the writing was on the wall. The imperial army was being withdrawn from Britain, Gaul, and Germania—an army by then composed of foreign conscripts with little loyalty to Rome itself. Then, in 476, the last of the Roman emperors, Romulus Augustulus, was deposed. The Dark Ages had begun, even though there would be even darker times ahead, when hordes of Vikings descended on Western Europe in the ninth century destroying the last vestiges of imperial civilization—as well as many Christian monasteries. This chapter is the story of monasticism's rapid growth, sudden destruction, and remarkable rebirth.

Pagan critics held Christianity accountable for Rome's collapse. The cross might have been a sign of victory for Constantine according to Eusebius, but in the West, Christianity was accused by its pagan critics of bringing Rome to its knees. Christianity, they said, weakened Rome's resistance by preaching meekness and forcing Romans to forsake their patron gods. Fortunately, in Augustine, the bishop of Hippo

---

4. From the preface to Hildegard's visionary *Scivias*, a trilogy of books calling for the moral reform of the church; quoted in Flanagan, *Hildegard of Bingen*, 41.

(a small town near Carthage in North Africa), Christians had an astute theologian who was able to respond to the challenge. Before his conversion to Christ, Augustine had been a student of philosophy under the spell of Neoplatonism; he was well versed in the intellectual culture of pagan Rome; and, in addition, he was for a time attracted to Manicheanism, a Persian gnostic movement. In other words, he was well-informed about the intellectual and spiritual currents of the day. But his conversion changed the direction of his life as well as the development and character of Christianity in the West.

In shifting focus from the East to the West, we need to keep in mind that while monasticism was beginning to evolve in Western Europe, it was flourishing throughout the Eastern Orthodox world as it began to stretch north beyond the Balkans. There were at this time at least eighty-five monasteries in Constantinople alone, baffling Western observers by what Peter Brown calls their "over-production of the holy."[5] Monasticism lay at the heart of Orthodoxy in a way that was different from in the Catholic West. It would also remain much the same through the ensuing centuries, unlike in the West, where it was regularly reformed.

We do not know exactly when the first monastic community was formed in the West, but by the end of the third century there were wandering ascetic prophets, influenced by Coptic and Syrian monastics, traveling across the Mediterranean and spreading the story of what was happening in the East. As a result, monastic-like cells began to form and proliferate in parts of Italy and Gaul. Then monasticism received a major boost. Athanasius, the bishop of Alexandria, was exiled to Rome in 339 during the Arian controversy, where he told the story of Anthony and the first Coptic hermits.

Later, in 356, after the death of Anthony, Athanasius wrote his *Life of Antony* which, as William Clebsch tells us, "quickly became the paradigm for . . . Christian hagiography."[6] It also became a textbook on monastic spirituality, especially after it was translated by Evagrius into Latin. Read alongside the Bible throughout this period and well into the Middle Ages, the *Life of Antony* shaped monastic life. More immediately, in answer to the prayers of his mother, Monica, it played a major role in the conversion of Augustine while he was still an agnostic student of philosophy enjoying the good life in Milan.

5. Quoted in Frend, *The Rise of Christianity*, 837.
6. Introduction to Athanasius, *Life of Antony*, xiv.

A Momentous Conversion

The history of Christianity is littered with conversions to Christ that had momentous consequences. That of St Paul on the Damascus road is probably the most paradigmatic. Not only did Paul become the apostle to the Gentiles and spearhead the expansion of the church in the Greco-Roman world from Asia Minor to Rome, but he also provided a theology for a post-Judaic and inclusive Christianity. Augustine took over the baton from Paul and became in the West what Origen had become in the East. He was an apologist for Christianity against its pagan critics, who blamed it for the fall of Rome. Deeply influenced by Neoplatonism, and something of a mystic, Augustine also established one of the first monastic communities in the West and provided an outline for what eventually became the Augustinian *Rule*. He then single-handedly fought and won what some have called a Pyrrhic victory over Pelagianism, a heresy that moralized faith and undermined grace, but has long persisted despite Augustine's efforts.

Augustine tells us about his conversion in his *Confessions*, a book written around the year 400 and destined to become a spiritual classic and favorite among Western monastics. One day, he recounts, a fellow African, Ponticianus, came to visit him and his friend Alypius in Milan. Ponticianus noticed some of St Paul's writings lying on a nearby table. Expressing his delight, he confessed that he was a Christian. Augustine tells us what then happened:

> When I had told him that I had given much attention to these writings, a conversation followed in which he spoke of Anthony, the Egyptian monk . . . whose name . . . up to that time was not familiar to me. (He then gave) an account of this eminent man . . . We all wondered—we, that these things were so great, and he, that we had never heard of them. From this, his conversation turned to the multitudes in the monasteries . . . and to the teeming solitudes in the wilderness of which we knew nothing at all.[7]

To his astonishment, Augustine then learned from Ponticianus that there was even a monastery under the care of Bishop Ambrose (339–397) outside the walls of Milan. (The ruins of this monastery still lie somewhere beneath the ancient church of St Ambrose, close by the great Renaissance monastery designed by Bramante.) Ponticianus also told them that while

---

7. Augustine, *Confessions*, book 8, chapter 6, 166–67.

he and two friends were wandering in a forest near Trier, a German city on the River Moselle, they came across a small hermitage in whicfh they found a copy of the *Life of Antony*. On reading it, the two friends, who in their time were equivalent to present-day secret service agents, immediately decided to join the community of hermits. Ponticianus was deeply moved, and congratulated them on their decision, but decided not to follow them. However, both their fiancées did follow them, and thereby "dedicated their virginity" to God.[8]

It was shortly after this, in 386, that Augustine's own conversion occurred, while he was sitting in a garden, probably attached to Ambrose's monastery, and reading from St Paul's Letter to the Romans. In a well-known passage in his *Confessions*, Augustine compares his experience with that of Anthony. Hearing a chant from nearby, "Tolle lege" ("Pick up and read"), Augustine opened the Bible and read the first passage he came across.[9]

> For I had heard how Anthony, accidently coming into church while the gospel was being read, received . . . as though addressed to him: "Go and sell what you have and give it to the poor . . . and come follow me." So . . . I snatched it up (the apostle's book), opened it and in silence read the paragraph on which my eyes first fell: "Not in rioting and drunkenness . . . but put on the Lord Jesus Christ, and make no provision for the flesh to fulfil the lusts thereof."[10]

Instantly, Augustine goes on to say, "there was infused in my heart something like the light of full certainty and all the doom of doubt vanished away."[11]

As Augustine's conversion was also influenced by the preaching of Ambrose, he undoubtedly shared what had happened to him with the bishop, and enquired about his experiment in monasticism.[12] So it is not surprising, that after Augustine returned to Carthage in 390, he established a small monastic community in nearby Tagaste, where he lived for the next few years, studying the Bible, engaged in theological reflection, and providing spiritual direction. It was also during this time that he

---

8. Augustine, *Confessions*, book 8, chapter 6, 168.
9. Romans 13:13.
10. Augustine, *Confessions*, book 8, chapter 12, 175–77.
11. Augustine, *Confessions*, book 8, chapter 12, 176.
12. Augustine, *Confessions*, book 5, chapter 13, 110–11.

opposed Manichaeism, a gnostic sect that had previously attracted him, rejecting its dualistic view of the world and denigration of the body. And then, somewhat reluctantly, he accepted ordination and was soon after made bishop of Hippo. There he relocated his monastic community as a center for training priests, and he established a convent for women.

Based on this experience and his growing knowledge of what was happening elsewhere, Augustine wrote his treatise *On the Work of Monks* in 401. This, together with a rudimentary draft of what became known as *The Rule of St Augustine*, was also influenced by the writings of Basil the Great, the most important monastic influence in Eastern Orthodoxy, along with John Cassian and Evagrius, the preeminent interpreters of the Eastern desert monastic experience for Christians in the West. But Augustine was by no means solely preoccupied with monasticism. The fall of Rome required that he also respond to the criticism that Christianity was responsible for the catastrophe.

The City of God

The argument against Christianity, later repeated in more detail by Edward Gibbon in his *History of the Decline and Fall of the Roman Empire* (1776), was that Christianity had weakened the Romans' will to defend the empire and made them more interested in the afterlife than the present. After all, since the time of Constantine, when the empire gave up relying on its pagan gods and espoused Christianity, it had been assumed that the Christian God would ensure the security of the empire. Even Ambrose made that argument. So, if the true God was on Rome's side, critics asked, why had the city fallen to the barbarians, among whom were many Arian heretics?

Augustine rose to the occasion by writing his famed *The City of God*. It is a remarkable tour de force, in which he weaves together ancient classical writings and biblical tradition, along with Greco-Roman philosophy and Christian conviction, to demonstrate the providence of God at work in human history. Central to the narrative are the cities of Babylon and Jerusalem: the one, a symbol of inevitable ruin, and the other, of redemption. For Augustine, the root cause of the fall of Rome was the fall of Adam. What happened in the garden of Eden, whether you read the story as history or myth, was the original or primordial sin that inevitably led to the fall of the tower of Babel. That same pattern, repeated in the subsequent decline of other empires, was now the fate of Rome.[13]

Rome fell for many reasons. Among them were pandemics, economic depression, a lack of patriotism and civic virtue, deep social divisions, and a reliance on conscripted soldiers from conquered territories. But Augustine probed more deeply. Rome, like Babylon, fell because it had become corrupt and unjust. The root cause was human arrogance and pride, the deadliest of sins because it makes us desire to be "like God," determining what is good and evil according to our own self-interest.[14] Interpreting Augustine, Hans von Campenhausen puts it succinctly. Rome fell, he says, because "the real basis of life, justice, which upholds men and kingdoms, was absent, and in its place came impious pride, the *superbia* [pride] of man."[15]

If *superbia* was the underlying cause, Christians were unwittingly also to blame for having claimed that by adopting Christianity the empire would automatically have the protection of God. Christians may not have caused the fall of Rome, but they should not have believed that God was on the side of the empire, irrespective of what the empire did, in the first place. The God of Jesus Christ, Augustine's God, is not a tribal god existing to protect one's own town, nation, or empire whether right or wrong. The God of Augustine holds so-called Christian nations accountable to God's law, even more so than pagan empires, because they should know better. This was exactly what the ancient prophets of Israel had told their people. In a memorable passage, Augustine writes:

> Set justice aside then, and what are kingdoms but fair thievish purchases. For what are thieves' purchases but little kingdoms, for in thefts the hands of the underlings are directed by the commander, the confederacy of them is sworn together, and the pillage is shared by the law among them?[16]

He goes on to say that "those ragamuffins," once they have achieved power, use it to subvert the law because they make themselves the lawgivers.[17] In other words, lawlessness reigns under the guise of law when those who have power grasp absolute control. So, the civic and imperial

13. Augustine, *The City of God (De Civitate Dei)*, book 14, chapter 28, 2:58–59.
14. See Genesis 3:1–7.
15. Campenhausen, *Tradition and Life in the Church*, 209.
16. Augustine, *The City of God*, book 4, chapter 4, 1:115.
17. Augustine, *The City of God*, book 4, chapter 4, 1:115.

pride that leads to greatness turns to arrogance, a sanctioning of greed and corruption, and a disregard for justice, which undermines civil society. For that reason, all empires fall, and only the city of God remains, for only the kingdom of God is eternal.

What Augustine wrote in *The City of God* connects him to what he had read years before in the *Life of Antony*. For there, Athanasius describes how Anthony left the corrupt city behind when he went into the desert, overcame the temptation of pride by living humbly before God, and attracted many followers. Thus, a new city grew and flourished in that barren land, a foretaste of the "new Jerusalem come down out of heaven."[18] The monastic city was set on a hill to give light to the world.[19] As Athanasius wrote:

> For how is it that he [i.e. Anthony] was heard of, though concealed and sitting in a mountain, in Spain and Gaul, and in Rome and Africa, unless it was the God who everywhere makes his men known who also promised this to Anthony in the beginning? For, even though they act in secret, and may want to be forgotten, the Lord shows them like lamps to everyone.[20]

In the end, Augustine did not equate the kingdom of God with the church.[21] But the true *ecclesia*, though sometimes hidden within the church, is also the visible household (*oikos*) of faith and love that is always being renewed in the life of the world.[22] The *ecclesia* of God is God's universal household or *oikumene*, which anticipates the eternal city, the new Jerusalem, among the ruins of Rome.

Augustine's theodicy does not resolve all the problems or answer all the questions raised by human and historical tragedy (no theologian from Job onwards has succeeded in doing that), and it could be argued that his pessimistic view of human nature did not inspire action to right all wrongs. But his diagnosis of the underlying problem, namely, the lack of will power to do what is right, or what Luther, following Augustine, would call "the bondage of the will," has remained pertinent ever since.[23] People and politicians, among them many Christians, may know what

---

18. Cf. Revelation 21:2.
19. Cf. Matthew 5:14.
20. Athanasius, *Life of Antony*, 99.
21. See Elshtain, *Augustine and the Limits of Politics*, 92.
22. See Milbank, *Theology and Social Theory*, 398-408.
23. Romans 7:14-25. Luther, *Martin Luther's Basic Theological Writings*, 173-226.

needs to be done but too often lack the will to do it. Despite promises and good intentions, we allow self-interest to determine our actions. So, for Augustine, the conversion of the will of the individual ruler or citizen was the key to serving the common good. But to what extent could the church be involved in politics, and to what extent should the church allow the state to influence its life?

By the time Augustine wrote *The City of God*, the church in the West was in a good institutional position to serve the needs of society. Not only did it have the political authority, but mirroring the imperial structures in its own organization, it was well organized to do so. As Richard Fletcher writes: "All the diverse services which today we would classify under the heading of 'welfare' came to be the responsibility of bishops—poor relief, public works, education, health care, hospitality for travellers, prison visiting, ransoming of captives" even "the provision of public entertainments and spectacles."[24] But God aside, where did ultimate political authority lie, and how was it to be exercised? Who had the authority to appoint bishops and convene synods, and who had control of the monasteries—the local abbot, abbess, or bishop, the prince, the emperor, or the pope?

The key figure in developing the basis for church–state relations in the West was Ambrose, Augustine's mentor and a strong supporter of monasticism. Ambrose trained as a lawyer. Before his conversion to Christ, he was governor of the province of which Milan was the capital city. After he became bishop in 374, he continued his relationships with political leaders and tried to mediate between the West and the East. But he was always a fierce advocate of the independence of the church. Most famously, he excommunicated Emperor Theodosius, a friend of his, for the massacre of innocent civilians after a riot in Thessalonica in 390, thus establishing a precedent in church–state relations. Monasticism especially was an irritant. On one occasion Theodosius threw up his hands in perplexity and demanded to know from his friend Ambrose, "What am I to do with these fanatical monks?"[25] This question would be asked time and again by emperors and other rulers through the rest of Christian history. Anthony the hermit would probably have replied, "A time is coming when men will go mad, and when they see someone who is not mad, they will attack him saying, 'You are not mad, you are not like us.'"[26]

---

24. Fletcher, *The Conversion of Europe*, 51.
25. Cochrane, *Christianity and Classical Culture*, 269.
26. Ward, trans., *The Sayings of the Desert Fathers*, 6.

The danger facing the church as an institution in Christendom was, as Ambrose was fully aware, that the church would become an agent of the state and begin to act in ways that mirrored not only its structures but also its methods, and so be seduced by its values. For the more the church began to act on behalf of the state, the greater the danger that it would act like the state; and the more the church depended on the state to protect its interests, whether in fighting heresy or securing property, the more likely it was that the church would accept its methods. That is why the development of monasticism and the monastic insistence on independence from the state, and not least from bishops appointed by the state, was so critical. This was one reason why bishops like Ambrose and Augustine, and popes like Gregory the Great (540–604), recognized the importance of monasticism and supported its development. Monasticism, they believed, had the potential to keep the church true to its vocation as a witness to the kingdom of God, which transcends all other kingdoms.

Indeed, by the Middle Ages monasteries and monastics wielded considerable political power from Salisbury in England to Kiev in Russia. The fact of the matter is that after the fall of Rome and the demise of the empire in the West, the only credible authority was the papacy. And as many popes were themselves monks, there was always a close relationship between the monasteries and the papacy. Even the establishment of the Holy Roman Empire in 800 with the coronation of Charlemagne by Pope Leo III in Rome did not diminish the spiritual authority of the papacy, or much of its temporal power. And, as we shall see, the monasteries became a crucial agent for the far-reaching social reforms instituted by Charlemagne.

The struggle between church and state, and especially the question of investiture (that is, whether emperors, monarchs, and princes had the authority to appoint popes and bishops), would continue for a long time. Much of it had to do with the balance between lay and clerical control of the church, and the role of the church in influencing political policy even where there was a theoretical division between church and state. The problem is complex. Sometimes monarchs and states may well serve the church better than its own leaders if the latter fail to provide moral leadership. Certainly, after the establishment of the Holy Roman Empire, Charlemagne played a good and critical role in the reorganization of both the church and the monasteries at a time when they were in disarray. But the power of the emperor fluctuated, and its relationship to the power of the papacy reached a new low when in 1077 the monastic Pope Gregory VII brought Emperor Henry IV to his knees in the snow at Canossa.

The problem of the relationship between church and state has continued through the centuries. It played a critical role at the time of the Protestant Reformation when nation-states challenged the authority of the papacy, established their own state churches, and dissolved the monasteries. And, of course, the relationship between church and state at this monastic moment has to do with speaking truth to power whether in a democracy or a more totalitarian state. This is certainly a critical issue if, as Thomas Merton says, the future of monasticism has to do with its prophetic witness in society.

The Triumph of Grace

Shortly before the Goths razed Rome, an austere British monk called Pelagius (354–418) fled the city for Carthage, en route to Palestine. Once in Africa he expressed his feelings about Augustine's theology. He was especially repulsed by a prayer in the *Confessions*: "Give what you command and command what you will."[27] For Augustine, this had to do with the personal choice he had to make about celibacy, but for Pelagius it promoted the repugnant idea that God did not know what he was doing when he gave us the freedom to choose.[28] Pelagius's comments incensed Augustine. He knew from experience as well as the Bible that it is not we who choose God but God who chooses us. To think otherwise was heresy being promoted by a monk who should have known better.

Pelagius's starting point was his rejection of Augustine's doctrine of original sin. We humans are not born in sin, he insisted, but in innocence, and God has given us the ability to choose between what is good and bad, and the freedom to follow Christ or not. Our salvation depends on whether we use that freedom rightly and decide to live according to God's will. Even if grace provides us with the means to be saved, we must choose to follow the way of Christ, which leads us to eternal life. Making that choice and living a moral life that pleases God is our responsibility. It all sounds eminently sensible—in fact, something I learned in Sunday school. But, for Augustine, it contradicted the gospel of God's saving grace that precedes any effort of our own to save ourselves.

27. Augustine, *Confessions*, book 10, chapter 27, 225.
28. See Bettenson, ed., *Documents of the Christian Church*, 74–75.

We are "conceived in sin," as Psalm 51 tells us, Augustine reminded Pelagius, and we are therefore sinners from birth.[29] St Paul also tells us that even if we want to do what is good, we cannot, for we are always inclined to do what is wrong.[30] The sorry saga began when Adam freely chose to disobey God. Whereas God had created him free, with the ability not to sin, once he had sinned, he was unable not to sin. In other words, his choice embedded sin in our spiritual DNA. According to the Genesis saga, that set off a train of events that led Cain to kill his brother Abel and subsequently to all manner of evil, including the collapse of the tower of Babel and the fall of Rome. The only antidote to this predicament is God's free, prevenient grace, for our redemption depends totally on God. That is why Christ died on the cross and was raised to life, and that is the good news Christians proclaim: the triumph of grace.

Combatting Pelagianism occupied a great deal of Augustine's time, though far less that of Pelagius, who was not interested in debate and soon withdrew into monastic seclusion with Jerome in Bethlehem. Pelagianism was condemned as a heresy by a council made up largely of African bishops held in Carthage in 412, but it remained influential in a modified form known as Semi-Pelagianism, though it might equally be called Semi-Augustinianism, which is probably the position of most Christians today. Later, at the Council of Orange in 539, Semi-Pelagianism was also condemned, but its influence continued, not least in Western monasticism. While all this might seem to be splitting hairs, it was a watershed in the development of Christianity in the West. As von Campenhausen remarks, Augustine's "anti-Pelagian dogma marks a theological boundary... behind which Latin Christianity... could never fall back to the level of pre-Augustinian moralism and rationalism." From then on, God's prevenient grace or predestination, became "the central idea of Latin theology."[31] Augustine, as the seventeenth-century painter Claudio Coello (1642–1693) portrayed him, was triumphant. He was a father of the Latin Church and a Catholic saint whose imprint on the church and monasticism in the West would have lasting consequences.

Not only has Augustine's doctrine of predestination been a very divisive doctrine in the Western Church, separating Luther from Erasmus, Calvinists from Arminians, and, in South Africa, ultra-Calvinists

---

29. Psalm 51:5
30. See Romans 7.
31. Campenhausen, *The Fathers of the Latin Church*, 255.

from Andrew Murray Jr., but it has perplexed and bothered many ordinary Christians who are rightly repulsed by the idea that God chooses some but not all to be saved. Certainly the fourteenth-century anchoress Julian of Norwich was among them, and her *Revelations* or *Showings* have gained considerable contemporary attention. She did not deny God's foreknowledge in saving humanity, but insisted that God's is "the most tender and maternal providence that loved humanity before he created it, and that continually works through mercy and grace, to save and not condemn."[32] The more recent popularity of Matthew Fox's *Original Blessing* is another indication of the desire to find an alternative to the deeply entrenched Augustinian tradition.[33] And Fox, of course, draws deeply from monastic sources in developing his "creation spirituality," including the writings of Meister Eckhart, the fifteenth-century mystic, and Hildegard of Bingen, whom we will meet later.

Augustine may be a revered Catholic saint, but he is not a favorite Eastern Orthodox one; in fact, he is generally regarded as the theologian largely responsible for the eventual division of the Catholic and Eastern Orthodox Churches. Certainly, his views on predestination are regarded by Orthodoxy as fundamentally flawed. The error lies, as Vladimir Lossky says, in "transposing the mystery of grace on to a rational plane" and therefore making grace and works two mutually exclusive concepts. By arguing against Pelagius on the latter's own terms, Augustine compounded the problem.[34] And as his teaching on "grace and the freedom of the will developed and spread across the West," becoming more accentuated in the process, says Lossky, it lost contact with the Eastern tradition, which has "always asserted simultaneity in the synergy of divine grace and human freedom."[35]

Nevertheless, who cannot but be moved by Augustine's prayer, which is a far better exposition of the triumph of grace than his more scholarly, polemical treatment:

> Too late have I loved you, O Beauty so ancient and so new. Too late have I loved you! You were within me, but I was outside myself, and there I sought you! I heedlessly ran after the beauty of the things you have made. You were with me, but I was not with

---

32. Rolf, *Julian's Gospel*, 294.
33. Matthew Fox, *Original Blessing*.
34. Lossky, *The Mystical Theology of the Eastern Church*, 198.
35. Lossky, *The Mystical Theology of the Eastern Church*, 199.

you. These things kept me far from you—things that only exist because they exist in you! You called and cried out aloud and pierced my deafness. You radiated forth and shone brightly and chased away my blindness. You breathed out your fragrance, and I breathed it in. Now I yearn for you. I tasted, and now I hunger and thirst for you. You touched me, and I burn with desire for your peace.[36]

Monastics have revered Augustine's *Confessions*, sermons, Bible commentaries, and teaching on the love of the triune God, rather than his polemical scholastic treatises. As Jean Leclercq says, the influence of Augustine on monastics has mainly been on inner illumination and the knowledge of God and the self, on mysticism rather than on scholastic speculation.[37] And, in this regard, Augustine was also closer to Eastern Orthodoxy, which reflects the influence of Neoplatonism on both. So maybe we should remember him above all as a profoundly spiritual pastor-bishop. His life ended as the Vandals invaded North Africa. Standing in solidarity with his clergy, who were tempted but forbidden to flee, he cared for the refugees that flooded into Hippo, melting down the golden vessels in his church "to alleviate their misery."[38]

The Goal of Monasticism

If Augustine laid the foundations for Western monasticism, it was John Cassian who best interpreted the Eastern monastic tradition within the West. Cassian, who was ordained a deacon in Constantinople, became a protégé of Evagrius, then a monk in Bethlehem, following which he joined the Coptic hermits in the Egyptian desert. Finally, he settled in a monastery in Marseilles. It was largely due to Cassian that Gaul, and especially Provence, soon became the center of monasticism in the West. From there it spread rapidly across western Europe. By the sixth century there were about two hundred monasteries in Gaul, the most influential being in Lerins and Arles.

Cassian's legacy has been handed down through his *Institutes*, written to help monastics achieve Christian perfection, and his *Conferences*,

---

36. Augustine, *Confessions*, book 10, chapter 27, 224. I have modernized this translation.
37. Leclercq, *The Love of Learning and the Desire for God*, 221.
38. Campenhausen, *The Fathers of the Latin Church*, 275.

which are reports of his discussions with hermits in Nitria and Scete in the Egyptian desert.[39] These are the source for much of what we know about the desert fathers and mothers today. Owen Chadwick sums up Cassian's character and significance: "No one who reads Cassian for long can doubt that this is a prayerful and pious mind," but Cassian also was gifted with "a powerful mind, integrated and constructive. This is one of the leading Fathers of the ancient church, though too long unrecognized as such except by Benedictine monks."[40]

Cassian it is who sets the direction for the evolution of monasticism in the West by integrating the austere asceticism of the desert into the evolving monastic pattern that would characterize medieval monasticism. He is the pioneer of the "middle Way," or monastic "balance," and therefore his work, says Chadwick, was "a protection against excess, and a constant call to that primitive simplicity where Eastern spirituality met Western."[41] It is Cassian who lays the foundation for "the medieval idea of the fusion, or interpenetration, between corporate psalmody and private aspiration; prayerfulness enriching worship in church, worship in church lending a structure and a series of ordered moments to prayerfulness."[42]

In the first of his *Conferences*, Cassian recalls what he learned from Abba Moses in the desert in Scete where there were "hermits of highest repute and spiritual perfection."[43] His question to the venerable abba concerned the monk's goal. The final goal is to achieve the kingdom of heaven, but the more immediate goal, said the abba, is purity of heart. It is, he said, "for this end . . . that we do and endure everything."[44] And this purity of heart is nothing less than perfect love. All spiritual disciplines only serve this purpose. If this goal is not their aim, they are of no value. Asceticism then becomes selfish and unworthy. That is why monasteries are not meant to be places in which to escape from the world, but places of retreat to serve the world better, and therefore havens of hospitality for those in need. Thus, with Cassian, followed later by Benedict, hospitality becomes a central and determining feature of monastic life.[45] Every

---

39. See Merton, *Cassian and the Fathers*, 71–80.
40. Introduction to Cassian, *Conferences*, 2.
41. Introduction to Cassian, *Conferences*, 36.
42. Cassian, *Conferences*, 19.
43. Cassian, *Conference 1*, 195.
44. Cassian, *Conferences*, 41.
45. See Kardong, *Benedict's Rule*, 431–35.

person who knocks on the door of the monastery, Benedict would say, is to be welcomed with courtesy and love as if he or she were "Christ, for he himself will say: *I was a stranger and you welcomed me*" (Matthew 25:35).[46]

Equally important is Cassian's attempt to balance prayer and work, and in doing so he rejects the notion that only the former is spiritual. For him, the active and the contemplative life had to be integrated. If you pray without working you starve, and if you work without praying, says Cassian, you might as well be a farmer—though he would have also encouraged farmers to pray. In a similar vein, Cassian stressed balance in all matters. He was an advocate of the ascetic life but an opponent of fanaticism. He was respectful of miracles but more concerned about charity and humility. In sum, he was a practical mystic with both feet on the ground—a respecter of the saints and martyrs, but an opponent of superstition attached to their relics; a critic of intellectualizing the faith, but also an advocate of true learning in which there is a reciprocity between heart and mind. Above all, reading and meditation on the Bible was meant to touch the heart, not just inform the mind. As Chadwick observes, Cassian stressed the need for exercising discretion in all matters, that is, avoiding extremes and finding the middle way.[47] In reading Cassian, I am reminded of Bonhoeffer's comments in his *Ethics* on the need to avoid both radicalism and compromise in seeking to do the "will of God," because:

> Radicalism hates time. Compromise hates eternity.
> Radicalism hates patience. Compromise hates decision.
> Radicalism hates wisdom. Compromise hates simplicity.
> Radicalism hates measure. Compromise hates the immeasurable.
> Radicalism hates the real. Compromise hates the word.[48]

Cassian, then, is a key figure, not only in interpreting the legacy of desert monasticism in the West, but also in helping us connect the desire for God with the love of learning and the struggle for justice. And yet, although at first he was an acknowledged saint in the Catholic Church, he was eventually downgraded and declared a heretic because of his Semi-Pelagianism. That was surely an unfair accusation, demonstrating how easy it is to judge people without understanding them. For Cassian

---

46. Benedict, chapter 50, verse 1 (*RB 1980*, 255; italics original).
47. Cassian, *Conferences*, 21–23.
48. Bonhoeffer, *Ethics*, 156.

acknowledged the priority of grace in seeking a balance between faith and good works.

We are saved by grace and cannot choose rightly without the grace and the help of God, but that does not mean we are not free to choose, or that we should not be disciplined in trying to do so as we strive for perfection. So, in *Conference* 1, Cassian discusses the "goal or objective of the monk," based on his conversation with Abbot Moses in the desert. That object is to "enter the kingdom of God," and the means to that end is a "pure heart." That is why, says the abba, "we must practice the reading of the Scripture, together with all other virtuous activities, and we do so to trap and to hold our hearts free of the harm of every dangerous passion and in order to rise step by step to the high point of love."[49]

To illustrate his point, Cassian refers us to Jesus's parable of the prodigal son, who, in the pigsty, came to the realization that he was not worthy to be called a son of his father. He then recognized the horror of his situation and how much better it would be back home, even as a hired hand. So, he turned to go back to his father, who "rushed forward to meet him," embraced him and "restored him to his former rank as son."[50] This illustrated what is, for Cassian and, following him, Benedict, and later Bernard of Clairvaux, the fundamental monastic vow, namely, the "conversion of manners." This is the journey towards the Father that requires an ongoing conversion of the will (*metanoia*), a continual turning towards God.

This, also called the "ladder of divine ascent"[51] by John Climacus (579–649), a monk of Mount Sinai, is not simply an inward journey, for it requires works of charity, and the disciplines necessary to achieve perfection are inseparable from the struggle for justice. So writes Cassian, reflecting the wisdom of the desert fathers:

> Their workings here would not be required were it not for the superabundant numbers of the poor, the needy and the sick. These are here because of the iniquity of men who have held for their own private use what the common Creator has made available for all. As long as the inequity rages in the world, these good works will be necessary and valuable to anyone practicing

---

49. Cassian, *Conferences*, 21–23.
50. Cassian, *Conferences*, 145.
51. John Climacus, *The Ladder*.

them and they shall yield the reward of an everlasting inheritance to the man of good heart and concerned will.[52]

Only when inequity and injustice are finally overcome will we contemplate the divine love, which is the true knowledge of God. It is then that the "pure in heart see God,"[53] for then good works will have passed away and only love will endure.[54]

In a letter to his friend John Harris, an English schoolteacher, Merton tells us that Cassian wrote down everything that the desert fathers "could be cajoled into saying, for none of them was very talkative." But, when he went to Marseilles, Cassian's book became a monastic best seller. Even though he was suspected of heresy, no one stopped reading him for that reason. After all, says Merton, "the heresy is just one little sentence he quoted from an old Desert Father one hundred years old . . . who could not be perfectly accurate on the fine shades of the doctrine of grace!"[55] And there we must, at least for the moment, leave the never-ending debate about faith and works, God's grace and human freedom, and turn to Benedict, who found help in Cassian's middle way while writing his famous *Rule*.

A School for Disciples

By the sixth century, with political authority in tatters, the only stability left in the West was the papacy. Fortunately, this was also the time of one of the greatest popes, St Gregory the Great, a key figure in the development of Western monasticism. Gregory was himself a monk; a great Bible teacher; a far-sighted overseer; and a contemplative influenced by the desert fathers, by Basil, Cassian, and Dionysius, as well as by Augustine. He was also the biographer of Benedict, and virtually all we know about Benedict is what we are told by Gregory in his *Dialogues*.[56]

Benedict, Gregory tells us, was born in Norcia, a small town northeast of Rome where he was later educated and experienced the immorality of the age. In reaction he decided to become a hermit and live in solitude in a cave in nearby Subiaco. But soon a community began to

52. Cassian, *Conferences*, 45.
53. Matthew 5:8.
54. 1 Corinthians 13:8.
55. Merton, *The Hidden Ground of Love*, 397.
56. Gregory the Great, *The Life of St Benedict*, 1993.

gather around him, which led him to form twelve monasteries of twelve monastics each, mostly laymen, with himself as abbot. Eventually, the locals forced him to move. So, in 525, taking his sister Scholastica (480–543) and all the monks with him, he went to Monte Cassino where he established what became the most famous of all Benedictine monasteries. The monastery at Monte Cassino eventually became an enormous "city on a hill," featuring an extensive library of manuscripts and books, many of them unique. Over the centuries it was sacked by succeeding invaders (among them Saracens and Normans) and destroyed by an earthquake, but always rebuilt, as it was after being bombed by the Allies during the Second World War.

It was at Monte Cassino that Benedict wrote his famous *Rule*, drawing on those of Pachomius, Augustine, Basil, Cassian, and Columbanus (543–615), a Celtic monk and saint who had settled in Gaul. Most directly, Benedict based his *Rule* on the anonymous collection known as the *Rule of the Master*, probably written a few decades before he wrote his own.[57] This was an extensive document of detailed regulations; but unlike most others, it also provided theological reasons and spiritual counsel. Its ninety-five chapters begin with a long introduction comprising a prologue, and a parable "of the spring" based on Jesus's saying, "Take my yoke upon you and learn from me, for I am meek and humble of heart."[58]

Benedict's *Rule* is much shorter and closer to Cassian's in spirit. He excludes many details about observances and adapts much in the light of his own experience as a monk and abbot.[59] The prologue opens with an admonition: "Listen carefully to the master's instructions and attend to them with the ear of your heart."[60] All else follows from this, especially the "labor of obedience." The *Rule* then instructs us to pray about what we are doing, asking God for guidance, to control our tongues, turn away from evil, and pursue peace. This is the way of life we should follow "with the Gospel for our guide." But we will never arrive in God's kingdom "unless we run there by doing good deeds." We must struggle against the "evil one" and learn to live by God's grace, as we daily translate the Lord's teaching into action. Benedict insists that he is not asking for anything "harsh or burdensome." But he does not downplay the cost of

57. See Preface, in Earle, trans., *Rule of the Master*, 8, and Pfeifer, "The Rule of St Benedict," 70–72, 79–83.

58. Matthew 11:29.

59. Pfeifer, "The Rule of St. Benedict," 90–96.

60. Benedict, prologue, verse 1 (*RB 1980*, 157).

discipleship, for monks are engaged in a "battle of holy obedience," and the road to life "is narrow," especially "at the outset." Yet it is "the road that leads to salvation." So, while the costs involved might not be "possible to us by nature," we should ask the Lord for the "help of his grace."

Benedict ends his prologue by telling us that the monastery is "a school for the Lord's service." He only uses the word *scholia* once in the sense of a school or workshop for attaining wisdom rather than gaining knowledge. The monastery is not an academy but a house of formation. Monastics are meant to study the Scriptures to be faithful disciples of Christ. Their practice of *lectio divina* was not a critical reading of the Bible but a contemplative discerning of what the Spirit of Christ is saying to us as disclosed in Scripture and woven into the daily rhythm of prayer, silence, work, and study.[61] Holding it all together is a lifelong commitment made at profession, to a life of stability and celibacy within a particular monastic community, obedience to Christ and the abbot, who represents Christ, and the daily conversion of life worthy of the gospel and the monastic calling, that is, the "conversion of manners." Taken together, these vows as they are commonly named, are, as Merton says, a commitment to Christian discipleship.[62]

There has been much debate about what the phrase *conversatio morum suorum* ("conversion of manners") meant for those who first read Benedict's *Rule*, and what it might mean today. But it is undoubtedly best understood as an ongoing changing of attitude and behavior.[63] Many people within the framework of Christendom who are brought up as Christians baptized in infancy have an "evangelical conversion" sometime later in life, often during adolescence, as happened to me. But that is only a fresh beginning of their lives as lived more consciously committed to Christ, though sometimes it can be as dramatic as was the conversion of Augustine. However, and whenever it happens, it is not an end, but only a significant part of our journey in the knowledge and grace of Christ. My Methodist grandparents knew this when they quoted St Paul on the flyleaf of the Bible they gave me when I was baptized as a baby.[64] By "conversion of manners," Benedict is telling us precisely the same: the Christian life is a process of never-ending conversion of life in Christ

---

61. See, Draper, *Listening to God*.
62. See O'Connell's introduction in Merton, *The Life of the Vows*, lxvi, lxxi.
63. See the discussion in Pfeifer, "Monastic Formation and Profession," 457–66.
64. 2 Timothy 2:1

through the Spirit. This, indeed, is what *metanoia* or repentance really means, the ongoing transformation of life which, as Merton tells us, is really what the monastic life is all about.[65] And for him, that meant both an inward and an outward journey.

With that in mind, Benedict provides practical monastic guidance for meals, sleeping, hospitality, making decisions, maintaining silence at specific times, going on retreat, the treatment of artisans working at the monastery, private ownership, traveling beyond the monastery, and looking after tools. Everything monastics do matters, for life cannot be easily separated into the secular and sacred, because it is all interconnected and related. How you behave in the kitchen or at meals is as important as how you pray and worship, and how you look after your tools in the workshop is as important as the way you look after the chapel. Most important is the election and the responsibilities of the abbot, for much is left to his discretion as the one who must interpret the *Rule* according to the needs of each monastic as well as the community. This makes humility and obedience indispensable in the life of the monastery. All of this has to do with the "conversion of manners."

Overall, in comparison with the *Rule of the Master*, in the spirit of Cassian, Benedict puts more emphasis on mutual love between monastics, on the community as a family. His *Rule*, it has been said, "manifests a certain liberalism and humanism" in the original sense of these terms. Benedict "knows that human persons and actions are of infinite variety and complexity," with different strengths and weaknesses. He wants to ensure that each monastic under his care grows fully as a Christian according to his or her own character and the circumstances under which they are living.[66] So Benedict eschews legalism in favor of flexibility; he is realistic and patient, and essentially evangelical, for everything hinges on the gospel.

The *Rule*, as Benedict insists, is only a beginning; it points the way forward. Being historically conditioned, it is open to fresh interpretation in different contexts. Those "hastening on to perfection in the monastic life," he writes, should consult the fathers and other monastic writers, such as Cassian, but especially the Old and New Testaments, which are the "truest guides for human life."[67] Purity of heart is the goal, for it is

---

65. Merton, "Marxism and Monastic Perspectives," 340.
66. Pfeifer, "The Rule of St Benedict," 93.
67. Benedict, chapter 73, verses 2–3 (*RB 1980*, 297).

only once we have overcome inner turmoil and outer distraction, and surrendered self-will, that we can listen to what the Spirit is saying, and that takes us beyond *Rules* and structures into evangelical freedom. In sum, "St Benedict's monks are indeed disciples under a master, come to the *scholia* to be trained, but they are also brothers to one another, bound together by ties of mutual charity and support."[68] This is the core of the *Rule*, for keeping all the rules and rhythms of monastic life without love is not meaningful.[69]

Benedict's *Rule* was written specifically for his monastery at Monte Casino. He did not envisage that it would have a universal and lasting impact on church or society. But it did so because it provided a guide for maintaining stable communities during a period when instability was endemic across European society. It was recognized as gathering up the best in monastic practice from earliest times; it was less austere and more balanced than most other *Rules*; it was better suited to the Roman/Latin cultural legacy of the empire than Celtic, Greek or Coptic *Rules*; and, not least, Benedict's *Rule* was strongly advocated by Pope Gregory the Great, who placed the monasteries under his patronage. It remains the definitive guide for Benedictine monastics with the gospel as their final authority.[70]

Many books have been written on the perennial value of St Benedict's *Rule*—not only for monastics, but for other Christians as well. One such book that has helped many people is Esther de Waal's *A Life-Giving Way*, in which she writes:

> This short and simple text has become a source and spring to which I return time and again. I have found that it is ancient wisdom ever new, and that, as I come to it with fresh questions and demands, so it continues to yield up its riches. Through the *Rule* I have been helped to deepen my understanding of my Christian faith and to strengthen Christian discipleship.[71]

Benedict, de Waal continues, "accepts the frailty of our human nature and works with that . . . He is never looking for blind obedience or outward observance . . . but to the interior motive and intention, to the inner disposition of the heart. It is this, above all, that I have seen as the central

68. Pfeifer, "The Rule of St Benedict," 93.
69. See especially Benedict, chapter 72, verses 3–8 (*RB 1980*, 295).
70. See Rees, *Consider Your Call*, 49.
71. De Waal, *A Life-Giving Way*, xix.

thread running through the *Rule*."[72] In a world that was fast descending deeper into the chaos of the Dark Ages, Benedict, like Noah, built an ark, "which lasted not only for one troubled century but for fifteen," and this ark still has "the capacity to bring many safe to land."[73] A guide that we likewise need at this monastic moment.

Celtic Monks & Pilgrims

Given that the monastery was for Benedict a place of hospitality, it is not surprising that Benedictine monasteries have long been major centers of pilgrimage, often situated on the crossroads from Canterbury to Rome, Paris to the Holy Land, and along the many routes of the Camino de Santiago de Compostela. Of course, pilgrimages were sometimes undertaken for the wrong reason. Early on St Basil warned against the danger of regarding pilgrimage as a way of obtaining divine merit.[74] But undertaken for the right reason it was, and remains for many, an opportunity to know oneself better and in the process come to a fresh understanding of God. Pilgrimages remind us of our journey into the mystery of God.

Going on pilgrimage, or *peregrenatio*, was also close to a monastic's heart because it was associated with ascetic "homelessness." As the Letter to the Hebrews puts it, "here we have no lasting city."[75] Abraham's wanderings and Israel's journey through the wilderness were the prototypes of pilgrimage as a means for finding one's way in life, an expression of faith in God's guidance and providence for the journey. The model pilgrim was St Martin, the bishop of Tours (316–397), who set up his cell in a foreign land far from home and travelled a great deal until he finally settled in Poitiers. He then founded a monastery at Ligugé in Gaul from where monasticism began to spread elsewhere.

But the most intrepid of all were the fearless Celtic pilgrims, who in the sixth and seventh centuries traveled back and forth across Europe, from Ireland to Egypt, before settling down in Gaul, Germania, or Rome. What was striking about these Celtic monastic missionaries was, as William Dalrymple comments, that "they deliberately sought out the most

---

72. De Waal, *A Life-Giving Way*, xix.
73. De Waal, *Seeking God*, 15.
74. See Campenhausen, *Tradition and Life in the Church*, 237–39.
75. Hebrews 13:14.

wild and deserted places... where they could find the solitude that, they believed, would lead them to God."⁷⁶

Monasticism, associated with St Patrick (390–460), the "apostle of the Irish," was well established in Ireland and the islands on the west coast of Scotland by the fourth century. Indeed, it played a much greater role in the life of the church in Ireland than probably anywhere else, and the Irish church was widely known for its monastic asceticism. It was from Ireland that monks first set out on missionary journeys across Anglo-Saxon Britain and Europe, most notably Germany. St Columba (521–597), a nobleman trained in Irish monasteries, who founded Iona Abbey around 563, was instrumental in the evangelization of Scotland; he was followed by St Columbanus (543–615), who first settled in southern Gaul. Columbanus's strict asceticism did not win him many friends, so he soon moved on and established monasteries in northern Italy. These became well-known centers of learning, and there Columbanus wrote many influential tracts, including several *Rules* for monks.

So austere was the first Celtic missionary sent from Iona to convert the Anglo-Saxons, a little known Celt by the name of Corman, that he was forced to abandon his mission because he found the English too obstinate and barbaric, totally unwilling to accept any discipline, let alone the gospel.⁷⁷ It was then that Iona sent St Aidan to do the job of converting the English, and it was he who established the "Holy Island" of Lindisfarne, on the northeast coast. This soon became an educational and missionary center for converting the Anglo-Saxons until its destruction by Viking marauders in the ninth century. But well before then, the Irish and Scottish monks remaining on Lindisfarne left for Iona because they rejected the new discipline that was being imposed on them by the Synod of Whitby in 664.

The events that led up to the Synod of Whitby, a significant turning point in English church history, are graphically described by St Bede (673–735) in his famous *Ecclesiastical History of the English People*, written in 731—the earliest of all histories of the English. The main point of controversy was the dating of Easter, though behind that lay the question of the authority of the pope and therefore of the preeminence of the Roman Church. A minor issue was that of the style of a monk's tonsure, which may seem a trivial matter to us, but which was obviously

---

76. Dalrymple, *From the Holy Mountain*, 106.
77. The story is told in Mitton, *Restoring the Woven Cord*, 13.

important for some at that time. Nevertheless, Bede praises the austerity of the monks at Lindisfarne, and comments that they "were so free from all taint of avarice that none of them would accept lands or possessions to build monasteries, unless compelled to by the secular authorities."[78]

But the Roman Church won at Whitby largely because by then Catholic Christianity was gaining ground across England following its reestablishment by Pope Gregory the Great at the end of the sixth century. To reestablish Catholic Christianity, Gregory sent a team of Benedictine monks led by a later-day Augustine (d. 605) to establish the church in Canterbury and to reorganize the church in England. The subsequent influence of Benedictine monasticism in England was enormous. Not only did it largely replace Celtic Christianity, but its growth was exponential.[79] Invariably succeeding generations of English bishops, St Dunstan (909–988) being one of the outstanding examples, were monks, and some were prominent public leaders. Among them were also remarkable Anglo-Saxon nuns who pioneered monasticism among women in England, namely, St Hilda (614–680), the abbess of Whitby, and St Etheldreda (d. 679) of Ely.[80] Both Hilda and Etheldreda were superiors or abbesses of "double monasteries"—that is, monasteries of both women and men, which were common in England until the Viking raids in the ninth century.

Despite the victory of Benedictine Christianity at Whitby, the Celtic spirit lived on in various parts of the British Isles. Ian Bradley, who has done much to interpret Celtic spirituality, speaks of seven revivals of interest in Celtic Christianity over the past thirteen hundred years. During these centuries, he says, "it has been invented and re-invented to suit the agenda of successive generations of Christians."[81] What is of particular interest to me is that Bradley connects Celtic Christianity to Bonhoeffer's "new monasticism" and the development of intentional communities today,[82] as I discovered in conversation with Bradley himself when he visited our community at Volmoed in 2019. Among these is the Northumbrian Community, located not far from Lindisfarne, whose *Celtic Daily*

---

78. Bede, *The Ecclesiastical History*, 161.
79. See Farmer, ed., *Benedict's Disciples*.
80. Bede, *The Ecclesiastical History*, 210–14.
81. Bradley, *Following the Celtic Way*, 7.
82. Bradley, *Following the Celtic Way*, 142.

Prayer book Isobel and I first used in 1998.[83] Celtic Christianity has too often been romanticized in the modern West, or regarded as an equivalent of Catholic, Orthodox, or Coptic Christianity, or as a denomination of some kind. But it cannot be conflated with the former or confused with the latter. It is, rather, a type of Christian spirituality that is demanding, countercultural, and essentially monastic.

Just as Celtic monks were the first to evangelize Britain, they were also the pioneers who evangelized western Europe. And they were as courageous as they were austere. However, they were essentially hermits by nature, rather than ecclesiastical organizers, so the early evangelization of Europe was a piecemeal affair. Even the Benedictine from Devon, St Boniface (680–754), and those missionary monks who followed him to Germany in the late seventh and early eighth centuries, were not guided by any comprehensive missionary strategy. In addition, pockets of paganism meant tough resistance to Christianity's spread in Europe. So, "the acceptance of Christianity . . . was mostly slow, uneven and faced powerful and stubborn resistance and hence many setbacks." Moreover, the very concept of mission, unlike in the first centuries of Christianity and our own, did not "have the same connotations."[84] The life and structure of the church needed a great deal of renewal and reorganization if it was going to fulfill its missionary task in the new Holy Roman Empire that emerged to unite Western Christendom after the collapse of the Roman Empire. No one knew this better than Charlemagne (768–814), who was crowned emperor by Pope Leo III in Rome on Christmas Day in 800.

Medieval Splendor

To achieve the unity of Christendom under the dual authority of himself as emperor and of the pope, Charlemagne introduced comprehensive social and ecclesiastical reforms, which became known as the Carolingian reforms. In fact, Charlemagne demonstrated the benefits of Christendom if the ruler involved had the insight and commitment necessary to implement good governance in the state and the church. Charlemagne also had an interest in theological matters, and he assembled many able

---

83. Raine and Skinner, comps., *Celtic Daily Prayer*; see also Northumbria Community, "Story of the Community" (web page) (www.northumbriacommunity.org/who-we-are/story-of-the-community/).

84. Tellenbach, *The Church in Western Europe*, 7.

clerical scholars, including some from Constantinople, to assist in making and implementing policy. Most important of these reforming scholars was the English monk Alcuin (735–804), an archetypical Christian humanist from York, whose influence was far-reaching on many levels.[85] Among these reforms were the reestablishment of the hierarchy, church discipline, the unity of the liturgy, the clarification of doctrine, and the education of clergy.

The monasteries were a key element in implementing these reforms, but they themselves needed to be reformed to fulfill this role. Too many were lax in discipline, the subject of popular derision and prophetic condemnation. Their reformation required that they should all more strictly follow the same *Rule*, namely, that of Benedict; use the same liturgies; diligently maintain the Catholic faith; and remain loyal to the papacy and emperor. The key figure in helping to achieve this goal was St Benedict of Aniane (750–821), a rigorous ascetic and interpreter of Benedict's *Rule* who initiated the reforms, starting in his own monastery in Languedoc, before doing so across much of the rest of the empire.

But parish and monastic bells, which had become common across Europe during the Middle Ages, were already sounding an alarm throughout the empire. In 793, shortly before Charlemagne's coronation, the island monastery of Lindisfarne was brutally attacked by Vikings, literally "sea-raiders." For the next two hundred years waves of Scandinavian pagan warriors, whose chief god Odin demanded human sacrifice, wreaked havoc from Ireland to Spain and North Africa, and from Gaul and Italy to Russia. Villages were burned, churches and monasteries destroyed, and priests and monastics put to the sword.[86] Even as late as 1013, London was overrun, and a Dane, Sven Forkbeard, was declared king of England.

Following the Battle of Chartres in 911, the Franks negotiated peace with the Vikings, granting them land on the west coast which became known as Normandy, a decision with far-reaching consequences for the Vikings, the Franks, and England. Within the next century, the descendants of the Vikings (among whom were my paternal ancestors) were "Christianized, Romanized, and feudalized,"[87] before engaging in the conquest of England in 1066. These Norman converts to Christianity

85. Knowles, *The Evolution of Medieval Thought*, 72–73.
86. Latourette, *A History of the Expansion of Christianity*, 2:107–8. On Vikings and Christianity, see Price, *The Children of Ash and Elm*.
87. Tellenbach, *The Church in Western Europe*, 13.

may not have understood what Christian faith and discipleship really meant any more than did the people who followed Constantine into the church in the fourth century. But accepting baptism was part of the peace negotiations—and, at least, peace meant that the Carolingian reforms could restart. The Normans became party to the process, monasteries were restored, and a new era of monastic growth began.

The famous Benedictine monastery at Cluny in Burgundy was founded in 909 even before peace had been achieved. But it was only under St Odo (879-942), its second and most notable abbot, that many new monasteries, estimated at more than two thousand, were established. It was only then that Cluniac reforms, supported by the pope, were able to be introduced, which, writes Steven Ozment, "brought a new religious discipline and sense of purpose to the western church at the papal, episcopal and parochial levels."[88]

Indeed, Cluny became the center of a wide network of great medieval monasteries, having a lasting effect on the revival of monasticism during this period.[89] In the process, monasticism became centralized and uniform in character. Monastic spirituality was contemplative rather than active, at the heart of which was the *lectio divina*. The hours of prayer in the chapel were regularized and routinely kept according to the *Rule of St Benedict* and aided by new breviaries. The *scriptorium*, which housed and preserved biblical and patristic manuscripts, became the center of monastic activity rather than agriculture. Monastics spent many hours copying manuscripts, which then generated a flowering of scholarship not seen before, as monastic scholars studied the Bible and the recently discovered writings of the ancient Greek fathers. In short,

> A great Carolingian abbey, was a vast establishment ... It might be surrounded by a town whose life was dominated by the monastery ... supported by large tracts of land worked by serfs ... the life of the monks was highly ritualized: many additional psalms and prayers were added to the Benedictine *opus dei* ... A monastery was an image in miniature of the empire itself, the earthly kingdom of God.[90]

But the development of the monasteries, Basil Pennington tells us, was not always for the good. Not only did they lose "their autonomy,"

---

88. Ozment, *The Age of Reform*, 4.
89. Leclercq et al., *The Spirituality of the Middle Ages*, 106.
90. Pfeifer, "The Rule in History," 123.

but they also lost "the balance of liturgy, sacred reading and personal prayer, and work which gave the Benedictine life its strength and characteristic simplicity."[91] The "camel's nose was already under the tent-flap."[92] The monastery was no longer just as a city set on a hill; it was an empire. What had begun as an ascetic flight from a corrupt world was now compromised through engagement in divisive political and intellectual conflicts. The liturgy reflected an elaborate courtly ceremony rather than the simplicity of the upper room, and monks, increasingly more clerical and studious, were somewhat distant from the lay brothers who tilled the fields and maintained the fabric. While monastics continued to seek God through prayer and asceticism, and some were hermits, the monastery had become an ecclesiastical institution and economic hub, much like a business or corporation. And the abbot, who now had to be an efficient administrator, often played a crucial role in the balance of power between the empire and the papacy.

If they had returned to visit these medieval monasteries, not only the ancient desert hermits, but also Cassian and Benedict, would have been astounded by what had evolved from their humble beginnings. No wonder Harnack exclaims, "what a chasm divides the silent anchorite in the desert, who for a life-time has looked no man in the face, from the monk who imposed his commands upon a world!"[93] It was this ambiguity that led Merton to warn of the danger of romanticizing monasticism. We can love it, he said, but we should understand that what we are cherishing is Christendom, indeed "the Romanitá of the Medieval and Renaissance Christian world."[94]

Perhaps it was inevitable that the grandeurs of Cluny, reflected in the many monasteries established under its jurisdiction, eventually led to a hunger among some monastics to return to the poverty and simplicity of the desert. As a result, several new orders arose, each seeking to return to a stricter life. The first was the Carthusian, established by St Bruno (1032–1101) at Grande Chartreuse in the French Alps in 1084. Bruno required that his monks vowed to keep silent, each living in his own cell within the monastery where they devoted many hours to prayer and study, and only meeting as a community for daily mass and feast day

91. Pennington, "The Cistercians," 205.

92. Pfeifer, "The Rule in History," 123.

93. Harnack, *Monasticism*, 12.

94. Merton, "Marxism and Monastic Perspectives," 340. Merton gave this lecture in Bangkok, Thailand, on December 10, 1968.

meals. This, the most austere of all monastic orders, chose as its motto *Cartusia nunquam reformata quia nunquam deformata*—"Carthusians never need to be reformed, for they have never been deformed"![95]

A second development was the Cistercians, founded by Robert of Molesmes (1027–1111). He was the founding abbot of the monastery at Molesmes, but in 1089, he and several brothers left it behind to build a new monastery in a wilderness area south of Dijon known as Citeaux.[96] Robert and some of the brothers later returned to Molesmes, but others remained at Citeaux. In their endeavour to return to the simplicity of the desert, the Cistercians strictly observed Benedict's *Rule*, and sought greater simplicity in liturgical practice and in the architecture of their monasteries. They insisted on maintaining the balance between prayer, the *lectio divina*, and manual labor, and rejected any dependence on feudal society. And soon their white habits were as ubiquitous as the traditionally black ones of the Benedictines.

But as Citeaux began to flourish, its lands were greatly extended. To cope with both their daily monastic life of prayer and study and the need to work the land, the monastery recruited lay brothers who took simplified vows and became a monastic labor force. Over time new monastic houses were established, one of the earliest being that at Clairvaux, where hundreds of new monks were attracted to the Cistercian way of life, not only from France, but from across Europe, becoming known as Cistercians of the Common Observance.

In 1662, further and even stricter *Rules* of silence were introduced at the monastery of La Trappe and its monastics were known as the Cistercians of the Strict Observance. This led to the formation of Trappist monasteries, such as Thomas Merton's Gethsemani, and one that was established at Marianhill in KwaZulu-Natal in South Africa in the nineteenth century, whose abbot at one stage came from Gethsemani. Founded by some ardent Austrian and German Trappists under the controversial but remarkable leadership of its founding abbot, Franz Pfanner, Marianhill grew into one of the largest monasteries of the Trappist Order in the world. But after struggling to be true to its *Rule* of silence while increasingly evangelizing and educating the Zulu people, the monastery left the Trappists early in the twentieth century and established its own

---

95. Quoted in Maguire, *An Infinity of Little Hours*, 1.
96. See the introduction in Matarasso, trans. and ed., *The Cistercian World*, xi–xvi.

order to fulfil its apostolic mission.⁹⁷ Sadly, to add a footnote, during the COVID-19 pandemic, ten elderly sisters at Marianhill convent succumbed to the virus.

Another monastic reform parallel to that of Cistercian simplicity and severity in the eleventh century was the foundation of the Camaldolese order of hermits founded by St Romuald (950–1027) at Camaldoli near Arezzo in Italy. Over time it accepted the need for community life, and so monasteries alongside hermitages were established as at Fontenbuono in 1102, generally following the *Rule* of Benedict. The Anglican Order of the Holy Cross, of which the St Benedict's Priory at Volmoed is part, has an association with the Camaldolese through the community at New Camaldoli in the United States. Much more can be said about each of these monastic reforms, but let me shift focus and conclude this chapter by highlighting the life and contribution of three of the great, archetypical monastics of the Middle Ages.

A Theologian, a Feminist, & a Mystic

Monastics prefer obscurity to publicity. Some withhold their names from the books they write and most have simply got on with being monastics—praying, studying, working, as required by the *Rule*. But a good number have become legendary, like those desert hermits whose lives are still celebrated. Medieval monasticism certainly produced many remarkable mystics, reformers, scholars, writers, and builders, among them astute abbots, abbesses, bishops, and counselors of the powerful. Let me name a few: Dunstan of Glastonbury, who later became archbishop of Canterbury, William of St-Thierry (1089–1148), Aelred of Rievaulx (1109–1167), Mechthild of Magdeburg (1210–1280), and Bridget of Sweden (1303–1373). After her husband died on a pilgrimage to Santiago de Compostela, Bridget founded a women's order at Vadstena and played an important role in ending the Avignon exile of the papacy. For me, three best represent the high point of medieval monasticism: a theologian and bishop, St Anselm; a feminist, author, scientist, and musician, St Hildegard; and a mystic and activist, St Bernard.

St Anselm (1033–1109) was born in Val d'Aosta in Italy. While still a boy, he entered the monastic school at the famous Cluniac monastery established at Bec in Normandy. Later, he became a monk and studied

---

97. Green, *For the Sake of Silence*.

under Lanfranc (1010–1089), who was one of the most illustrious of all Benedictine abbots, transforming Bec from one of the least to one of the greatest monasteries. Lanfranc eventually became counselor to William the Conqueror, duke of Normandy, and eventually was appointed archbishop of Canterbury. There he rebuilt the cathedral, founded a library, and wrote a constitution for the monastery. But Anselm, his protégé, would become equally famous as a scholar, teacher, spiritual director, and theologian before he, too, followed Lanfranc as archbishop of Canterbury in 1093, where he remained for five years.

Anselm was arguably the most renowned theologian between Augustine and St Thomas Aquinas (1225–1274), the illustrious Dominican Doctor of the Catholic Church. Anselm thus provides a bridge between the theology of the Patristic period, during which monasticism was born, and the Scholastic theology that emerged during the late Middle Ages, producing a genuinely Christian humanism that made the Reformation possible.[98] Arguably the most famous of his several important theological works is *Cur Deus Homo*, or "Why Did God Become Human?"[99] His answer is that, as God alone can save humanity, and yet human beings must pay the price for their sin, God becomes a human being to satisfy the righteous demands of God. In other words, in Christ, God takes our place on the cross to satisfy God's justice. This "satisfactory" doctrine of the atonement would become dominant from Anselm's time onwards. It was adopted by the Protestant Reformers and is still widely held by Christians today. We will come across it later when we consider Luther's struggle to satisfy the demands of a holy God.

But many would argue that Anselm's greatest theological achievement was his *Proslogion* in which he argues that "God is that beyond which nothing greater can be conceived." Sometimes misleadingly called the "ontological proof" for the existence of God, it has been endlessly debated ever since Anselm penned his reflections. While it is not beyond criticism, it still carries considerable weight. But what is perhaps of more importance for us is Anselm's approach to theology as such, for it brings together the two sciences or ways of knowing, the scholastic and rational on the one hand, and the monastic and contemplative on the other.[100]

---

98. Zimmermann, *Incarnational Humanism*, 117–24.
99. Anselm, *Basic Writings*.
100. See Leclercq, *The Love of Learning and the Desire for God*, 214.

Whereas the first has to do with intellectual inquiry, the second is the knowledge of lived experience that leads to wisdom.

In fusing these two ways of knowing, Anselm builds on Augustine's comment in his *Confessions* that "unless we believe we will not understand."[101] By this Augustine meant that faith in God's revelation in Christ is not only reasonable but also the prerequisite of knowing God. Anselm went one step further. Faith, by its very nature, he said, desires to know God; it is an act of responsive love that leads us into the mystery of God, recognizing that God is always greater than we can conceive. As Karl Barth, who was profoundly influenced by Anselm, states, it is "not the existence of faith, but rather . . . the nature of faith, that desires knowledge."[102] It is our desire for God that awakens in us that love for knowledge of the truth that is divine wisdom. In sum, Anselm helps us connect faith and reason, contemplation and critical reflection, the desire for God and the love of learning, in such a way that prayer becomes theology and theology prayer. For prayer is faith discerning God's will, and theology is faith seeking to understand it.

Anselm's arguments may not be flawless, but his insight is fundamental to Christian faith. Faith is not the opposite of reason, nor is theology the opponent of critical thought. Just as discipleship is not a flight from the world into the desert, but a different way of relating to the world, so faith in Christ is not a flight from reason, but a different way of engaging philosophy and science that leads to both knowledge and wisdom. Faith does not absolve us from rational thought and understanding; it makes such understanding possible. With Anselm in mind, Barth therefore insists that "prior to any desire or ability to find theological answers is the question of dedication on the part of the theologian himself." He goes on to say:

> What is required is a pure heart, eyes that have been opened, child-like obedience, a life in the Spirit, rich nourishment from Holy Scripture, to make him capable of finding these answers.[103]

Nothing represents monastic theology better than that, suggesting that the great Reformed theologian was closer to the theological spirit of monasticism than we might think. Indeed, through Barth, Anselm provides a bridge between Reformed and monastic theology.

---

101. Augustine, *Confessions*, 119, book. 6, chapter 5.
102. Barth, *Anselm*, 18.
103. Barth, *Anselm*, 34.

Hildegard of Bingen (d. 1179) was a visionary from an early age, but when she was about forty, she began to write down her visions. As a result, her reputation soon grew across Germany. But she was far more than a visionary. She was a Bible commentator, a systematic theologian, a natural scientist, a contemplative, and a great organizer whose ascetic common sense enabled her monastery to flourish. She was also physician to the emperor, an author, a musician, and a composer—in fact, a humanist, feminist, and mystic all wrapped up together. If it were not for the fact that she was a woman, it would not be necessary to mention that she was also invited to preach in cathedrals and monastery chapels, nor that she was not confined to her convent but traveled a great deal to give counsel and settle conflicts. As she tells us, she was directed in her visions "to visit certain religious communities of men and women, to reveal openly to them the words that God had shown" her, "and following God's instructions" to settle "internal quarrels."[104] Indeed, "prelates and princes, priests and religious, communities of nuns, all begged for her prayers and asked for her advice," and she was not "afraid to speak plainly and to reprove iniquity, thus actively contributing to the reform of the church."[105]

Those achievements would, on any count, mark Hildegard out as a remarkable person, equal to any other monastic of note, and certainly exceptional among women of her period. But I also like Sara Maitland's description that she was "wonderfully eccentric," as well as an author of "a string of remarkably original works, both about her own interior life, and about the world more widely," among them a "mystery play with an all-women cast, except for the devil who is male and, because of his fall from grace, cannot sing."[106] In speaking out against the historic "oppressive alienation" of women in the church, Jürgen Moltmann cites Hildegard as one of those exceptions who prepared the way for what became "feminist theology" in the twentieth century.[107] She not only had to overcome illness, but in a patriarchal world that both virtually and often literally confined women to the enclosure of a convent she achieved far more than many of her male counterparts. And she did so not least because she believed that God had called her and had given her the ability and authority to do so. In her own words,

---

104. Quoted from her *Vita* in Flanagan, *Hildegard of Bingen*, 172.
105. Leclercq et al., *The Spirituality of the Middle Ages*, 177.
106. Maitland, *A Book of Silence*, 258.
107. Moltmann, *Experiences in Theology*, 12.

> What I write in the vision, I see and hear, and set down no other words than those I hear, and in unpolished language I bring them forth, just as I hear them in the vision. For in this vision I am not taught to write as the philosophers write. And the words in the vision are not like the words that sound from the mouths of human beings, but like a vibrating flame and like a cloud moving in pure air.[108]

We have come a long way from Syncletica in the desert to Hildegard in her monastery on the River Rhine north of Cologne, but there is a striking spiritual and intellectual bond between them and the many other women monastics, who in recent times have beaten the odds in making a significant contribution to the life of the church and the world. And the church can neither be transformed nor serve the world if their leadership is sidelined or their voices silenced. When I was a theological student, I learned much about Anselm but nothing at all about Hildegard. But it is her voice, and that of those who follow her, that we need to hear and heed more at this monastic moment, not least when it comes to the reformation of the church and its witness to the world.

If Hildegard is the most famous abbess of her time, Bernard is undoubtedly the most famous abbot, though not everything about him attracts us. A close friend of Pope Eugenius (d 1153), who was himself a Cistercian monk under Bernard before becoming pope, Bernard was a political force to be reckoned with. The downside was that he persecuted heretics, was a misogynist, and misguidedly inspired the disastrous Second Crusade. Too late he discovered that the Crusade, which he thought would be a pilgrimage to achieve peace, did the very opposite. But, despite his failures and faults, according to David Knowles, whose knowledge of this period surpasses most, Bernard "on the great web of medieval religious thought and sentiment, changed and formed more patterns than any other man of his century." He was not only a "great intellectual power"—indeed, the "last of the Fathers"—but also "a literary genius."[109] Above all, however, Bernard was an ascetic of deep mystical piety, and a monastic reformer—indeed, a "puritan" Cistercian, calling monastics back to the simplicity and austerity of the desert. Late in his life, Martin Luther would say Bernard was "an example for everyone else, and I know no one among the monks who wrote or lived better than he."[110]

108. Quoted in Sölle, *The Silent Cry*, 71–72.
109. Knowles, *The Evolution of Medieval Thought*, 147.
110. Luther, *Sermon on the Mount and the Magnificat*, 283.

Bernard, who is sometimes called the Marian Doctor of the Church, had a special love for the Virgin Mary. Popular devotion to Mary stretched back to the third century, anticipating her acknowledgment as the "Mother of God" (*theotokos*) at the Council of Ephesus in 431, at the same time as monasticism was developing. But it was during the Middle Ages that the "cult of Mary" developed ever more strongly in the Catholic Church with the support of the monasteries, and notably under the influence of Bernard, who introduced among other innovations the chanting of the *Salve Regina* after compline. At the same time, Bernard's mysticism was strongly christological and, following a tradition that can be traced back to Clement of Alexandria, he spoke of Jesus as nurturing mother, often in erotic terms. This was typical, in fact, of medieval monastics such as Aelred of Rievaulx, Catherine of Siena (1347–1380), and Julian of Norwich.[111] Indeed, Julian, in writing about "our Lady" as "our mother," and the "mother of all who are saved in our saviour," continues by saying, "our saviour is our true Mother, in whom we are endlessly born and out of whom we shall never come."[112]

Christ-centred eroticism certainly strikes readers in Bernard's celebrated sermons on the Song of Songs. But those sermons also reveal, above all else, his struggle to be fully committed to Christ and engaged in the world at the same time. "It is hard," he writes,

> for the lover to divide himself equally between Christ and the world, hard indeed to have outside cares invade the purlieus [environs] of love and the world's turmoil disturb the converse of heaven.

He continues:

> So it is with perfect justice that the Bride seeks out a chamber with her beloved, where she might devote her untrammelled attention to him and where, present to him in spirit, she may enjoy him fully and, in quietness of heart, embrace him without reserve.[113]

He is, of course, writing here about the contemplative life of those who, like Mary of Bethany, "sit at Jesus's feet," unlike Martha, who was

---

111. See Rolf, *Julian's Gospel*, 513–14.
112. Julian of Norwich, *Showings*, 292.
113. Sermon 11 in Matarasso, ed. and trans., *The Cistercian World*, 217.

"troubled about many things."[114] But, he says, it is love that brings "those with a common way of life under the same roof" and "inclines and unites the human spirit to God."[115] The contemplative and the active life belong together as they are, of course, in the Virgin Mary, a subject to which I will return.

In parenthesis, I must include here a reference to Bernard's leading role in breaking up the famous love affair between the Parisian theologian and musician Peter Abelard (1079–1142) and his student Heloise d'Argenteuil (1100–1164). Heloise was an established scholar before she met Peter, and has a significant place in the history of French feminist literature. And Abelard is a scholar of equal importance in the history of theology—indeed, "the most controversial of the first generation of scholastic theologians."[116] I introduce their story partly because it illustrates Bernard's authority and passion to defend the truth and protect the purity of the church, and partly to illustrate that the history of monasticism is not just one of passionless saints and mystics, but also of many who have struggled with personal relationships and human sexuality at an intense level.[117]

Bernard was scandalized equally by Abelard's illicit love life and his theology. For, contrary to Augustine, Abelard emphasized human free will and natural goodness, and contrary to Anselm, he rejected the satisfactory doctrine of the atonement. Instead, he argued that God's love revealed in Christ's death on the cross saves us by awakening within us a response of faith and love. In the end, Bernard had his way. Peter became a monk, eventually an abbot, and finally a hermit, and Heloise, in turn, a reluctant nun, and the inconsolable abbess of a convent in Champagne. But looking back, we might say that while Bernard won the battle, he did not win the war of popular acclaim, for Abelard's theology remains persuasive for many today, and the romantic fate of Abelard and Heloise continues to be held against him. Maybe David Knowles's summation of their relationship is the most apt: "as a teacher and master who for forty years could draw a multitude with his magic wand, Abelard was

---

114. See Luke 10:39–41 (KJV).

115. Sermon 11 in Matarasso, ed. and trans., *The Cistercian World*, 218.

116. Ozment, *The Age of Reform*, 5.

117. See Waddell, *Peter Abelard*; Knowles, *The Evolution of Medieval Thought*, 116–30.

unsurpassed; his only rival, in a field that bordered upon his own, was the great abbot of Clairvaux."[118]

Despite this sad episode, Bernard's stature as a profound thinker and mystic has not only survived but was immortalized by Dante Alighieri (c. 1265–1321), for whom Bernard was the greatest of all who have desired God and glimpsed something of the reality of God's glory. And that, after all, is the chief end of all monastics. In her introduction to Dante's *Paradiso*, Barbara Reynolds tells us that in the *Divine Comedy* "we find affirmed with the utmost clarity and consistency the fundamental Christian proposition that the journey to God is the journey into reality. To know all things in God is to know things as they really are."[119] And so *Paradiso* ends with Bernard's "Beatific Vision," the vision of God, which is the desire of all who seek the love that "moved the sun and other stars":

> But as my sight by seeing learned to see,
> The transformation which in me took place
> Transformed the single changeless form for me
>
> Thither my own wings could not carry me,
> But that a flash my understanding clove,
> Whence its desire came to it suddenly.
>
> High phantasy lost power and here broke off;
> Yet, as a wheel moves smoothly, free from jars,
> My will and my desire were turned by love,
> The love that moves the sun and the other stars.[120]

---

118. Knowles, *The Evolution of Medieval Thought*, 130.

119. Introduction by Dorothy L. Sayers to Dante Alighieri, *The Comedy of Dante Alighieri, the Florentine*, 3:16.

120. Dante, *The Comedy of Dante Alighieri*, 3:346–47 (canto 33, lines 139–45: St Bernard's Prayer).

3

IN A REFORMING WORLD

A safe stronghold our God is still,
A trusty shield and weapon;
. . .
and though they take our life,
goods, honor, children, wife,
yet is their profit small;
these things shall vanish all:
the city of God remaineth.
—MARTIN LUTHER[1]

Verily there is that which is more contrary to Christianity . . . than any heresy, any schism, more contrary to all heresies and schism combined, and that is to play Christianity.
—SØREN KIERKEGAARD[2]

We must not exclude the possibility [that monasticism was] a highly responsible and effective protest and opposition to the world, and not least to a worldly church . . . Do we not see in these movements of retreat a sign of the power and vitality of the church?
—KARL BARTH[3]

---

1. *Ein' feste Burg.* Paraphrase of Psalm 46, translated by Thomas Carlyle (1795–1881).
2. Kierkegaard, *Attack upon "Christendom,"* 8.
3. Barth, *Church Dogmatics* IV/2, 13.

Monasticism is often understood as "Christianity for the few," as an affirmation of sacred life in a sacred realm, the little, holy, self-contained, world-denying world of the monastic enclosure ... [But] this institution of a little, perfect world in the midst of an imperfect world, which is implicitly or explicitly denied, ends up being also an affirmation of the world itself.
—THOMAS MERTON[4]

WE SHIFT FROM THE European Dark Ages and the bright lights of the High Middle Ages to the late Middle Ages, an age of dissent and reform. If the High Middle Ages were years of stability, scholastic achievement, and monastic flourishing, the late Middle Ages were characterized by uncertainty and anxiety as penitential pilgrims hurried from one holy place to the next in search of salvation and assurance. But they often walked, as Ozment portrays this *kairos* moment in Western history, "through the valley of the shadow of death."

> The greatest famine of the Middle Ages struck in the second decade of the fourteenth century, and an estimated two-fifths of the overall population of Europe died when bubonic plague, or the Black Death, following the trade routes, erupted in midcentury.[5]

In addition, war between England and France lasted throughout the fourteenth and fifteenth centuries, leaving towns, villages, and countryside in ruin, while "agrarian and urban revolts by the poor rent the social fabric in both town and countryside." To crown it all, "religious and moral foundations were shaken by a schism in the church that produced no less than three competing popes and colleges of cardinals by 1409."[6]

This social, economic, and ecclesiastical *kairos* was, more fundamentally, a crisis of faith. The Scholastic synthesis of faith and reason so carefully and majestically crafted by Thomas Aquinas, together with the Franciscan theologian in Oxford, Duns Scotus (1265–1308), at the height of the Middle Ages, was undermined by a new generation of scholars led by another Franciscan in Oxford, William of Ockham (1285–1347).

4. Merton, *Conjectures of a Guilty Bystander*, 179.
5. Ozment, *The Age of Reform*, 8.
6. Ozment, *The Age of Reform*, 8.

Ockham's *via moderna*, in contrast to the *via antiqua*, the "old way" of the Scholastics, was based on a nominalist critique of universals. By this was meant that generalizations or abstract concepts exist in name only (*nomino*, "to give something a name"): that is, they are not real, but mental abstractions. What is real is the particular, *this* man or woman, not humankind in general. Only these particularities can be verified by experience and confirmed by Scripture. This radical change of perspective undermined the whole edifice of Neoplatonic conviction on which medieval Christendom had been built, including our understanding of God and the self and, not least, of salvation.

Clearly, the future of European Christendom lay in the balance, its reality more notional than the muscle-flexing emerging nation-states, which were able to take on both pope and emperor, and win. Indeed, confidence in the authority of the papacy to provide leadership and assurance in such uncertain times had been seriously undermined by its moral failures as well as its own schism and captivity in Avignon. The schism, which began in 1378 with the appointment of two antipopes representing nationalist interests, was a huge scandal. But this did not mean that the entire church was corrupt, even if corruption in the Roman curia seeped into church life at every level. The situation was, after all, of great concern to many bishops, theologians, parish priests, monastics, and friars alike. It was also of concern to Christian princes, for whom the well-being of the state was contingent upon the unity and health of the church.

The papal schism was finally resolved at the Council of Constance (1414–1417), at the insistence of Emperor Sigismund. But hopes that the conciliar process would thereafter continue to reform the church more broadly were soon dashed, as succeeding popes of the Renaissance refused to be subject to the decisions of councils, and corruption within the papal curia continued to plague the church.[7] It was only at the Council of Trent (1545–1561) that widespread reforms would be introduced. By then, it was too late to do anything to prevent the Reformation, set in motion by an angry and disillusioned monk and professor of theology, Martin Luther (1483–1546). This happened publicly when, on October 31, 1517, Luther nailed Ninety-Five Theses to the door of the castle church in Wittenberg to provoke debate on some of the critical issues that dismayed him. There were two in particular: the most immediate was the sale of indulgences; the second, the theology that gave legitimacy to the practice.

---

7. Spinka, ed., *Advocates of Reform*, 91.

I have a beautiful parchment bought by my non-Catholic mother in Rome on my behalf in 1955, signed by Pope Pius XII and granting me "plenary indulgence" for my sins. I do not know what she paid for it but, if I were a devout Catholic in the Middle Ages I would have been overjoyed, because it meant that I would be saved from years in purgatory and, what is more, I would have been helping the pope build St Peter's Basilica in Rome. For Luther, this was a travesty of true repentance and the gospel of God's amazing grace and forgiveness. Without pulling any punches, he asked:

> Why does not the pope empty purgatory for the sake of holy love and the dire need of the souls that are there, if he redeems an infinite number of souls for the sake of miserable money with which to build a church? The former reasons would be most just; the latter is most trivial.[8]

The underlying problem, as Luther argued in his *Heidelberg Disputation* (1518), was that Scholastic theology had become a theology of glory that gave legitimacy to the power of a triumphalist papacy to act in this way.[9] Against this Luther placed Paul's theology of the cross, which proclaims the true wisdom and power of God in saving the world.[10] The triumph of the risen Christ is always the triumph of the suffering Christ, never that of a triumphant church or nation.

The failure of the conciliar movement and the indulgence controversy may have sparked off Luther's reformation, but there were many other antecedents that fed its eventual eruption. His disillusionment with the state of the papacy, with Scholastic theology, and with the general condition of the church, was widely shared by many whose pastoral commitment to the church and its witness in the world mirrored his own. But Luther had the prophetic charisma as well as his monastic and theological credentials to lead the attack. So, when the sale of indulgences reached his neighborhood, he went on the offensive, even if only by way of a long list of academic propositions. But they were explosive enough to provoke a stern counterattack such as had often occurred in the suppression of what was deemed dissent and heresy.

---

8. Thesis 82, "The Ninety-Five Theses," in Luther, *Martin Luther's Basic Theological Writings*, 28.

9. "Disputation against Scholastic Theology," in Luther, *Martin Luther's Basic Theological Writings*, 13–20.

10. 1 Corinthians 1:18–25; see Loewenich, *Luther's Theology of the Cross*.

Forerunners of Reformation

The late Middle Ages was a period of religious and spiritual dissent, often occurring within the monasteries and religious orders. Among them were the Franciscan Spirituals, who in the spirit of Anthony and St Francis of Assisi (1181–1226) attacked the wealth of the church and suffered severely at the hands of the Inquisition. There were also well-educated priests who, disaffected with ecclesiastical corruption, spoke their mind, among them Peter Valdes of Lyons (1140–1205) and his followers, the Waldensian Brotherhood; John Wycliff (1330–1384) and the Lollards in England; and Jan Hus (1369–1415), whose Bohemian Brethren would later be known as the Moravian Brotherhood. Excommunicated by the pope and persecuted by the Inquisition, these groups bore a family resemblance to the first desert monastics, who protested the worldliness and triumphalism of the Constantinian church, except that these reformers were forced out, usually against their own volition.

There were also other monastic-like lay reforming movements that managed to remain in the church, such as the Beguines in the Netherlands, a loosely organized movement of women who lived on the periphery of society, caring for the sick and living a life of contemplation. From their ranks came the mystic Mechthild of Magdeburg (1210–1280) and her contemporary Hadewijch of Antwerp. Then there was the *Devotio Moderna* movement, also emerging in Holland, whose leader, Gerard Groote (1340–1384), was influenced by the Carthusians, and who spoke about salvation by grace, faith and Scripture alone, long before Luther. Significantly, in establishing his Brethren of the Common Life, Groote revived an interest in a simple monasticism, which had a remarkable influence on many. Among them was Thomas à Kempis (1380–1471), whose book *The Imitation of Christ* greatly influenced Luther, as did the writings of the Dominican mystics Meister Eckhart, Johan Tauler, and the anonymous *Theologia Germanica*.[11] Bonhoeffer would later also show great appreciation for the monk Thomas' *Imitation of Christ* which significantly contributed to his understanding of discipleship, the *ecclesia*, and his "theology of the cross."[12]

At the same time, theologians like Luther began rediscovering the writings of the early Greek fathers, which had been so carefully preserved in the monasteries, and now provided fresh inspiration and insight.

11. Hoffman, *Luther and the Mystics*.
12. Frick, *Thomas a' Kempis and Dietrich Bonhoeffer*.

Luther was reading Athanasius when still a novice, and it was Eusebius's history of the early church that convinced him that while the pope in Rome might have primacy in the West, that did not apply to the whole church. But the real source of Luther's theology was the Bible, which he could now read in the original Hebrew and Greek thanks to the labors of Christian humanists. The prince of these was Desiderius Erasmus (1469–1536), a product of the Brethren of the Common Life and for a time an Augustinian monk like Luther. Without Erasmus's labors the Reformation might not have begun in the way it did. For it was while reading Erasmus's Greek New Testament that Luther discovered that repentance, that is *metanoia*, did not mean "do penance," as translated in the Latin Vulgate[13] and then misused to promote the sale of indulgences, but conversion to Christ.

I first became aware of this important linguistic discovery when as a student I read Roland Bainton's biography of Luther titled *Here I Stand*, which remains as good an introduction to the reformer as any.[14] Luther scholarship may have moved on since the 1950s when it was published, but it remains a good account, and there is never a dull moment in reading it. This is especially true of Bainton's account of Luther's decision to become a monk and what that meant at that *kairos* moment in the late Middle Ages.[15]

Leaving the Cloister for the World

Luther's decision to become a monk was made suddenly in July 1505. At the time he was studying law in obedience to his father's wishes at the University of Erfurt. While walking through a forest one day he was struck down by lightning. In a moment of desperation, Luther vowed to St Anne, the mother of the Virgin Mary, that he would become a monk if his life was spared. A few days later he turned his back on the world, his father's plans for him, and his friends, and entered the monastery of the Augustinian Eremites in Erfurt.

The Augustinian Eremites were founded in 1256 as a mendicant teaching order, which strictly observed the *Rule of St Augustine*. One of its greatest theologians was Gregory of Rimini (d. 1358), an Ockhamist

---

13. Matthew 4:17
14. Bainton, *Here I Stand*, 88.
15. Bainton, *Here I Stand*, 21–36.

philosopher whose writings were especially influential in the order. As the word *eremites* suggests, the Augustine monastics were rigorous in their monastic disciplines, striving for perfection. For many of them, as for the young Luther, this was the reason for becoming a monk—to enter the kingdom of heaven. And yet, the Augustinians, like the Dominicans, were established to serve the world through education.

As Augustine had written in *The City of God*, the chief rule in life was to obey "God's holy precepts" and "keep the faith, the true path of salvation." There are, he added, "three kinds of life, active, contemplative, and the mean between both," and it is possible "to keep the faith" in all. There is, however, he said, "a difference between the love of truth and the duties of charity." Indeed, Augustine went on to say,

> One may not be so given to contemplation that he neglect the good of his neighbour, nor so far in love with action that he forget divine speculation. In contemplation one may not seek for idleness, but for truth; to benefit himself by the knowledge thereof, and not to grudge to impart it to others.[16]

Bernard, whose desire for God, love of learning, and reformist actions embodied Augustine's teaching was, for Luther and his generation of monastics, the model monk.[17] But as Augustine taught and Luther soon learned, there was always a tension between seeking personal perfection and serving the world.

At Easter 1507 Luther was ordained a priest. A year later, he was sent to study in Wittenberg, at another Augustinian foundation, where he obtained his doctorate in theology in 1512 and became a professor of biblical studies.[18] Both the universities in Erfurt and Wittenberg were centers of reformist ideas. As a student at Erfurt, Luther was strongly influenced by the *via moderna* and the prevailing humanist scholarship, which helped him to read the Bible with fresh eyes. But all the time he did so within the context of the daily life of the monastery, strictly keeping the hours of prayer, and like the desert hermits struggling against demons and the temptations of the devil, whether then in his cell, or later in the isolation of Wartburg Castle, where he hid after his excommunication in 1521.

Luther had an acute sense of the cosmic struggle between God and the devil, but his worldview was not apocalyptic in the same sense as that

---

16. Augustine, *The City of God*, book 19, chapter 19, 2:256.
17. Dickens, *The German Nation and Martin Luther*, 84.
18. Oberman, *Luther*, 138, 178.

of Joachim of Fiore (1132–1202), the Cistercian mystic whose interpretation of history was so influential during the Middle Ages. Nevertheless, Augustine's *The City of God* together with the writings of Bernard of Clairvaux made Luther fear that the world was on the edge of an abyss. With many monastics and mystics, Luther also concluded that the pope was the antichrist foretold in the book of Revelation.[19] No matter how much he was influenced by the *via moderna* or anticipated the birth of modernity, he remained a late medieval monk.[20] Indeed, his superior, Johannes von Staupitz, a mystic in his own right and later a Benedictine abbot, thought the young monk too ardent in trying to "work out his own salvation."

Although Luther was an Augustinian, his understanding of salvation was Semi-Pelagian and legalistic. As Anselm taught, just as the holy wrath of God towards sinners was satisfied by the blameless suffering and death of Christ on the cross, so sinners in turn had to satisfy God's justice through acts of penitence to gain eternal bliss. In Heiko Oberman's words, "Luther knew himself unworthy to appear before the holy God," so his "intense asceticism and mortification was informed by the conviction that only by striving for perfection could one even hope to exist before God."[21] Luther may have been a professor of theology, but as a monastic his aim was spiritual perfection not peer-applauded treatises. As he learned from Augustine, theology is about faith seeking understanding, and such faith is not a mental construction or abstract principles but learning to trust Christ in the daily struggle between God and the devil, between hope and despair.

A great deal happened between Luther's entry into the monastery and the fateful day he was told by Staupitz, his friend and confessor, that he had to leave. This included a visit to Rome when he was still the vicar of a dozen Augustinian monasteries in Wittenberg. He was appalled by the decadence he observed. Then, shortly after, during his semester-long lectures on the Psalms and Paul's Letter to the Romans, Luther became convinced with Paul that we are justified by faith alone, not by any works of our own, and certainly not by buying indulgences. That conviction was the basis of his Ninety-Five Theses, but it was also the reason why he was charged with heresy at the Diet of Worms, a conference convened by Emperor Charles V in 1520. Luther refused to recant, and so, on January 3, 1521, Pope Leo X excommunicated him from the Catholic Church.

19. Oberman, *Luther*, 67–74.
20. Oberman, *Luther*, 104 et al.
21. Oberman, *Luther*, 137.

That act, and Luther's defiance, soon divided Europe into two increasingly theologically irreconcilable and politically warring factions with devastating consequences for Christendom. More personally, it meant that Luther, the heretic, had to leave the cloister, which had been his life. The monastery door was shut behind him, and monasticism would play no positive role in his future. Moreover, many other Augustinian monks and nuns would follow his example, crippling the order in Germany.

But, just as Luther, like Merton centuries later, discovered that he had not really left the world behind when he became a monk, the question must be asked: did he really leave monasticism behind when he returned to the world? My sense is that, long after, even when he was married with a family, and daily engaged in the work of the Reformation, strong vestiges of monasticism remained in his psyche. He was, I surmise, a monk at heart, and a monastic rather than a scholastic theologian, by vocation. After all, the monastery had provided the biblical, patristic, and humanist tools with which he was able to attack indulgences and prepare for his career as reformer.[22] And he continued to wield those tools once he left the cloister.

To understand Luther as a monk even after his excommunication, it is useful to compare him to Erasmus, the prince of Christian humanists. Luther was not a Christian humanist preparing the way for the modern world but a medieval monastic living on the cusp of modernity. Erasmus became a monk because he wanted the space and solitude to study and pursue his scholarly interests and only left, with papal consent, when that was no longer convenient. Luther became a monk to save his soul, and he only left because he was forced out by excommunication and then had to find his vocation in the world rather than the cloister. Erasmus had more confidence in reason than Luther, but Luther had a greater sense of the awesome holiness of God. Erasmus wanted to keep the gospel simple enough for the common person to understand, not full of paradoxes like Luther's theology of the cross, which forced him to journey more deeply through the "dark night of the soul." For Erasmus, living according to the Sermon on the Mount was essentially what it meant to be a Christian, whereas for Luther, the Sermon on the Mount drove him to despair of his own righteousness and forced him to cling to Christ alone. For Luther, Erasmus was really a Semi-Pelagian; for Erasmus, Luther was too much of an Augustinian eremite. And whereas Erasmus renounced his vows

22. Oberman, *Luther*, 129.

with papal dispensation, Luther was forced to do so by papal decree. We do not really know if he would have done so if the pope had decided otherwise.

The break between Luther and Erasmus followed the latter's 1524 attack on Luther's teaching on original sin, predestination, and the bondage of the will.[23] In other words, on Luther as a disciple of Augustine. Luther would have none of this, and so responded with his equally incisive and bombastic treatise *On the Bondage of the Will* (1525). This led to the parting of the ways between Luther and Erasmus, but this was not the only factor in the separation. Erasmus believed that it was more important to maintain the unity of the church and the peace of Christendom than to pursue far-reaching reforms. That tension, between unity and reform had been an "acute problem in the late medieval church long before the time of the Reformation," but now, for Luther, "the goals of reform proved to be incompatible with the desire for unity."[24] For Luther, Christian unity was not based on allegiance to the pope, but on faithfulness to the gospel, so the real heretics were the papists who had already divided the church with their false teaching.

Yet we must not lose sight of the fact, noted by A. G. Dickens, that Luther always reacted and constructed his reforms and theology "within a Catholic framework," and his works "reveal many positive debts to his Catholic origins."[25] He had no desire to start a new church; his passion was to reform the old one. But this required recovering the true meaning of the gospel and therefore the path to salvation. It was to answer that question that Luther entered the monastery, and it was in discovering the answer and its consequences that he finally had to leave.

What, then, was the true gospel for Luther and, therefore, the basis on which everything else followed? It was quite simply that it is the "righteousness of God" revealed in Christ crucified that "makes us righteous," not our deeds.[26] In other words, while we do not have to satisfy God's justice, for God has already done so in Christ crucified, we must still respond through acts of penitence. This understanding of the atonement, known as the satisfaction theory, was first developed by Anselm in *Cur Deus Homo*, to which I previously referred. This had become the accepted dogma in the West from then on and was woven into the fabric

---

23. Winter, ed., *Erasmus–Luther: Discourse on Free Will*.
24. Oberman, *Luther*, 134.
25. Dickens, *The German Nation and Martin Luther*, 98.
26. Luther, *Lectures on Romans*, 116–17.

of its penitential theology and practice. For it was through penitence that we humans access the merits of Christ's death on the cross for us and for our salvation.

Anselm's teaching held sway for Luther, but he concluded from Scripture and his own experience that we access the merits of Christ's death not through penitential acts but through faith alone. Our righteousness is imputed, not earned by us, whether through martyrdom, monastic vows (regarded as a "second baptism"), not through acts of penance, and certainly not by buying indulgences. This did not mean that "good works" were unimportant, but they were deeds of gratitude—the love of God working in and through us in the world, not deeds by which we gain God's favor. In this Luther was not saying anything that others, including Bernard of Clairvaux and Gregory of Rimini, had already said. Even before he left the monastery, in his lectures on Paul's Letter to the Romans (1516), Luther had, like many other reforming monastics, attacked the hypocrisy and legalism of monks who identify Christianity with outward observances while disregarding the "commandments of God and faith and love."[27] That is why monastic vows had to be taken for the right reason, namely, for love of God, and taken in faith, "not because it is necessary for salvation but from a spontaneous will and out of a sense of liberty."[28]

Luther's rejection of monasticism, it is important to stress, was centered on the nature of monastic vows and their abuse, not on monastic community as such. This is evident in his lengthy treatise—some might say diatribe—on *The Judgment on Monastic Vows,* written in 1521, with considerable passion and pulling no punches, shortly after he had left the monastery. The making and keeping of monastic vows was for Luther at the center of his rejection of monasticism both theologically and existentially. Breaking his vows was no easy matter, for he had made them not only before his superiors but also before God. In writing his *Judgment,* he also had in mind the many other monks and nuns who in following his example were likewise struggling with their consciences. Were they at liberty to renounce what they had so solemnly professed? And, while it is highly unlikely that this lengthy, and repetitive, document has been widely read among subsequent generations of Protestants, it spelled out the theological—if not political—rationale for the renunciation of

---

27. Romans 14:1–13; Luther, *Lectures on Romans,* 382–83.
28. Luther, *Lectures on Romans,* 383.

monasticism, at the heart of which was liberation from obedience to the pope.

Luther makes it clear that his attack on monastic vows is not an attack on the great monastic saints from Anthony the hermit to Bernard of Clairvaux. After all, there were no monastic vows to be taken in Anthony's day, and Bernard, whom Luther so admired, certainly kept his Benedictine vows, and encouraged others to do the same, for the right reason. His vows were taken in faith for the sake of love.[29] Even so, in Luther's experience, that was not how the system worked, nor was this the understanding of most monastics. For them, the keeping of the vows of poverty, chastity, and obedience—each of which Luther discusses in considerable detail—was for the sake of achieving perfection or, as Luther says, earning "a halo in heaven."[30] In other words, the keeping of the vows was a way of gaining salvation, the way of "works" rather than of "faith alone."[31] Indeed, taking the vows had become a "second baptism," which not only separated monastics from other Christians, making monastics a superior class, but led to self-righteous hypocrisy and a lack of social responsibility. What monk could claim to be "poor" while living as part of a well-endowed monastery? And did not the exaltation of celibacy, lapses aside, not downgrade the sanctity of marriage?

For Luther, all Christians are called to be committed disciples of Jesus Christ, irrespective of whether they are monastics, clergy, or laypeople. He says as much in his sermon on Jesus's Sermon on the Mount (1532), drawing heavily on St Augustine, where he speaks about the "pope's monks," who claim to be more perfect than other Christians but are full of "greed, pride, and finally every kind of evil."[32] In fact Luther goes further and often says that while some people may have gifts that others lack, all Christians are equal—"man or woman, young or old, learned or unlearned, noble or ignoble, prince or peasant, major or minor saint" because there is "only one kind of Christ" and one kind of faith and baptism.[33]

Quite apart from his own experience as a monk, often weighed down by the burden of a guilty conscience, as the superintendent of monasteries

29. Luther, *The Judgment on Monastic Vows*, 253, 363, 290, 292, 325, 354.
30. Luther, *The Judgment on Monastic Vows*, 264.
31. Luther, *The Judgment on Monastic Vows*, 274, 281.
32. Luther, *Sermon on the Mount and the Magnificat*, 6.
33. Luther, Postscript to *Sermon on the Mount*, in *The Sermon on the Mount and the Magnificat*, 286.

while still a monk, Luther had an insider's knowledge of the monastic life. Not only did he know about the faults and failures of monks, as well as widespread corruption in some places, but he also knew about the struggles of diligent monks to keep their vows with a good conscience. Indeed, he knew the bitter pangs of soul-destroying guilt that too often accompanied the endless and impossible struggle for perfection.

And yet, Luther conceded, if vows are regarded neither as eternally binding nor as a means for achieving salvation, they could be helpful. If you are already "saved," vows freely taken and "led inwardly and wondrously by the Spirit of Christ" are good and sometimes necessary.[34] To "sum up the whole argument," Luther says,

> Whatever is contrary to love can in no circumstances be imposed, nor can any law be interpreted to work against love, for no case of hardship or necessity works against love. To put it another way, whatever is not against love is a matter of free choice, permissible and sanctioned, especially in cases of necessity.[35]

Indeed, if you do choose to be a monk, then, says Luther, you should do so for "love's sake" not because you are desperate or in despair, nor to save your soul.

Merton would later acknowledge the rightness of Luther's critique of monastic self-righteousness, and the need for "*the conversion of the good to Christ*," adding that this was something that Kierkegaard, Barth, and Bonhoeffer also saw.[36] But it is not only Luther's critique that is important; it is also his emphasis on love as the essential ingredient of any rule that might be adopted in the life of the Church. In stressing this, Luther was not saying anything new. The First Letter of John, as well as the sermons of Bernard of Clairveaux, make the same point. But, equally, in drawing up his regulations, Benedict tells us in his prologue, they are intended "to safeguard love."[37] If there is going to be a *Rule*, love must be its foundation, purpose, and guiding principle. We will return to this later when we consider the *Rule, or Covenant, of Love* that should guide us as we contemplate the "new kind of monasticism"[38] necessary for today.

---

34. Luther, *The Judgment on Monastic Vows*, 304, 315.
35. Luther, *The Judgment on Monastic Vows*, 393.
36. Merton, *Conjectures of a Guilty Bystander*, 170 (italics original).
37. Benedict, prologue, verse 47 (*RB 1980*, 165).
38. See Bonhoeffer, *London*, 284–85.

Following Luther's example and his *Judgment on Monastic Vows*, many monastics, especially those belonging to the Augustinian Order, abandoned their monasteries, and some monks, like Luther himself, married former nuns. But although among them there were some feisty nuns, the Reformation was largely a patriarchal affair.[39] A notable exception was Katherine Schütz (1497–1562) in Strasbourg, who married a renegade priest in 1523, and wrote scathing attacks on the hypocrisy of Catholic bishops, as well as chiding Luther and Huldrych Zwingli (1484–1531) because they could not agree on the Lord's Supper.[40] Another was Argula von Grumbach (1492–1554), a Bavarian woman of noble stock who had no inhibitions about challenging the Reformers in her lobbying princes on behalf of the Reformation.[41] But neither Schütz nor Grumbach, nor any other women, especially former nuns, had much good to say about monasticism, or any desire to be part of it. Though it must be said that the migration from being a nun to becoming a housewife was not necessarily altogether favorable. Leaving the convent and getting married did not often mean freedom in the patriarchal environment of the Reformation. After all, some nuns, especially abbesses, exercised considerable authority, not only in the convent but more generally in society.

The fact that patriarchy reigned in the Reformation churches, with women having to "remain silent" as if they were still in a convent,[42] may be connected to the negative attitude of most of the Reformation leaders to the Marian cult. But this was not true of Luther himself. Luther's devotion to the Virgin Mary as the Mother of God (*theotokos*), which is expressed so well in his sermon on the Magnificat preached in 1521 in Wittenberg, was lifelong.[43] But Luther's praise for Mary centered on her humility and willingness to be available for God's work of grace; he did not exalt her at the expense of God's grace, for that, he says, does not honor her at all, as it is contrary to her own openness for God. Calling her "Queen of Heaven," Luther writes, "is a true enough name and yet it does not make her a goddess." Some monastic and popular Marian devotion transgressed that boundary.[44] Luther's views were shared by Huld-

---

39. Stjerna, *Women and the Reformation*.
40. Fernández-Armesto and Wilson, *Reformation*, 58.
41. See Matheson, *Argula von Grumbach*.
42. See 1 Corinthians 14:34; 2 Timothy 2:12.
43. See Luther, *The Sermon on the Mount and the Magnificat*, 326 n26.
44. Luther, *The Sermon on the Mount and the Magnificat*, 327.

rych Zwingli (the reformer in Zurich) and John Calvin (1509–1564) in Geneva, the two patriarchs of the Reformed tradition; both Zwingli and Calvin insisted that to honor the Virgin Mary most highly is to honor Jesus, as she herself did.[45]

Calvin, it should also be noted, wrote at length on monasticism in his *Institutes of the Christian Religion,* and largely followed the same line as Luther. Like Luther, he approves "ancient monasticism," that of the desert monastics. Drawing on the writings of Gregory of Nazianzus, Basil the Great, St Chrysostom (307–347), as well as Augustine, he commends the first monastics for their rigorous piety, and contrasts that with "our present-day monks," who "find in idleness the chief part of their sanctity."[46] But, worse than their idleness was, and here he quotes Bernard, their sexual "incontinence and vice."[47] Most of Calvin's objections, like those of Luther, are not about monasticism as such, but about the morality of "present-day" monks, especially the abuse of monastic vows and the idea that there are two brands of Christians—the perfect and the rest. Indeed, Calvin supports Augustine's "kind of monasticism," which enables the "duties of piety enjoined on all Christians," and especially commends Augustine's view that "brotherly love" is really "its chief and almost its only rule."[48]

Despite his criticisms of monasticism, as late as 1537, when Luther wrote the *Smalcald Articles,* he still recognized the potential role of monasteries, just as he continued to express his admiration for Anthony the first hermit, and for Bernard of Clairvaux. Monasteries should be abandoned, he said, only if they do not serve their good intentions of Christian formation and spuriously claim "to be superior to the ordinary Christian life and to the offices and callings established by God."[49] But, as time passed, it also appears that Luther had some regrets that he had not taken the monastery with him into the Reformation church to serve its educational and missionary outreach. The human resources in the monasteries were no longer available. Dietrich Bonhoeffer brings Luther's possible regret to our attention in a book review he wrote of Friedrich Parpert's study of monasticism and the Protestant church. Bonhoeffer

45. See Stephens, *The Theology of Huldrych Zwingli,* 109 n3.
46. Calvin, *Institutes,* 4.10, 1264.
47. Calvin, *Institutes,* 4.3, 1257, n6.
48. Calvin, *Institutes,* 4.10, 1264.
49. Article 3, The *Smalcald Articles* in Luther, *Martin Luther's Basic Theological Writings,* 510.

writes that according to Papert, "Luther had a difficult time separating himself from the monastery," and, when he "saw his own new church becoming alienated from all monastic ideas, he himself reached back for the genuine wealth he believed was still hidden beneath the ruins of the monasteries."[50] Luther was discovering to his great disappointment that it was easier to denounce corrupt institutions than to create new and incorrupt ones. Maybe it would have been better to preserve continuity with what had been established and seek its renewal rather than contribute to its demise.[51]

More seriously, however, was that Luther's rejection of monasticism and his reliance on civil authorities to take the lead in dissolving monasteries proved disastrous. This began in earnest in England, where King Henry VIII, influenced by Luther, broke with Rome in the 1530s to become head of the Church of England. Following that, in a massive and shameful landgrab by the crown, monasteries and abbeys were dissolved, and the spoils were distributed among the nobility. Pilgrimage shrines were also destroyed, and practicing anything considered popish became a punishable offense, which meant at least imprisonment if not beheading.[52]

In a recent study of what happened, Richard Ovenden refers to the dissolution of the monasteries in Europe and in England in particular as a crime against humanity not unlike the more recent destruction of cultural sites by ISIS in the Middle East. After describing the bloody butchering of the saintly abbot of Glastonbury by the king's agents, Ovenden recounts the destruction of the abbey, which was plundered within a few days, and its extensive library virtually destroyed. And this was, he says, "just a fraction of the violence and destruction that the Reformation would bring to the British Isles and Europe."[53] Jaroslav Pelikan is right: Luther's "introduction of the civil authorities as the proper agency for presiding over the dissolution of the monastic institutions was part of a fateful process in many areas of church life."[54] Greed cloaked in "reformatory zeal," to use Pelikan's words, is not a pretty sight.

---

50. Bonhoeffer, *Barcelona, Berlin, New York*, 408–10; Parpert, *Das Mönchtum und die Evangelische Kirche*.

51. Pelikan, *Spirit versus Structure*, 75–76.

52. Dickens, *The English Reformation*, 197–228.

53. Ovenden, *Burning the Books*, 54.

54. Pelikan, *Spirit versus Structure*, 62.

Restoring Ecclesia

Martin Luther did not want to destroy Christendom; his desire was to reform the Catholic Church, as many others had tried to do. But the support he received from some German princes inevitably undermined the unity of both the church and the empire. Christendom was necessary whether for Luther in Germany, Zwingli in Zurich, Calvin in Geneva, or those who followed them. They had to depend on the support of princes and magistrates to pursue their objectives, and accordingly argued that the authorities had the divine duty to protect the church and further the objectives of the Reformation. For this reason, they are often referred to as the magisterial Reformers as distinct from those designated radical Reformers, who are normally grouped together as Anabaptists—those who rejected Christendom in their attempt to restore the apostolic *ecclesia*.[55]

The Anabaptist movement first emerged in Zurich within Zwingli's domain but soon formed its own congregations. Zwingli's reforms, necessary as they were, were considered inadequate, and the Anabaptists were not prepared to wait for the city council to approve their own demands.[56] What was needed, they insisted, was a return to the *roots* of the New Testament *ecclesia* (hence they are called the *radical* Reformers) and the restoration of its original, apostolic pattern. Their rejection of infant baptism in favor of believer's baptism (for which reason they were called rebaptizers, or *anabaptists*, by their opponents) was an affirmation of costly discipleship and a break with a worldly church, a break as radical as taking monastic vows. And often the discipline exercised within their communities was similar to monastic discipline. Their condemnation and persecution, by the Reformers as heretics and by the authorities as subversives, led to widespread martyrdom, graphically documented in the seventeenth-century *Martyrs' Mirror*. Persecution also resulted in the spreading and splintering of Anabaptism across Europe, as its followers sought refuge in Holland—where they became known as Mennonites—and in other tolerant states.

Radical Protestants in England, who had come under Anabaptist influence while in exile in Holland, were known as Separatists, because they took seriously the biblical injunction to "come out from among" and "be separate from" the heathen.[57] Some took the name Baptist, though

---

55. Williams, *The Radical Reformation*.

56. The story is told in the Hutterite *Chronicle* (1525) in Williams, ed., *Spiritual and Anabaptist Writers*, 41–46.

57. 2 Corinthians 6:17

not all Baptists trace their origin to the Anabaptists, and others were known as Independents and later as Congregationalists, but all suffered persecution. That is why several hundred Congregationalists eventually went into exile across the Atlantic to establish the Commonwealth of New England in 1620. Then, after the passing of the Act of Uniformity in 1662, all those Puritan ministers remaining in the Church of England who did not accept episcopacy and the Book of Common Prayer were also ejected from their livings. Most of these were Presbyterian and some Congregational in outlook. From then on, they were known as Nonconformist Puritans, because they were committed to keeping the church pure through godly discipline.

In tracing the Puritan ancestry of Congregationalism, Geoffrey Nuttall refers to "similarities of a general kind between monasticism and Puritanism," namely, the Nonconformist ideals of "sincerity, simplicity, purity," and separation from the world. He goes on to say,

> By St Benedict and his disciples, as by Calvin and his, obedience was given a high place in the scale of values; then, as if in check upon the dangers lurking wherever obedience to God is to be expressed through obedience to man, one may watch institutions developing in which authority and responsibility are shared.[58]

Nuttall then refers to Cistercian monasticism, in which every abbey is "self-sufficient and self-governing," and described by one of their own historians as "independent congregations" or "self-governing entities within the church."[59] Of course, English Nonconformists would have repudiated any connection with Catholic monasticism, and vice versa, but on reflection, they might have said: "Well there are similarities because we all try to recover the New Testament *ecclesia*—and central to that endeavor is the need to produce committed disciples who have separated from the world in order to follow Christ from this life to the next."

No one described this better than the Baptist preacher John Bunyan (1628–1688) in *Pilgrim's Progress*. Bunyan wrote his allegory in a Bedford prison where he spent twelve years because he refused to conform to the ecclesiastical demands of the king. *Pilgrim's Progress* has played a remarkable role in Protestant history, much like the part that Athanasius's *Life of Antony* has played among Catholic monastics. In the nineteenth century,

---

58. Nuttall, *Visible Saints*, 3.

59. Nuttall, *Visible Saints*, 3–4. Quoting Knowles, *The Religious Orders in England*, 153.

it was even brought to Zululand by American Congregational missionaries. The story of *Pilgrim's Progress* obviously made an impression on their converts. Indeed, the father of Albert Luthuli, a distinguished leader of the African National Congress and Nobel Peace Prize winner, was baptized John Bunyan Luthuli.[60]

The story of Bunyan's pilgrim named Christian certainly reminds us of those early hermits who went in search of God in the desert. He leaves family, friends, and home, turns his back on the world and the established church and, setting off alone, soon faces all the temptations that assailed the desert fathers. Evagrius and Cassian would immediately recognize Bunyan's Christian, the demons that assail him, and the "heavy burden" he carries on his back. Puritan as he is, Christian is a semi-Pelagian, like most monks were. Even though at the cross his burden was lifted, and it is God's grace that saves him, Christian still has to "work out his own salvation in fear and trembling," "fleeing the wrath to come" and "fighting the good fight" with all "the armor of God."[61]

Puritan pilgrims share much in common with Celtic monks and Coptic hermits, and some commentators even liken John Bunyan himself to Anthony.[62] They all believed that the Christian life is a journey from this world to the next, and that the only way to gain the heavenly prize is to follow Christ faithfully and resist the temptations of the flesh. And both Puritan pilgrims and Coptic hermits, even if they sometimes travel with companions along the way, travel much of the time in solitude. As Owen Chadwick observes, the desert monastics "were the puritans of a church which in capturing society had partially jettisoned its puritanism."[63] I was not surprised, then, when a Coptic bishop told me that the best Bible commentaries in English were those written by Matthew Henry, a seventeenth-century Welsh Puritan and Nonconformist.

Whatever the similarities between the Pilgrim Fathers who settled in New England and the desert fathers, the comparison falters in at least one important respect. The desert fathers went into the wilderness to seek God and find themselves; the Pilgrim Fathers settled in the wilderness of New England to establish a "godly commonwealth," not a monastery. Or we might say that the towns they established were meant to be communities of saints, that is, like monasteries. But, in the process,

---

60. Hofmeyr, *The Portable Bunyan*.
61. See Philippians 2:12; Luke 3:7; 2 Timothy 4:7; Ephesians 6:11, 13.
62. Athanasius, *The Life of Antony*, xiv–xv.
63. Chadwick, ed., *Western Asceticism*, 13.

they and their descendants became Christian triumphalists, claiming the land as God's providential gift to them alone, believing that they were an elect people and favored nation, Christendom restored. This soon meant that Native Americans were forced to leave their ancestral homes and journey into the alien West. The American defense of Christianity today is often simply the attempt to preserve European triumphalist Christendom, as did those who in South Africa defended apartheid in the name of Christianity.

If we compare *Pilgrim's Progress* and Geoffrey Chaucer's *Canterbury Tales,* written two hundred and fifty years earlier, we find ourselves in two different worlds. Bunyan's allegory is set in Restoration England and is Puritan in substance, recounting the spiritual experience of many believers. Chaucer's *Tales* are medieval and Catholic, graphically capturing what must have unfolded on countless pilgrim routes from Glastonbury to Canterbury, and beyond to Rome and Jerusalem, to venerate the relics of saints. But there are differences as well as similarities. Today, you may have to travel on your own along the Camino to Santiago and prefer to remain in solitude, but invariably you have company along the way, find hospitality in monasteries, and can share your tale with others at an evening meal. Like the tellers of Chaucer's *Tales,* Camino pilgrims cover the whole gamut of human experience, a diverse and even motley crew, not necessarily intent on following Jesus to the cross, whose stories range from the holy to the lewd.

In 1993, while in Edinburgh, Isobel and I attended a performance of *Pilgrim's Progress* as an opera set to music by Ralph Vaughn Williams. A bishop was sitting in front of me, and I sensed, as he confirmed afterwards, that we were both more attracted by the music and worldly goings-on in Vanity Fair than by the austere, lonely, and pious journey of Christian from the godless world to the "heavenly city." It was as though a Puritan descendent of the Reformation, which began when Martin Luther left the monastery and its flagellations to reenter the world, marry a former nun, and enjoy beer, had now turned his back on that world. Even the "middle way" of Cassian and Benedict seemed forgotten in favor of the austere desert hermits and Carthusian monks. I am sure the Puritans in New England both feasted and fasted, and they certainly spoke about an "inner joy" even if it was not always written on their faces. But Chaucer was right. Pilgrims need companions, they need a hospice to welcome them at the end of the day; they need to break bread and drink wine with those who share the journey; they need to turn the heaviness of being into a lightness that accompanies laughter.

Of course, Bunyan's Christian did find companions and guides along the way, but he cuts a lonely figure. There is no real *ecclesia* in the story, no community. But then Bunyan wrote in prison, and sometimes, like him, we all must travel alone and find God and our true selves in solitude. Certainly every pilgrim who has also been a prophet, like Jeremiah, and every pilgrim prisoner of conscience, like Bunyan and Bonhoeffer, knows that the journey to resurrection life goes via the cross. And in the end, we all face death, hopefully surrounded by family and friends, but still on our own. "Mr Worldly-Wise" told Bunyan's "Christian" that he was mad to choose the "narrow way," reminding us that Anthony the desert father once said that people call monks mad, and Luther thought that is how it should be. But maybe monastics are sometimes the only sane people around. The same might be said of Søren Kierkegaard (1813–1855), whose solitary journey from aestheticism through moralism to ascetic discipleship continues to challenge us, and offers us another reason to revisit monasticism.[64]

A Navigation Buoy

A journalist, amateur philosopher, and Christian layman, Kierkegaard was a thorn in the flesh to the established Danish church and scathing in his attack on its nominal Christianity, which assumed that every Dane by birth and baptism was a disciple of Jesus. No one since the Anabaptists challenged the Christendom captivity of established Protestantism more than Kierkegaard. He also believed that monasticism was necessary to save the soul of his native Lutheran Denmark. But unlike the desert hermits, Kierkegaard did not flee the world; he attacked it from within with an evangelical zeal equal to that of Luther. Today, Kierkegaard's statue stands outside one of Copenhagen's prestigious churches, and to that extent he has been honored as a prophet in his own country. But, perhaps more significantly, some sixty years after his death, his writings played a formative role in radically reshaping Protestant theology in the twentieth century.

Kierkegaard would have been at home among the desert fathers even if he did not choose to leave the city and dwell with them. Consider what he wrote in his *Journal* on Easter Monday 1848, the day of the Battle of Schleswig when the Danes tried to counter Prussian troops three times their number, resulting in enormous casualties. He was thinking about

64. See Coates, *The Aesthetics of Discipleship*.

what it meant to be a Christian in a comfortable "Christian" world now at war with itself, and particularly about the misuse of the Bible in supporting the established status quo:

> Fundamentally a reformation which did away with the Bible would now be just as valid as Luther's doing away with the Pope. All that about the Bible has developed a religion of learning and law, a mere distraction . . . As a result it does immeasurable harm; where life is concerned its existence is a fortification of excuses and escapes.[65]

And, again, it "is high time that Christianity was taken away again from men in order to teach them to appreciate it a little."[66] Then, in a collection of his writings titled *Attack on Christendom*, Kierkegaard asks:

> What then is "Christendom"? Is not Christendom the most colossal attempt at serving God, not by following Christ, as he required, and suffering for the doctrine, but instead of that by "building the sepulchres of the prophets and garnishing the tombs of the righteous[?]"[67]

For Kierkegaard, as for the first monastics, Christendom is all about the expansion of Christianity, an increase in numbers, mass conversions, triumphalist and nominal Christianity. And too often it is so because kings supported by court theologians demand, not the making of disciples, but servile subjects whose religion makes them so. In the process, Christianity is abolished with the help of a Christian state, and we end up with a Christian world, by which we even try to hoax God, but in which there is not one single Christian. Then, on another occasion, Kierkegaard, intriguingly remarks that there can be no doubt that Protestantism "may need the monastery again, or wish it were there," because it is "an essential dialectical element in Christianity . . . a navigation buoy at sea in order to see where we are."[68]

Kierkegaard often used pseudonyms in his attacks on Christendom. Significantly, one of them was Johannes Climacus, the monk whom we met earlier and who wrote *The Ladder of Divine Ascent*. The choice of the name goes back to Kierkegaard's childhood. The reasons for the choice need not detain us, but they have to do with his developing understanding

65. Kierkegaard, Journal entry 1848, in *The Journals of Søren Kierkegaard*, 150.
66. Kierkegaard, *The Journals of Søren Kierkegaard*, 153.
67. Kierkegaard, *Attack Upon "Christendom,"* 121; Matthew 23:29
68. Quoted on the frontispiece in Maguire, *An Infinity of Little Hours*.

of the Christian faith—an understanding that puts him at odds with Christendom and contemporary philosophy, and in both respects connects him with the protest of the first desert hermits.[69] Under the name Climacus, Kierkegaard gives his fullest analysis of monasticism, in his *Concluding Unscientific Postscript*. But it is in a sermon in his *Edifying Addresses*, the first to be translated into English and published as *Purity of Heart*, which was meant to be a preparatory guide for the office of confession, that we discover Kierkegaard the pilgrim and secular monk:

> When we are thinking of divine things, the deeper the stillness the better. When the wanderer comes away from the much-travelled noisy highway into places of quiet, then it seems to him . . . as if he must examine himself, as if he must speak out what lies hidden in the depths of his soul.[70]

Kierkegaard, who is sometimes described as the father of modern existentialism, attacked Christendom and the established church in Denmark because it had cheapened both Christ's call to costly discipleship and the need for individuals to decide to follow Christ rather than the cultured crowd. But Kierkegaard, like Bunyan, said little about the need for a committed Christian community, the *ecclesia*, that was more than a conglomerate of individual disciples. For that, we must look to Karl Barth who fell under Kierkegaard's spell during the First World War when Christendom finally collapsed in the trenches of France. It was Kierkegaard, in fact, who inspired Barth's attack on liberal Protestant theology in Germany because of its nationalist support for Kaiser Wilhelm II's war policy.

A Powerful Impulse

Reformed theology, as distinct from Lutheran, has focused relatively more on the doctrine of the church than it has on "justification by faith"—that is, on the community of faith rather than on the person of faith. Luther spoke a great deal about the church as a fellowship of believers, but his ecclesiology was essentially Catholic in structure. By contrast, the fathers of the Reformed tradition, following Zwingli and Calvin, wanted to reconstruct the church from the ground up. They replaced bishops with presbyters and synods, gave power to laypeople and relative autonomy to congregations, encouraged greater direct participation in the liturgical

---

69. Lowrie, *Kierkegaard*, Vol. 2, 29–37.
70. Kierkegaard, *Purity of Heart*, 42.

life of the church, and emphasized what Calvin called the "third use of the law," that is, church discipline. The congregation, not just the monastery, was meant to be "pure," a community of "visible saints," modeled on the New Testament *ecclesia*.

Among Reformed theologians of the twentieth century, no one expressed this better than the Swiss professor in Zurich, Emil Brunner (1889–1966), Barth's contemporary and sometimes sparring partner. As a student I devoured his book *The Misunderstanding of the Church*, which clarified the relationship between the church as a necessary worldly institution and the *ecclesia* as the community (*koinonia*) of believers in Christ who share a common life. Much of my life as a pastor and theologian has been informed by this understanding of the church, which is as much Catholic as it is Reformed, because it is ecumenical and monastic. From this perspective, denominationalism is an ecclesial aberration or heresy.

The churches of the Reformation cannot be antimonastic in principle, for their founding was to embody the *ecclesia* in the life of the world. Thus, as Brunner reminds us, throughout the history of the churches of the Reformation, groups have emerged within them (he refers to them as Brotherhoods) attempting to recapture the life and spirit of the New Testament *ecclesia*. I previously mentioned some of these that emerged at the time of the Reformation. More recent examples Brunner refers to are the Iona Community (in Scotland), the Sisterhoods of Grandchamp and Gelterkinden (in Switzerland), the Taizé community (in France), as well as Anglican monasteries in England, though these are more obviously Catholic in character.[71] The point Brunner is making is not about whether these groups have always been successful, but that neither monastic-like communities nor religious orders are foreign to Reformation ecclesiology. They are a reminder or signpost of what the *ecclesia* is meant to be.[72] That is why Brunner concludes with words that every monastic would affirm:

> The Word of Jesus, "Whosoever would keep his life will lose it, and he who loses it for my sake will find it," must in such fashion become the norm of the Church that it never loses sight of the maxim *ecclesia reformata semper reformanda* ("a Church reformed and ever willing to be reformed") and understands ever more clearly that it is there for the world's sake.[73]

---

71. Brunner, *The Christian Doctrine of the Church*, 83.
72. Brunner, *The Christian Doctrine of the Church*, 83.
73. Brunner, *The Christian Doctrine of the Church*, 84.

If Brunner so strikingly reminded the Reformed churches of their need to be the *ecclesia* that is always being reformed, it was Barth who inspired a new generation of theologians across the ecumenical spectrum to take the Bible more seriously, to engage the world more intensely, and to listen more carefully to what the Spirit was saying to the church through the witness of the Word. Indeed, without Barth, there would have been no Confessing Church opposing Nazism, no Barmen Declaration, and not the Bonhoeffer we now know. For if Bonhoeffer had not met Barth, he would probably not have written about the need for a "new monasticism."

Bonhoeffer met Barth in person for the first time in the summer of 1931 in Bonn, where Barth was a professor. In a letter to Erwin Sutz, a Swiss Reformed pastor and former fellow student in New York, who had introduced him to Barth, Bonhoeffer tells us what happened. "Barth lectured at seven this morning. I spoke with him briefly. Tonight there is an evening of discussion at his house with people from Maria Laach."[74] The "people from Maria Laach" were Benedictine monks. That Bonhoeffer met them on the day he first met Barth is a remarkable coincidence. What did they talk about? Undoubtedly the emerging ecumenical movement, the biblical renaissance underway, and the changing political landscape. Probably they also discussed the place of monasticism in the modern world. On the same day, July 15, Bonhoeffer visited the Maria Laach monastery with the monks, and they developed a good relationship.[75] From then on, the monastery had a special significance for Bonhoeffer, as Eberhard Bethge told me when we visited the monastery together on two occasions many years later.

Barth was initially wary of monasticism, as we would expect, just as he was about the House of Brothers that Bonhoeffer established at the seminary in Finkenwalde a few years after their meeting in Bonn. In a lengthy letter to Bonhoeffer, he expressed reservations about his encouragement of "scriptural meditation" (*lectio divina*) rather than serious biblical study. More generally he was bothered "by the smell . . . of monastic eros and pathos." At the same time, Barth acknowledged that what Bonhoeffer was attempting might "represent new possibilities" even if he himself had "no use for it at the time."[76] That suggests that he accepted the possibility that a time might come when it might be useful. That it did

---

74. Bonhoeffer, *Ecumenical, Academic and Pastoral Work*, 34.
75. See Bonhoeffer, *Ecumenical, Academic and Pastoral Work*, 34 n2, 36.
76. Bonhoeffer, *Theological Education at Finkenwalde*, 268–69.

seems apparent from what Barth says in the final volumes of his *Church Dogmatics* where he discusses monasticism first, critically, and then, at greater length, positively.

Christians, he writes, irrespective of tradition, might try to "flee the world," but we can never escape because "the most dangerous representative of the world," namely, our "self," goes with us into the desert, the monastery, or on our pilgrimage. Moreover, if we do attempt to flee, we cannot say we are imitating God if God loves the world so much that in Christ he became embodied in it. Barth also warns against the misuse of monastic vows and certain forms of asceticism.[77] These sentiments are not new. Luther said as much, and they have been echoed by monastics themselves over the years. As Merton acknowledged, the Reformation attack on the theory and practice of the vows can serve "as an invitation to a thoroughgoing re-examination of the nature and function of the vows."[78]

Having expressed some reservations, Barth then shows considerable appreciation for monasticism. Let me use italics to highlight what he says. The "*lasting* significance" of monasticism is that it reminds us that we must not conform to the values of the world. Indeed, monasticism is "a *highly* responsible and *effective* protest and opposition to the world, and not least to a worldly church." It offers "a *new and specific* way of combatting it . . . a retreat in fact, for the purpose of more effective attack." Barth even asks whether there is "*any other way*" for the church to respond to the world unless through "an equally genuine retreat?"[79] For this reason, monasticism can be understood as "*a movement of the Spirit*" which expresses "the power and vitality of the church."[80] The historical proof is seen "in the concrete and influential movements of reform" that have resulted.[81] Monasticism is, in fact, "an *impressive*" attempt in the struggle for Christian perfection, even if it separates the religious and secular spheres. So we cannot judge it negatively for "demanding a particular vigilance and strictness in these spheres."[82] Indeed, "*it is a weakness of Protestantism that it has not taken monastic asceticism seriously.*"[83]

---

77. Barth, *Church Dogmatics* IV/2, 14.
78. Merton, *The Life of the Vows*, lxvii.
79. Barth, *Church Dogmatics* IV/2, 14 (italics added).
80. Barth, *Church Dogmatics* IV/2, 13 (italics added).
81. Barth, *Church Dogmatics* IV/2, 13–14.
82. Barth, *Church Dogmatics* IV/2, 15 (italics added).
83. Barth, *Church Dogmatics* IV/2, 16 (italics added).

The Reformers were right to criticize monastic abuses and monasticism's sometimes un-evangelical theology, but this did not apply to all monasteries and monks. There were many good ones that were "never the den of arrogance and tyranny that the majority of Protestants imagine." Indeed, Barth refers positively to the *Rule of Benedict*, which, he says, "displays an extraordinary knowledge of life and the soul and humans" and "is also characterized by a true fear of God."[84] The "normal monk" has always been "occupied with spiritual and physical labor, with all kinds of arts and serious scholarship, with the exercise of hospitality and charity, even with preaching and pastoral work among the people, with social work and teaching, and above all with the supremely monastic *opus Dei*."[85] Indeed, Barth concludes, the monastic life is an attempt to embody "the *sanctorum communio*," and is therefore "*an example* to both church and the world."[86] In fact, "*monasticism derives from faith*" and has to do "with discipleship, sanctification, concretion, brotherhood and love." That it can become perverted is no reason to reject it. So whatever reservations we might have, we must give it "our *serious consideration in detail*."[87] In doing so, we are not "leaving the ground of the Reformation but *following a powerful Reformation impulse*."[88] That is a remarkable statement.

Around the same time that Barth expressed these views on monasticism, he welcomed the changes in thinking about the "religious life" being adopted at the Second Vatican Council (1962–1965). This, he said, indicated both an affirmation of and an openness to the adaptation of traditional monasticism to meet contemporary challenges.[89] Though it must be said that it was difficult for Vatican II to be proscriptive about this because of the many modifications and varieties that had developed over the centuries within Catholic monasticism, especially with regard to its apostolic character.[90] Yet Barth supported the general direction and spirit adopted and, in turn, Catholic theologians and bishops acknowledged his contribution to the renewal of the church. Thus shortly after

---

84. Barth, *Church Dogmatics* IV/2, 17.
85. Barth, *Church Dogmatics* IV/2, 16.
86. Barth, *Church Dogmatics* IV/2, 17 (italics added).
87. Barth, *Church Dogmatics* IV/2, 18 (italics added).
88. Barth, *Church Dogmatics* IV/2, 19 (italics added).
89. See *Lumen Gentium*, article 9 in Vatican Council (2nd: 1962–1965), *The Documents of Vatican II*, 472–73.
90. See Wulf, "Decree on the Appropriate Renewal of the Religious Life," 353.

the Council ended, the abbot of the Benedictine monastery in Montserrat in Spain, Gabriel Brasó, invited Barth to address his fellow monks on the nature of the monastic life, the role of monastics today, and possible directions that monasticism should take following the Council.[91] Barth happily agreed, and told the monks that "such special communities of brothers or sisters were *especially* dependent on free grace and that their task and significance was to be 'in exemplary fashion' the brothers and sisters of *all* Christians" as well as *all* people.[92] But he also spoke specifically, and significantly, of the monastic life as "an event."

Barth always distinguished between the church as an institution and as an event. He fully acknowledged the necessity of the former but insisted that it is not of the essence of the church. What is of the essence is that through the Spirit and the Word, God continually calls the church into being and upholds it in its witness to Christ. And this, said Barth, is especially true of monasticism, the reason why its ministry is fruitful when it is persistent in fulfilling it. That is why, to repeat Barth's insistence, we Protestants have to learn that monasticism "derives from faith, it has to do with discipleship, sanctification, concretion, brotherhood and love."[93] And it is precisely because monasticism at its best lives by faith, grace, and love, relying on God's mercy, that it fulfils such a necessary role in the life of the church and in its service of the world.

Bonhoeffer as Monastic Theologian

As we have noted, Vatican II both affirmed traditional monasticism and encouraged its development in fresh ways consonant with the overall spirit of the Council. In response to that encouragement, many New Monastic Communities began to appear within the Catholic Church. This was especially true in Italy, Spain, France, and the United States. In her detailed study of these communities, focusing especially on Italy, Stefania Palmisano says that they sought to renew "monastic life by emphasizing the most innovative and disruptive aspects" of the Council's theology. She notes that those involved were not members of existing monastic orders; the communities were gender inclusive; they accepted lay members "whether single, married or families," and did not live in enclosed

91. See Gioia, "Word of God and Monasticism in Karl Barth," 419.
92. Busch, *Karl Barth*, 482 (italics original).
93. Barth, *Church Dogmatics* IV/2, 18.

environments; they adapted the hours of prayer to allow outside labor and voluntary service; they engaged in evangelism; and they were ecumenically orientated and often involved in interfaith dialogue.[94] Among the most prominent, successful, and controversial of these New Monastic Communities Palmisano studied is that of Bose in the Commune of Magnano near Turin, founded by Enzo Bianchi in the mid-1970s.[95] But irrespective of where these communities are located, whether they are Catholic or ecumenical, they often refer to Bonhoeffer as the theologian who has inspired them most, making reference in particular to his *Life Together*, and his reflections on "a new kind of monasticism."[96]

The seeds of Bonhoeffer's interest in monasticism were already planted when, in 1924, as a young twenty-one-year-old student in Tübingen, he visited Rome for the first time.[97] Unlike Luther's visit centuries before when the Reformer was shocked by what he saw, Bonhoeffer was profoundly moved, especially by what he experienced there during Holy Week.[98] He describes this at length in his Italian diary, in which he notes that much of it was influenced by the monastic tradition.[99] This was his first taste of the rich catholic heritage that stretched back over the centuries and his first experience of the church as truly universal.

The theological foundations for Bonhoeffer's monastic reflections came a few years later when, now a student in Berlin, and already under the influence of Barth, he began working on his dissertation, *Sanctorum Communio*, which he completed in 1927. This was for Bonhoeffer more than the academic exercise of an aspiring theologian preparing for a future professorship. Though thoroughly scholastic to meet the rigorous demands of the university, his research and writing was also motivated by an existential desire to understand the essence of the church to which he felt called to serve as a pastor. After his visit to Rome, he found his own Prussian Protestant Church lacked the catholic diversity, liturgical vitality, and spiritual passion that had so enthralled him in the Eternal City. Setting aside the temptation to become a Roman Catholic, in *Sanctorum*

---

94. Palmisano *Exploring New Monastic Communities*, 2–3.

95. Palmisano, *Exploring New Monastic Communities*, 62–65, 148–53. Bianchi retired as abbot in 2015 and was later asked to leave the community by the pope over problems related to leadership succession.

96. Bonhoeffer, *London*, 284–85.

97. Bethge, *Dietrich Bonhoeffer*, 59–62.

98. Bonhoeffer, *The Young Bonhoeffer*, 88–93.

99. See Bonhoeffer, *The Young Bonhoeffer*, 528–29.

Communio he reimagined the Protestant Church as *ecclesia*, as a community of love in relation to but distinct from its sociological character as an institution. And he did so with the striking thesis, that the church is "Christ existing as a community of persons."[100] In his reaching this conclusion, the cornerstone was laid for all that was to follow.

But the catalyst that finally turned Bonhoeffer the "scholastic" into Bonhoeffer the "monastic" theologian happened during his year of study at Union Theological Seminary in New York in 1930-31. He implies as much when, soon after he began to form his House of Brethren at Finkenwalde in 1935, he recalls the influence of Jean Lasserre, a French Reformed fellow student at Union, and his experience of the African American church. It was then, he says, that he "discovered the Bible," and realized that while he had often preached, he had "not yet become a Christian."[101] Reading the Bible, especially the Sermon on the Mount, through Lasserre's eyes and those of African American Christians, made it clear to Bonhoeffer

> that the life of a servant of Jesus Christ must belong to the church, and step by step it became plainer to me how far that must go. Then came the crisis of 1933 . . . The revival of the church and of the ministry became my supreme concern.[102]

This was the beginning of Bonhoeffer's journey into the desert and his discovery of costly discipleship that informed his participation in the German Church Struggle, led to his monastic turn at Finkenwalde, and finally resulted in his martyrdom.

Much to Barth's dismay, in October 1933, amid the crisis facing the church in Germany, Bonhoeffer left the scene to become the pastor to two German expatriate congregations in London. But that retreat gave Bonhoeffer time to think more seriously about monasticism. In a letter dated June 1934, which Hardy Arnold wrote to his father Eberhard, the founder of the Bruderhof Community in Germany, Hardy mentions meeting Bonhoeffer and two friends in London. He tells his father that they were motivated to start "a sort of Protestant monastic community," and though their "planning was still a bit piecemeal," they had "good intentions of learning from others, from monasteries, from Gandhi's ashram, and *from us!*" He also tells his father that Bonhoeffer had "very

---

100. Bonhoeffer, *Sanctorum Communio*, 134-41, 189-92.
101. Quoted in Bethge, *Dietrich Bonhoeffer*, 205.
102. Quoted in Bethge, *Dietrich Bonhoeffer*, 205.

clear views . . . on the issues of violence and private property" and leaned "strongly toward *asceticism and self-denial*."[103]

Bonhoeffer's thinking was like that of Eberhard Arnold. But what he had in mind was not a community separate from the world in some rural space, like some monasteries, for his concern was for the renewal of the church *in the world*.[104] He was also of the opinion that a purely university training for pastors would no longer suffice. As he told his Swiss friend Erwin Sutz in a letter in September 1934:

> The next generation of pastors, these days, ought to be trained entirely in church-monastic schools, where the pure doctrine, the Sermon on the Mount, and worship are taken seriously—which for all three of these things is simply not the case at the university and under the present circumstances is impossible. It is also time for a final break with our theologically grounded reserve about whatever is being done by the state—which really only comes down to fear.[105]

So it was, that, four months later, in January 1935, Bonhoeffer wrote to his brother Karl-Friedrich, and mentioned for the first time in writing the need for "a new kind of monasticism." This is what he said:

> The restoration of the church must surely depend on a new kind of monasticism, which has nothing in common with the old but a life of uncompromising discipleship, following Christ according to the Sermon on the Mount. I believe the time has come to gather people together and do this.[106]

Soon after writing this, Bonhoeffer accepted a call to return to Germany to establish and direct a new Confessing Church seminary in East Prussia.[107] In preparation, he visited several Anglican and Free Church seminaries in England which provided additional or alternative forms of theological formation to those offered by universities. Among them was the monastery at Mirfield in Yorkshire, home to the Community of the Resurrection where Trevor Huddleston, the priest who would play a major role in the formation of Desmond Tutu, and who later founded the Anti-Apartheid Movement, enrolled a few years after Bonhoeffer's

---

103. Bonhoeffer, *London*, 161 (italics original).
104. See Bonhoeffer, *London*, 166 n5.
105. Bonhoeffer, *London*, 217.
106. Bonhoeffer, *London*, 284–85.
107. Bethge, *Dietrich Bonhoeffer*, 412.

visit.[108] Indeed, it was in the Community at Mirfield that Tutu learned both the disciplines of Christian spirituality and how these connected to the political struggle for justice.[109]

Once he had settled into his new life as director of the seminary at Finkenwalde, Bonhoeffer introduced his new vision of theological formation based on the monastic style of formation he had experienced in England. This was not easy for his students, who had already completed their university training and were not readily compliant to his seemingly monkish proposals. But Bonhoeffer was adamant. How could he and his students be faithful pastors in a world torn apart by nationalism and warmongering unless they became a community of committed disciples who not only believed in the doctrine of justification by faith but lived by faith and obedience? As he wrote in *Discipleship* around the same time, "*only the believers obey*, and *only the obedient believe*."[110] He also wrote, "whenever Christ calls us, his call leads us to death."[111] Which is precisely how the first monastics understood their retreat into the desert.

In virtually the same breath Bonhoeffer says that the cheapening of grace that had occurred in the churches of the Reformation was avoided in the Catholic Church *because of monasticism*, for there "on the boundary of the church, was the place where the awareness that grace is costly, and that grace includes discipleship was preserved."

> People left everything they had for the sake of Christ and tried to follow Jesus' strict commandments through daily exercise. Monastic life thus became a living protest against the secularization of Christianity, against the cheapening of grace.[112]

Bonhoeffer's main reservation about monasticism was the same as Luther's: costly grace can become "the extraordinary achievement of individuals, to which the majority of church members need not be obligated." Monastic "self-denial" then becomes "self-righteousness," and a monk's withdrawal from the world "a subtle love for the world."[113] But, says Bonhoeffer, Luther's return to the world was not to avoid costly discipleship, it was to embrace it, for he had come to believe that it was only

108. Huddleston, *Naught for Your Comfort*.
109. Battle, *Desmond Tutu*, 19–24.
110. Bonhoeffer, *Discipleship*, 63 (italics original).
111. Bonhoeffer, *Discipleship*, 87.
112. Bonhoeffer, *Discipleship*, 47.
113. Bonhoeffer, *Discipleship*, 47.

in the world that a Christian could truly follow Jesus. "Complete obedience to Jesus' commandments had to be carried out in the daily world of work."[114]

However, the net result of the Reformation was the reverse: "justification of the sinner in the world became the justification of sin and the world." It was a repeat of what I have called the triumphalist heresy when, in early Christendom, the world became nominally Christian.[115] This was a catastrophic self-deception for those descendants of Luther in Germany who, capitulating to Hitler, cheapened grace while claiming to follow Luther and affirming "justification by faith alone." But the truly "blessed" are those who

> by simply following Jesus Christ are overcome by this grace, so that with humble spirit they may praise the grace of Christ which alone is effective. Blessed are they who, in the knowledge of such grace, can live in the world without losing themselves in it.[116]

Bonhoeffer's monastic turn was therefore not about escaping the world, it was part of his turn "from phraseology to reality."[117] And reality was where God and the world connected in Christ.

Indeed, in a letter to his parents from Ettal monastery in November 1940, Bonhoeffer, now working for the Resistance, and therefore deeply and dangerously engaged in the life of the world, speaks very positively about monasticism. "This form of life," he writes, "is naturally not foreign to me, and I experience its regularity and silence as extremely beneficial for my work." He then goes on to say, that it "would certainly be a loss (and was indeed a loss in the Reformation!) if this form of communal life preserved for fifteen hundred years were destroyed, something those here consider entirely possible."[118]

But when Bonhoeffer became director of the Confessing Church seminary in Finkenwalde a few years earlier, his primary task was not to save monasticism; it was to prepare pastors for their work in Confessing Church congregations as Germany implemented its Final Solution of the so-called Jewish problem and increasingly prepared for war. The

114. Bonhoeffer, *Discipleship*, 48.
115. Bonhoeffer, *Discipleship*, 55.
116. Bonhoeffer, *Discipleship*, 46–56.
117. Bonhoeffer, *Letters and Papers from Prison*, 358.
118. Bonhoeffer, *Conspiracy and Imprisonment*, 87.

challenge was immense. A purely academic training was totally inadequate for what was happening. The *kairos* demanded something far more, indeed, nothing less than a monastic-type of environment, such as he had experienced in England.

The problem was that the ordinands coming to Finkenwalde were only meant to stay there for a semester or two, so it was necessary for them to become part of an existing community that understood what he was trying to do, thus providing continuity and stability. In other words, the seminary needed to be located within a stable, monastic type of community. That is why Bonhoeffer felt it necessary to establish the House of Brethren, composed of some ordinands who would commit themselves to stay at Finkenwalde for a longer period as well as commit themselves to a common life and the ministry of the church.[119]

To establish his House of Brethren, Bonhoeffer had to get the support of the relevant regional Confessing Church council, so he wrote to explain what he had in mind. His aim, he said, was "to produce a group of completely free, committed pastors" who could "preach the word of God for the sake of decision and discernment of the Spirit in the present and future struggles of the church, a group prepared for immediate service and proclamation whenever new emergency situations might arise." He went on to say that such a group

> must be prepared to make themselves available wherever their services are needed, under any circumstances, and without consideration of any financial or other privileges otherwise associated with the ministry. By being able to come from and return to a brotherhood, they will always have the home and the fellowship [*Gemeinschaft*] that they need for their ministry. The goal is not monastic isolation but rather the most intensive concentration for ministry to the world.[120]

After the Gestapo closed Finkenwalde in October 1937 the House of Brethren continued to function, but now as collective pastorates that enabled theological education to continue underground.[121] And it did so until November 1939 when Germany invaded Poland, right on the border near where Finkenwalde was situated. Bonhoeffer was then banned and joined the Resistance.

---

119. See Introduction in Bonhoeffer, *Life Together; Prayerbook of the Bible*, 17–20.
120. Bonhoeffer, *Theological Education at Finkenwalde*, 96.
121. Bonhoeffer, *Theological Education Underground*.

Bonhoeffer's classic study on Christian community, *Life Together*, in which he described the kind of community he tried to achieve at Finkenwalde, was written a year before the outbreak of war. *Life Together* is not a monastic *Rule* in the same sense as those produced by Augustine, Cassian, or Benedict, but like them it provides a vision, a rationale, and practical guidelines for life together in an intentional community. I will say more about its influence on new monastic communities in my next chapter. Since its publication, it has been a source of inspiration for many who have been engaged in establishing such communities, and widely read and appreciated by monastics, including the monks at Taizé. I first read *Life Together* in 1963, the year before I first visited Taizé, and my memory tells me that when I was there it seemed as if what I had read had come alive. *Life Together* was also influential when the Volmoed Community was established in the 1980s.

Taizé: A Monastic Parable

On our way to Chicago in 1963, Isobel and I, together with our young son Steve, passed through London and by chance visited St Alban's Abbey in Hertfordshire. Shrine to Britain's first martyr, St Alban's is the oldest place in Britain where Christians have worshiped continually since Saxon times. The present buildings date back to the eleventh century when, in 1077, the monastery was established and its first abbot was appointed by Lanfranc, the Norman archbishop of Canterbury, previously abbot of Bec. Dissolved by Henry VIII in the sixteenth century, the abbey now serves as a cathedral church. This was my first experience of a medieval monastic building. It was also the first time that I came across the name Taizé, when, in the Abbey bookstore I came across *This Day Belongs to God* by Roger Shutz, its founding prior.[122] On reading the book, I found, to my surprise, that Brother Roger was a Reformed pastor, so I felt an immediate affinity, and vowed to visit the community if ever given the chance.

That providential opportunity occurred a year later, in September 1964, on my journey home from the United States, after bidding farewell to Isobel and Steve, who went directly to Johannesburg. I arrived at the

---

122. Br. Roger, *This Day Belongs to God*; see also Br. Roger and the Community of Taizé, *The Rule of Taizé*; González-Balado, *The Story of Taizé*, 27; and Spink, *A Universal Heart*.

little train station below the village as a curious "theological tourist," but I was welcomed as a pilgrim. The brother assigned to care for me suggested that I go on a weeklong silent retreat. During the week I read *The Rule* of *Taizé*, written by Br. Roger, for the first time and thought about its possible significance for my life. I also discovered that *monasticism* is a synonym for a hospitality that welcomes all and provides space for each to discover why they have come.

Br. Roger was born in 1915 in a small French-speaking village in Switzerland. His father was a Reformed pastor, and his mother the daughter of another. Various influences that shaped his early life, among them a family openness towards Catholics and a concern for the poor, led him to study for the ministry at Lausanne. After the outbreak of the Second World War Roger decided that his future ministry should not be in comfortable Switzerland but in France where so many people were suffering hardship. This led him to visit Cluny in search of a house where he could shelter the homeless and serve refugees. He found such a place in the nearby village of Taizé, but the war situation prevented him from staying. So he returned to Switzerland, where he completed his dissertation on *The Idea of the Monastic Life before Saint Benedict and Its Conformity to the Gospels*. He then formed a small community of friends who shared his ideal of establishing an ecumenical monastic-style community of prayer and hospitality.

In 1944, Roger and his small group of friends returned to Taizé to start their monastic community, and at Pentecost 1948 they celebrated their first service in the somewhat derelict parish church which had been made available to them by the papal nuncio in Paris, the future Pope John XXIII. The community grew steadily, becoming more ecumenically diverse, and soon attracted Catholics. Taizé was warmly acknowledged by John XXIII when he became pope referring to it as "a little springtime." Such affirmation was also given by Paul VI as well as various Orthodox patriarchs, and many other ecumenical church leaders. And Br. Roger and a few other brothers were also special guests at the sessions of Vatican II.

The 1960s were years of ferment among young people across Western Europe. Traditional cultural norms and practices were radically challenged, religious faith was rejected, and sometimes the spirit of rebellion turned violent. Ironically, or better, providentially, but certainly unexpectedly, many thousands of young people began visiting Taizé, curious to find out what it was about. The number of brothers and visitors soon grew so large that the community decided to build a much larger church, as the old parish church was far too small. So it was that in 1962 the Church of Reconciliation was opened with many church dignitaries attending. And, as one commentator reports, "journalists and film crews" wanted "to know why so many young people were traveling to this little village to pray with a group of 'Protestant monks.'"[123] Young pilgrims, during 1974 alone, the year in which Taizé sponsored its first Council of Youth, numbered sixty thousand.

This also led to liturgical changes, most notably the introduction of a new style of singing at the three daily prayer services, a style that has now become widely associated with Taizé and adopted in many places, including Volmoed. Adapted from a form used for centuries at the Benedictine monastery at Montserrat to welcome pilgrims to the abbey, the songs were contemporary yet based on Scripture and connected to ancient monastic chants.[124] No one who has heeded the majestic summons of the Taizé bells and attended the daily services of prayer in the chapel can remain untouched as the sound of the songs gently spreads across the vast auditorium, interspersed with Scripture readings and prayers in many languages.

Towards the end of the 1970s, Archbishop Desmond Tutu visited Taizé, and while worshiping in the Church of Reconciliation, he had a vision of 144 young South Africans going there on a Pilgrimage of Hope.[125] This vision was fulfilled during 1980 when a racially diverse group visited Jerusalem and Rome, and then spent a week at Taizé to reflect on their lives, their country, and the gospel. Tutu could not lead them because he was prevented from doing so by the apartheid government; but for those who went it was a life-changing experience that opened new horizons and provided signposts for life back in South Africa. Among those hopeful pilgrims was our now late son Steve, who, while at Taizé, received his call to ministry.

Taizé not only became a place of pilgrimage, but the community also began to send brothers as pilgrims of "trust on earth" to many parts of the world, especially where there was great injustice and poverty. Br. Roger himself made pilgrimages to such places, including South Africa, until his untimely death in August 2005 when he was murdered by a mentally ill woman during evening prayer in the Church of Reconciliation. We at

123. Santos, *A Community Called Taizé*, 67.
124. Santos, *A Community Called Taizé*, 107–10.
125. See Tutu, "Review of *Taizé*."

Volmoed were privileged to receive his successor, Br. Alois, who spoke at our weekly Eucharist in September 2019, after the Pilgrimage of Hope in Cape Town.

Towards the end of the *Rule of Taizé* there is a passage that is read when brothers make their life profession.

> The Lord Christ, in his compassion and love for you, has chosen you to be in the Church a sign of brotherly love. He calls you to live out, with your brothers, the parable of community.[126]

A parable, like those Jesus taught, helps us see things differently and so discern the way towards the coming of God's kingdom. But the meaning of a parable is not always self-evident. Jesus's parables were often explained by the Gospel writers to help their readers, just as they are also interpreted by preachers in many contexts different from those in which Jesus lived. So, too, is the parable of the Taizé Community. It is a Spirit-led invitation to plant authentic communities of justice, peace, and reconciliation in our own contexts, by renouncing "all thought of looking back, and joyful with boundless gratitude, never fear to run with the dawn."[127] That is what true pilgrims have always done. Each day is a new day, and often before dawn they have begun to journey further into the future with God. That is the core meaning of the parable of Taizé; it is a story that points the way towards the kingdom of God.

Taizé began, as Jesus's parable has it, like a "mustard seed," when Br. Roger and his friends first prayed in a small apartment in Geneva for the guidance of the Spirit. This led him beyond his Swiss comfort zone across the border into war-ravaged France—a move no less significant than when those young and earnest Alexandrian Christians left the city for the desert in search of God. Roger went because he believed he was being called by God to leave home behind and begin a journey, for only in doing so would he come to know the God who meets us on the road, among the poor and the refugees The beatific vision, that is, Jesus's promise that the "pure in heart shall see God,"[128] is not simply a blessing beyond this life, for the "pure in heart" see God in everyone they meet along the road. Taizé was not a flight from the world but a journey deeper into its pain and suffering, and the first brothers traveling on that

---

126. See Br. Roger of Taizé and the Community of Taizé, *The Rule of Taizé* (2012 ed.), 117–18.

127. *The Rule of Taizé* (2012 ed.), 119.

128. Matthew 5:8.

journey bore a message of peace, justice, reconciliation, and hope. So it is that Taizé's commitment to the world has been enclosed in prayer for its needs. There is no boundary between prayer and the struggle for a more just world.

Today, as I write this chapter, I have browsed again through *This Day Belongs to God* and noted all the passages I had previously underlined. It is in many ways an *apologia* for Taizé, the reason for its foundation, the meaning of its *Rule* and its vocation as a monastic community pledged to serve the world. Brother Roger's understanding of ecumenism and its vital importance combine with a clear analysis of the problems we face as Christians seeking to serve Christ in the world. *This Monastic Moment* is about discovering that *this* day and every moment belongs to God, for it is *today* that we must listen to what the Spirit and the Word are saying to the church.

> The kingdom of God is justice and peace,
> and joy in the Holy Spirit.
> Come, Lord, and open in us,
> the gates of your kingdom.[129]

---

129. Community of Taizé, 2001

4

IN THIS TIME & PLACE

How awesome is this place! This is none other than the house of God, this is the gate of heaven.
—GENESIS 28:17

When I am tempted to run from an onerous task in the present, I am likely to picture past times that I now imagine to be better than they were, or to project myself into future events of which I can . . . know nothing. I am unable to see the grace that is available to me now, in this place and time.
—KATHLEEN NORRIS[1]

Though monasticism seems to be a bedrock of tradition, it has nevertheless changed a great deal. It has dialogued with many cultures simultaneously and . . . found permanence, not in its customs or observances, for these are many and varied; but it has found its identity in the charism of the Holy Spirit. God has freshly gifted the Church with monasticism through all the Church's times and expressions. This is our permanence.
—FRANCIS KLINE[2]

---

1. Norris, *Acedia & Me*, 39.
2. Kline, *Lovers of the Place*, 119.

Kathleen Norris recounts that a monk once told her, "We are still a great experiment after all these years, and we resist codifying." She goes on to comment that the "great experiment of Christian monasticism has taken so many forms that it is hard to characterize . . . Time will tell what works, and what doesn't; after a millennium and a half, Benedictines can afford to take the long view."[3] If Benedict's *Rule* encourages us to "hasten" towards the coming of God's kingdom, Benedict also tells us to do so with patience. Indeed, "love is patient," and God's love toward the world is infinitely so, "abounding in steadfast love and faithfulness."[4] Certainly, God's timetable seldom fits neatly into our own, which is why we need to take time out to discern how and where we are being led.

In telling the monastic story, I have highlighted key issues and players and placed them in their context. We have seen how monasticism developed in a variety of ways, guided by *Rules* shaped by experience, and inspired by the lives and teaching of remarkable men and women—some of them now officially designated saints, though none of them was perfect, as they themselves best knew. As the story has unfolded, I have explored continuities that hold it together and considered changes that have occurred over time. I have tried not to romanticize monasticism—like its saints, monasticism itself has by no means been perfect otherwise there would have been no need for the attempts to reform it. How could it be? Its quest is the vision of God, its hope is the coming of God's reign, and its means is the rule of love.

I now return to my initial question: How does this remarkable story inform our response to this present *kairos*? If this is a monastic moment, as I have argued, what is the Spirit and the Word saying to the church today as we reflect on it? Are we able, as Norris puts it, "to see the grace that is available" to us in monasticism "in this time and place?"[5] Or, to use Francis Kline's expression, what is God "freshly gifting" to the church in the world today through monasticism? If we are sensitive to the Spirit, as was John the Divine in writing his apocalypse, we will soon discern that we, like the first monastics, are engaged in a war of the Spirit, a struggle between justice and oppression, truth and falsehood, hope and despair, love and hatred, life and death.

---

3. Norris, *The Cloister Walk*, 18–19.
4. 1 Corinthians 13:4; Exodus 34:6.
5. Norris, *Acedia & Me*, 39.

The War of the Spirit

When the Berlin Wall fell in 1989, at virtually the same time as the collapse of the apartheid regime, the cultural historian Francis Fukuyama famously announced the "end of history," by this he meant that the globalization of democracy would bring about a new world order of liberty and equality, thereby preventing future major conflict. But Fukuyama acknowledged that human beings, "bored with peace and prosperity" could "restart history," even though modern science provided a "bulwark" against that possibility.[6] Little did he anticipate what happened on September 11, 2001, in New York when history began again, or the way in which, twenty years later, a disillusioned public in the United States would turn against its own democratic values, deny the importance of scientific data, and storm the Capitol. In both instances, religious extremism played a major role, further confounding those who anticipated a religionless world. We may live in a scientific age, but misguided and ill-informed religious beliefs combined with nationalist, racist, and sexist convictions remain a potent force affecting human behavior.

And now, as I finish writing this book, which I began as COVID-19 forced us into lockdown, we are threatened by new variants of the coronavirus and remain almost as isolated if not as silenced as Trappists. And, while Donald Trump has been dethroned, his legacy of crimes and misdemeanors remains to be exorcised. It seems as if a host of demons, which have long been lurking beneath the surface and periodically erupting, have been let loose on a terrifying scale, rivalling the Four Horsemen of the Apocalypse and revealing the structural injustices of modern society. Just as serious is the moral confusion and spiritual emptiness that pervades modern culture, the debasement of human values, and the loss of meaning that transcends the mundane. We all find it difficult to live with anxiety and despair, now made worse by a lockdown loneliness that struggles to handle either the enforced need to be alone, or to live in confined spaces with others. We are learning again that Fukuyama's projected "last man," humanity free and happy, is no different from the "first man" (Adam). Paradise regained has become a dream deferred rather than the reality pundits promised. The realists among us know that it will remain an illusion, as monastics have long known, even for those with enough money to create their own bubble of security and opulence.

6. Fukuyama, *The End of History*, 335–36.

The COVID-19 pandemic has undoubtedly evoked acts of great courage, dedication to the service of others, scientific advances, and a creativity that has led to remarkable innovations for coping with adversity and keeping hope alive. It has also taught us much about ourselves and the societies in which we live, the importance of healthy communities and serving the common good, and the danger of selfish individualism, whether driven by religion or secularism. Yet, as Fukuyama wrote:

> The decline of community life suggests that in the future, we risk becoming secure and self-absorbed last men, devoid of . . . striving for higher goals in our pursuit of private comforts. But the opposite danger exists as well, that we will return to being first men engaged in bloody and pointless battles, only this time with modern weapons."[7]

In identifying the decline of community, Fukuyama puts his finger on one important reason why *this* is a monastic moment. We desperately need to strive for higher goals than the "pursuit of private comforts," and build communities based on life-sustaining values. And we need models for doing so, just as we need models of leadership that point the way. That is why, already forty years ago, Alasdair MacIntyre wrote about the need for another St Benedict, who could help us form communities of mature human beings committed to the common good.[8] Such communities are not collectives in which the individual is absorbed in the mass, lacking freedom to be who they are or reach their potential. But, equally, they reject self-centered individualism that does not care about others or the environment and is incapable of developing enduring relationships and stable commitments.

The notion that individual freedoms or liberties are incompatible with the common good is false, dangerous, and unchristian, as Parker Palmer eloquently describes in *The Company of Strangers*. A Quaker social philosopher and theologian, Palmer draws on insights from Bonhoeffer and Merton to argue his case. He provides a compelling account of how, "in a culture of brokenness and fragmentation, of individualism and autonomy," private or personal and public life can be integrated.[9] Personal spirituality and social justice, he insists, are not polarities but complementarities. The struggle for justice, peace, and a sustainable

---

7. Fukuyama, *The End of History*, 328.
8. MacIntyre, *After Virtue*, 245.
9. Palmer, *The Company of Strangers*, 23.

planet arises out of, and is sustained by, a spiritual vision of what it means to be human and live together in community.

It is humbling for Christians that Fukuyama hailed the birth of global democracy, not Christianity, as the hope of the nations. Following Hegel, he regards Christianity as a "slave religion" that promises the masses a better life in heaven rather than a transformed life on earth. And, for some, that is what Christianity represents: fleeing the world for the sake of gaining paradise. It was the French Revolution we are told, that brought about an era of liberty and equality here and now. But even this utopia was short-lived, as it led to a reign of terror and endless wars that devastated Europe, and all but destroyed monasticism in its medieval heartland. Secularism replaced Christianity as the religion of modernity and the driving ideology of post-Christendom Europe.

But the secular, enlightened debunking of religion was no more successful in delivering lasting happiness than was triumphalist Christendom, which promised heaven to its obedient subjects. And while democracy may have belatedly become the best available form of government we have managed to construct, even its most robust forms can be undermined by nativist politics, economic interests, and social media. The truth is, no political platform or party can make or keep humanity happy, especially in times when fears overwhelm hopes for a new day of justice and peace.[10] History does not just start again; history repeats itself. And for that reason alone, the struggle of the Spirit continues, and will continue to the end of time, just as our own personal struggles remain to the end of our lives.

Fukuyama spoke of human hopes for a better world in terms of desire—not the desire for God or for wisdom, but the desire for justice, the desire of the oppressed to be recognized as fully human and given their rightful place in the sun. Yet Fukuyama also acknowledged that this will never be achieved without a struggle, a "war of the Spirit" he called it following Hegel, fought over conflicting desires: the desire for dignity and justice, on the one hand, and the lust for power and domination, on the other. Marxists describe this as a class war, and democracy, dependent on an informed civil society, seeks to deal with the problem according to the "will of the people" expressed through elections, and the rule of law. But neither democracy nor the myth of inevitable progress have brought paradisical happiness. Indeed, utopian myths, says Benedictine

---

10. See de Gruchy, *The End Is not Yet*.

Joan Chittister, "drive us like lemmings on the way to the sea, to our own destruction."[11]

Desire, as I have previously noted, has a distinctly negative connotation in the New Testament where St Paul tells us that God has handed us over to the false desires of our hearts.[12] Monastics from the desert hermits onwards, following Scripture, have long understood the heart as a site of struggle, for the heart is a metaphor for the deepest recesses of our humanity where desire resides. What happens in that struggle makes us who we are, the kind of people we are becoming in our lifelong journey. The heart is where the outward struggle is initially won or lost, for it is there that we are tempted to grasp after power and possessions that lead to our moral and social undoing. That is the wisdom of the desert, for it is in the heart that what Evagrius called the eight evil thoughts—which later became the seven deadly sins—have their origin. Sin is not a metaphysical concept but a worldly reality. That is why we cannot separate the struggles for justice and peace in the world from the inner struggle to overcome arrogance, envy, and grasping for what is not ours to possess. Acts of violence, hatred, and lust are certainly related to social and historical realities, but all of these are the outcome of sin, our alienation from the source of life, whether manifested as racism, rape, rage and fear, or economic plunder.

Of course, not all desires "of the heart" are false and destructive. In fact, desire has as much to do with our redemption as it does with our destruction—the desire for truth, goodness and beauty, the desire for love, justice and wisdom, and the desire for God.[13] Julian of Norwich desired self-knowledge, compassion, and a will for God.[14] Indeed, a twelfth-century Carthusian monk, Guido II, compared the desire for God with the taste for good wine[15]—a sentiment shared by the psalmist, who tells us to "taste and see that the Lord is good."[16] And Jesus tells us that we will only be happy when we "hunger and thirst for God's justice."[17]

---

11. Chittister, "Old Vision for a New Age," 89.
12. Romans 1:18–31.
13. Gorringe, *The Education of Desire*.
14. Julian of Norwich, *Showings*, chapter 2.
15. See Maguire, *An Infinity of Little Hours*, 3.
16. Psalm 34:8.
17. See Matthew 5:6.

The "war of the Spirit" is a struggle, then, between conflicting desires waged at a far deeper level than that of political policy or social ideology. It is the struggle between truth and falsehood, love and hatred, the common good and crude self-interest, despair and hope, the humanization and dehumanization of the world. Or, as expressed in the Bible, a struggle between the God of mercy, justice and love, and the gods of tribes, nations, and self-seeking individuals, that sanction and demand revenge, exclusion, and domination. Monastics and Jungian therapists describe it as a struggle against archetypal demons deeply embedded in our collective unconscious. But, however described, it is not simply a struggle "against enemies of flesh and blood," as the Letter to the Ephesians tells us, "but . . . against the spiritual forces of evil in the heavenly places."[18]

We may demythologize the language of spiritual warfare such as we find in the letter to the Ephesians or monastic writers, but we cannot escape the reality which, as Bonhoeffer says, "is laid bare" in *kairos* moments, when we suddenly recognize that "Shakespeare's characters are among us. The villain and the saint . . . arise from primeval depths and, with their appearance, tear open the demonic and divine abyss out of which they come, allowing us brief glimpses into their suspected secrets."[19] In a sermon preached in Barcelona on Remembrance Day, November 25, 1928, notably on a text from the Song of Songs, titled "Love is Strong as Death,"[20] a young Bonhoeffer referred to this "war of the Spirit" as a battle between love and death. He also called it a "battle without equal, one into which we are all drawn, a war between the highest powers: the war of death against love, of love against death, two foes worthy of each other in majesty." But, he concluded, love is ultimately stronger than death because death is subject to God, and "God is love, not death."[21] This is the mystery of faith in Christ, crucified and risen, that Christians proclaim.

Led into Mystery

The rejection of Christian triumphalism by the first monastics was not articulated in theological declarations or treatises. By turning their backs

---

18. Ephesians 6:12.
19. Bonhoeffer, *Ethics*, 76.
20. Song of Songs 8:6b.
21. Bonhoeffer, *Barcelona, Berlin, New York*, 538.

on the empire and a worldly church, they were responding to a deep human desire for a love that passes understanding. In doing so, they made a powerful theological statement with their bodies. They did not claim to be theologians, like Clement and Origen of Alexandria, or the Cappadocians, or articulate their thoughts with theological precision, but they were daily engaged in the war of the Spirit between life and death. The hermitage was a site of struggle between the God of imperial might and ecclesial splendor, and the God revealed in Jesus the Christ crucified, made known through the Word and Spirit. Their theological formation happened in the struggle against demons who continually tempted them to think and act otherwise, to doubt that love would triumph. It was a cosmic struggle made internal and personal.

Monastics were, nonetheless, inevitably often caught up in the ecclesial politics and theological debates that divided Constantinople from Rome, and Antioch from Alexandria. Even though they resisted theological scholasticism, they could not avoid the controversies about Christology and the Trinity that raged around them any more than they could flee the world. Heresy was a problem not because monastics were interested in splitting hairs, but because their life was dependent on their trust in the God who is revealed in Jesus Christ. Affirming the Nicene Creed mattered, because in doing so, they confessed that the God in whom they believed was love, truth and beauty, just as it matters to us at *this* monastic moment that the God in whom we believe is not the God of vengeance and violence, but of redemptive love and justice.

The attempt to describe this mystery we name God led to the doctrine of the Trinity formulated primarily by the Cappadocian fathers in the East and by Augustine in the West. Ever since, Christians have been trying to understand what the doctrine means. But words inevitably fail to express the mystery of God in abstract terms, a language unsuited to the task. Like all symbols, words can only point beyond themselves to something which, as Anselm said, is greater than we can conceive. So, let us not linger on the problem of linguistics but go to the heart of the matter.

The doctrine of the triune God means, in the words of the First Letter of John, that "God is love" (the Greek word is *agape*),[22] and that this love is relational and reciprocal, self-giving, creative, and redemptive. This contrasts with deism, which posits an impersonal divinity that exists

---

22. 1 John 4:16.

absolutely and in splendid isolation, a philosophical construct rather than One who is always seeking to embrace us in a community of love. That is why Augustine describes the Trinity in analogical terms—God is at one and the same time "the lover, the beloved, and love."[23] This cannot be reduced to mathematical formulae; it is a doxological statement about the nature of reality based on faith in Jesus Christ. It is, said Bonhoeffer in a sermon he preached in London in May 1934, a doctrine that is "immensely simple, so that any child can understand it."

> There is *truly only one* God, but this God is perfect love, and as such God is Jesus Christ and the Holy [Spirit]. The doctrine of the Holy Trinity is nothing but humankind's feeble way of praising the mighty, impetuous love of God, in which God glorifies himself and embraces the whole world in love.[24]

God alone loves absolutely. All other absolutes are idols.

According to the First Letter of John, in the war of the Spirit this divine love enables us to test the spirits, distinguishing between truth and falsehood, justice and oppression, to "see whether they are from God." This divine love is also the basis for life in the *ecclesia*, for if we do not love one another as God loves us, then Christ is not present among us. And it is this divine love that enables us to grow in Christian perfection, for to love fully is to become fulfilled in God.[25]

Many people who say they believe in the Trinity simply mean, however, that they accept the Creed; it does not mean that they live a Trinitarian life. In fact, some have misused the doctrine in defense of Christian triumphalism, nationalism, and white supremacy, as some did in South Africa in defense of apartheid. That is why Catherine LaCugna says that a "nontrinitarian theology of God," that is, a God of absolute power unqualified by love,

> opens the door to every kind of ideology or idolatry, whether it comes in the form of a self-sufficient masculine Father-God, or a plenipotentiary God who perversely wishes small children to die, or an apathetic God who does not mind if some people are always poor, or a violent, vengeful God who enjoys wars fought in God's name.[26]

23. Augustine, *The Trinity*, book 1:16; book 8:14, 76, 255.
24. Bonhoeffer, *London*, 363.
25. 1 John 4.
26. LaCugna, *God for Us*, 395.

In contrast to the triumphalist God, the Bible, says Bonhoeffer in his *Letters and Papers from Prison*, "directs people toward the powerlessness and the suffering of God," because "only a suffering God can help."[27] This is the power of God, as it is the basis for Bonhoeffer's worldly interpretation of Christian faith. As he tells his friend Bethge:

> God consents to be pushed out of the world and onto the cross; God is weak and powerless in the world and in precisely this way, and only so, is at our side and helps us . . . Christ helps us not by virtue of his omnipotence but rather by virtue of his weakness and suffering![28]

This is not a denial of God's omnipotence, but a redefining of that omnipotence in the light of the cross. The crucifixion is, for the Christian, the death of false images of God, a supreme iconoclastic action. Christ crucified is "the image of the invisible God,"[29] which means that the triumph of the risen Christ is the power of the "crucified God."

This is the God of Mary's Magnificat, who stands in solidarity with the struggling people of the earth, not the God who legitimates the power of the strong.[30] Consider what Bonhoeffer says in a sermon preached in London in 1933 on the song of Mary, the "oldest Advent hymn," which, he says, "is also the most passionate, the wildest, and one might almost say the most revolutionary Advent hymn that has ever been sung."

> This is not the gentle, tender, dreamy Mary as we often see her portrayed in paintings. The Mary who is speaking here is passionate, carried away, proud, enthusiastic. There is none of the sweet, wistful, or even playful tone of many of our Christmas carols, but instead a hard, strong, relentless hymn about the toppling of the thrones and the humiliation of the lords of this world, about the power of God and the powerlessness of humankind.[31]

This, says Bonhoeffer, places Mary among the prophetic women of the Old Testament. But Mary is more than one of the prophets. Seized by the power of the Holy Spirit, she "humbly and obediently lets it be done unto her as the Spirit commands her," and "knows better than anyone else what

---

27. Bonhoeffer, *Letters and Papers from Prison*, 479.
28. Bonhoeffer, *Letters and Papers from Prison*, 479.
29. Colossians 1:15.
30. Luke 1:46–55.
31. Bonhoeffer, *London*, 342.

it means to wait for Christ's coming." That is why Mary is the "Mother of God" for all Christians, even Reformed ones as Barth affirms.[32] In doing so, we acknowledge that the journey into the mystery of God is also a journey with Mary, the humble yet courageous young woman in whom action and contemplation are united in her witness to the son to whom she gave birth.

Indeed, our journey into the mystery of God at this time and place begins at a specific time and place: "when the fullness of time [*kairos*] had come, God sent his son, born of a woman."[33] In other words, our journey into the mystery of God is not a flight into a fantasy world, or even into a Neoplatonic moment of illumination, for it begins in Bethlehem, where the mystery is first disclosed to faith. We journey to Bethlehem because, as Bonhoeffer says,

> Mary knows the secret of his coming, knows about the Spirit, who has a part in it, about the Almighty God, who has performed this miracle. In her own body she is experiencing the wonderful ways of God with humankind: that God does not arrange matters to suit our opinions and views, does not follow the path that humans would like to prescribe. God's path is free and original beyond all our ability to understand or to prove.[34]

Our journey is therefore located within history, in the world as we know it, a world of strife, exclusion, massacres of the innocent, rape, and fleeing refugees. It is in this world, at this time and this place, that we hear and accept Christ's invitation to follow him into the mystery of the God who loves the world and seeks to redeem it through a baby born out of wedlock. And we do so, says Bonhoeffer,

> whether we, like the first disciples, must leave house and vocation to follow him, or whether, with Luther, we leave the monastery for a secular vocation, in both cases the same death awaits us, namely, death in Jesus Christ, the death of our old self caused by the call of Jesus.[35]

---

32. Barth, *Church Dogmatics* I/2, 138. See also McLoughlin and Pinnock, eds., *Mary Is for Everyone*.
33. Galatians 4:4.
34. Bonhoeffer, *London*, 343.
35. Bonhoeffer, *Discipleship*, 87–88.

For some that death means martyrdom, but for all it is dying to those values that in the war of the Spirit promote death rather than give and sustain life.

Today, in *this* monastic moment, we do not need a skull to be placed on our desk, as did Jerome in his cell in Bethlehem, to remind us that we daily face death. We only need to turn on the television or read the newspapers. Even as I write, the COVID-19 death count has broken all previous records across much of the world, and several people I know have personalized the statistics. Our time has become defined by death, just as it has been redeemed by the care and compassion of people who daily put their bodies on the line, as Mary did, in the struggle between the love of life and the pain of death. In doing so, they have entered the mystery of God without necessarily understanding it as such. Indeed, their anguished cry itself is a witness to the mystery: "Why, in God's name, is there all this suffering?"

This is the ultimate challenge to all our theologies, all our pious attempts to allay our fears, and all our inadequate attempts to justify God. But, as we discovered on the day our son Steve drowned in February 2010, and we started our painful journey into mystery in earnest, because God is love, death is always penultimate, never ultimate. And the Christ who was born in Bethlehem is the Christ who continually takes form in the world, leading us further into the mystery of God.

Christ Taking Form in the World

The first monastics discovered that seeking God in the solitude of a hermitage required belonging to a community of fellow seekers. If Anthony led the way into desert solitude, Pachomius formed the first community of monastics and provided a *Rule* to guide them. Jesus's call to follow him was, likewise, from the beginning, both personal and communal, for he formed his followers into a community, no easy feat given their personalities. After his death and resurrection, that community began to take on the form of Christ in the world through the Spirit, thereby embodying the trinitarian life of God long before that was described in dogma. It became what Paul called "the body of Christ," the *ecclesia*, or John's "beloved community," the community in which the love of Christ was expressed, because "they loved one another as Christ loved them."[36]

---

36. Bonhoeffer, *Sanctorum Communio*.

This was by no means how it really or always was, but how it was meant to be and sometimes miraculously was. That, in essence, is why Barth told the monks in Montserrat that "their task and significance was to be 'in exemplary fashion' the brothers and sisters of *all* Christians," indeed, of all people.[37]

Bonhoeffer would not have had monasticism in mind when, aged twenty-one, he attempted to describe the social reality of the church in his dissertation *Sanctorum Communio*, and concluded that it was Christ "existing as church-community." But anyone who wants to understand his "new kind of monasticism" must begin there. Barth would later call *Sanctorum Communio* a "theological miracle" because, for him, it was one of the finest theological treatises on the church to have been written.[38] The real miracle, however, is not Bonhoeffer's dissertation; it is when a community of sinners becomes a community of saints, and the new humanity is born amid the death that defines the old. For this is, says Bonhoeffer, "what the reality of Jesus Christ means"[39]—not a "religious community" composed of like-minded individuals, or an institution in which individuals surrender their personal identity in a mass movement, but the real presence of the risen, crucified Christ present through the Spirit in history, which is "*at the same time the norm for its own history.*"[40] By definition, it is a community that embraces the other in the love of God, so that we are "no longer strangers and aliens, but . . . citizens with the saints and also members of the household of God."[41] This is the mystery of God's love revealed in Christ.

But how is this possible? What transforms a community of sinners into a community of saints and enables it to be the body of Christ that embraces all in love? This is brought about by the Holy Spirit, the Spirit of the risen Christ who makes Christ present in the church-community.[42] What Bonhoeffer calls the "actualization of the essential church," that is, the church as *ecclesia*, the church as beloved community, is "accomplished by the Spirit-impelled word of the crucified and risen Lord of the

---

37. Busch, *Karl Barth*, 482.
38. See Barth, *Church Dogmatics* IV/2, 641.
39. Bonhoeffer, *Sanctorum Communio*, 153.
40. Bonhoeffer, *Sanctorum Communio*, 211 (italics original).
41. See Ephesians 2:11–22.
42. Bonhoeffer, *Sanctorum Communio*, 139, 143.

church."[43] This is the "life-principle" of the church, namely, "God's will to rule in love."[44] The church is therefore only the true church of the crucified and risen Christ when it embraces us all in the love of God. Or, as Parker Palmer puts it, the reconciliation of the world, including the unity of the church, "is not achieved through calculation and manipulation, but received through contemplation and vulnerability and self-giving."[45]

Over the years, Bonhoeffer became disillusioned about the institutional Protestant church, even the Confessing Church, but he never gave up on the church. Instead, it was precisely amid that disillusionment that he began talking about a "new kind of monasticism" that would enable the church to be "conformed to the unique form of the one who became human, was crucified, and is risen."[46] That is, Christ taking form here and now, in this place and at this time.

Compare what Bonhoeffer says in this regard with what we already know about authentic monastic formation:

> To be conformed to the one who has become human [means that] . . . all efforts to outgrow one's nature as human, all struggle to be heroic or a demigod, all fall away . . . Pretension, hypocrisy, compulsion, forcing oneself to be something different, better, more ideal than one is—all are abolished. God loves the real human being. God became a real human being.[47]

And again: "to be conformed to the crucified . . . means to be a human being judged by God . . . (to) die daily the death of sinners." At the same time, to "be conformed to the risen one . . . means to be a new human being before God." What could be more monastic than to say, with Bonhoeffer, that "we live in the midst of death; we are righteous in the midst of sin; we are new in the midst of the old."

> Our mystery remains hidden from the world. We live because Christ lives, and in Christ alone. "Christ is my life." As long as the glory of Christ is hidden, so the glory of the new life also is "hidden with Christ in God" (Col. 3:2).[48]

---

43. Bonhoeffer, *Sanctorum Communio*, 157.
44. Bonhoeffer, *Sanctorum Communio*, 264.
45. Palmer, *The Company of Strangers*, 27.
46. Bonhoeffer, *Ethics*, 93.
47. Bonhoeffer, *Ethics*, 94.
48. Bonhoeffer, *Ethics*, 95.

Those who are becoming conformed to the incarnate, crucified, and risen Christ in this way, Bonhoeffer says further, "are not concerned to promote themselves, but to lift up Christ for the sake of their brothers and sisters . . . they show themselves as those who have received the Holy Spirit and are united with Jesus Christ in incomparable love and community."[49] It is not in isolation that we experience the mystery of God's love in Christ, but in this community in this time and place. How, then, does the mystery of this God revealed in the crucified and risen Christ become embodied in Christian community today?

Worldly Ascetics & Educating Desire

Bonhoeffer wrote sections of his *Ethics* in the Benedictine monastery at Ettal where he spent several weeks in late 1940 and early 1941.[50] The previous Christmas, the monks had read his book *Discipleship,* so they were presumably aware of what he wrote in the chapter on "The Saints."[51] They would have agreed that, as Paul himself wrote, Christ "himself is our sanctification,"[52] and therefore, with Bonhoeffer, that "those who have faith are being justified; those who are justified are being sanctified; those who are sanctified are being saved on judgment day."[53] But they might not have agreed so readily with Bonhoeffer's view that some Christians are not more holy than others, or that ascetic disciplines do not make them so. And they would probably have been more bothered by Bonhoeffer's later reservations about *Discipleship,* which he expressed in a letter from prison to Bethge. In it he said, that while he stood by what he had written, he had not understood at the time that one could only follow Jesus "by living in the full this-worldliness of life."[54]

In telling Bethge this, Bonhoeffer recalled a conversation he had with Jean Lasserre, a French pastor and fellow student at Union Seminary, in which Lasserre told him he wanted to become a saint. Bonhoeffer was impressed, but replied that he would rather "learn to have faith," and

---

49. Bonhoeffer, *Ethics,* 94–95.
50. 17 November 1940 to 28 February 1941; 1–7 April 1941. See Bethge, *Dietrich Bonhoeffer,* 701–2.
51. Bethge, *Dietrich Bonhoeffer,* 453.
52. 1 Corinthians 1:30.
53. Bonhoeffer, *Ethics,* 280.
54. Bonhoeffer, *Letters and Papers from Prison,* 486.

do so "by trying to live something like a saintly life."[55] But, since then, he had stopped trying to make something of himself, "whether it be a saint or a converted sinner or a church leader (a so-called priestly figure!), a just or an unjust person, a sick or a healthy person" and threw himself "completely into the arms of God." This, he said, is what "this-worldliness means," namely, "living fully in the midst of life's tasks, questions, successes and failures, experiences, and perplexities," and no longer taking seriously "one's own sufferings but rather the suffering of God in the world." This, he added, "is faith; this is μετάνοια [metanoia]. And this is how one becomes a human being, a Christian. (Cf. Jer. 45!)"[56]

In an earlier letter to Bethge, Bonhoeffer made the same point: being a Christian means "being human . . . the human being Christ creates in us." It "is not a religious act that makes someone a Christian," he writes, "but rather sharing in God's suffering in the worldly life."[57] Instead of our trying to be religious, Christ demands of us a "mature worldliness." However, he stresses, this does not "mean the shallow and banal this-worldliness of the enlightened, the bustling, the comfortable, or the lascivious, but the profound this-worldliness that shows discipline and includes the ever-present knowledge of death and resurrection."[58]

Merton concurred with Bonhoeffer.[59] True Christian worldliness, he would write, "is an affirmation of life and humanity, of confidence and hope amid struggle, suffering and death."[60] Indeed, true Christian asceticism is a way of exercising Christian responsibility *for* the world, as the Catholic theologian Johan Baptist Metz says:

> What drives the Christian to the flight of asceticism and denial of the world is not, therefore, contempt for the world, but responsibility for it in hope—in hope for that world future as it is announced and sealed in the promises of God, against which we constantly harden our hearts in pride and despair.[61]

This means that as the Christian community engages in the war of the Spirit, the ascetic and active life need to be synchronized. The

---

55. Bonhoeffer, *Letters and Papers from Prison*, 486.
56. Bonhoeffer, *Letters and Papers from Prison*, 485–86.
57. Bonhoeffer, *Letters and Papers from Prison*, 480.
58. Bonhoeffer, *Letters and Papers from Prison*, 541.
59. Merton, *Conjectures of a Guilty Bystander*, 253.
60. Merton, *Conjectures of a Guilty Bystander*, 156–57.
61. Metz, *Theology of the World*, 102.

contemplative and the prophetic belong together. True Christian asceticism is, therefore, about engaging the world in ways that are loving, creative, redemptive, hopeful, and life-giving, and educating and disciplining our desires accordingly.

Timothy Gorringe suggests four ways in which this can be done.[62] The first stems from a recognition that whether the body is degraded or honored has to do with relationality. If our relations with others and with our own selves are just, loving, and caring, then the bodies of those involved are affirmed and made whole. Christian asceticism, in other words, is incarnational not gnostic. The second way is solidarity with the poor. If it is obscene, says Gorringe, to ask the poor to become ascetics because they are already "involuntary ascetics"; it is equally obscene for wealthier Christians not to help them in their need, both by sharing resources and by challenging economic systems and policies that make and keep them poor. Christian asceticism is socially and politically responsible. The third way is through expressing our desires in ways that are loving, just, and creative. In other words, Christian asceticism is active, not passive, caring not uncaring, and expressed in a polyphony of ways.

The fourth way, says Gorringe, is through the transformation of sexual desire. This was, of course, distinctive about monasticism from the beginning, for celibate chastity was a necessary requirement. It was also required by some early intentional Christian communities, such as the Shakers in America, an eighteenth-century sect loved by Merton for their Cistercian simplicity of life and their handicraft.[63] But taking a vow of chastity does not expunge sexual desire, any more than good intentions prevent gender-based violence. How, then, are we to understand the "vow of chastity" at *this* monastic moment, when such violence is rife even in societies which are sexually liberated?

Sexuality & the Polyphony of Life

The problem of sexuality is central to the Genesis myth of the fall.[64] This is clear when we recognize that the Hebrew word for "to know" God, or "to know" good and evil is the same word that describes sexual intercourse, that is, "to know" someone intimately. As soon as Adam and Eve

---

62. Gorringe, *The Education of Desire*, 97–99.
63. Merton, *Seeking Paradise*.
64. Genesis 3. See Bonhoeffer, *Creation and Fall*, 122–26.

eat the forbidden fruit of the tree of the "knowledge of good and evil," they become ashamed of their nakedness and hide from God. Then, we are told, Adam "knew" Eve, and she became pregnant.[65] To "know God" thus means to have an intimate relationship with God. It is not surprising, then, that the Song of Songs has always been a monastic favorite, the biblical book most read and commented on by monks. As Jean Leclercq says, "with its ardent language and its dialogue of praise, it was more attuned than any other book in Sacred Scripture to loving, disinterested contemplation."[66] It was even considered the complement to Benedict's *Rule* and understood as "the rule of love."[67]

The Genesis story also connects human sexuality to self-knowledge. Having tasted of the fruit of the tree of the knowledge of good and evil, so to speak, all our illusions about ourselves are stripped away. We see ourselves naked, not just in relation to each other, from whom we can still disguise ourselves, but before God, from whom we cannot hide. We cannot pretend to be what we are not. We may desire God, but we are forced to recognize that we are not God; we may still dominate others, but then we transgress the limits that keep us respectful of the other. Chastity properly understood, like not hugging the other during the COVID-19 pandemic, is a sign of respect. When that boundary is transgressed, our sexuality becomes "a *passionate hatred* of any limit," which, says Bonhoeffer,

> seeks to destroy the other person as a creature, robs the other person of his or her creatureliness, lays violent hands on the other person as one's limit, and hates grace . . . It is affirming oneself to the point of self-destruction. Obsessive desire and hate . . . are the fruits of the tree of knowledge.[68]

The fact that Adam and Eve, the mythic representatives of us all, became ashamed of their bodies—not because they had intercourse with each other, but because they rejected the limits that protect our humanity and relationships, means that they could no longer "know" God. Gender-based violence is therefore portrayed as symptomatic of a revolt against God, and at the same time, an expression of self-hatred. Instead of loving others as we love ourselves in loving God, we hate others because we hate

---

65. Genesis 4:1.
66. Leclercq, *The Love of Learning and the Desire for God*, 85.
67. See Leclercq, *The Love of Learning and the Desire for God*, 86, 273.
68. Bonhoeffer, *Creation and Fall*, 123 (italics original).

ourselves. Sexual desire is not the problem; self-hatred, which leads to the abuse of the other, is. Both the monastic vow of celibacy and those of Christian marriage thereby acknowledge the limit to sexual desire that derives from love of the other and recognizes that both are equally a God-given vocation.

Bonhoeffer and Bethge had an intimate friendship; some have even surmised that it was homosexual. That assumption derives from a failure in contemporary culture to appreciate the depth of real friendships, those commonly called Platonic.[69] Some monastics, like many nonmonastics, acknowledge that they are homosexual, and accept their sexuality as God-given. The persecution of homosexuals by certain Christians is often a hypocritical expression of a failure to come to terms with their own sexuality, and results from their obsessive desire to control the other. Gender-based violence and the persecution of homosexuals have the same pathology. At *this* monastic moment, Christians need to recover true friendship within the *ecclesia*, strongly oppose sexual hypocrisy and violence, and develop relationships of respect for people of all genders.

Bonhoeffer helps us to go further and understand our sexuality in relation to our knowledge of God. In a letter from prison to Bethge in May 1944, he discusses how the love of women and men for each other relates to their love for God. He writes, "There is a danger, in any passionate erotic love that through it you may lose what I'd like to call the polyphony of life."[70] Bonhoeffer uses this musical analogy to affirm life in the fullness of its many dimensions, not least the sensual and creative, in opposition to those who repress or deny it, as many critics claim, with some justification, that Christians have often done.[71] But God, says Bonhoeffer,

> wants to be loved with our whole heart, not to the detriment of earthly love or to diminish it, but as a sort of cantus firmus[72] to which the other voices of life resound in counterpoint. One of these contrapuntal themes, which keep their *full independence* but are still related to the cantus firmus, is earthly love.[73]

---

69. See de Gruchy, *Daring, Trusting Spirit*, 59–73.
70. Bonhoeffer, *Letters and Papers from Prison*, 393–94.
71. See Pangritz, *The Polyphony of Life*, 55–56.
72. The fixed melody that makes polyphony possible.
73. Bonhoeffer, *Letters and Papers from Prison*, 394 (italics original).

Bonhoeffer then refers to the Song of Songs and says that we cannot really "imagine a hotter, more sensual, and glowing love than the one spoken of here (cf. 7:6!)."[74]

The Song of Songs is clearly a sensuous poem of human passion and, surprisingly for a biblical book, a text in which the word *God* does not appear. Yet it is in the Bible, and, as I have said, it is a favorite of monastics and mystics. Why is this so? The only reason is surely, as Bonhoeffer as well as Barth recognized, that divine, self-giving love, or *agape*, and sexual love, or *eros*, inform each other.[75] They are complementary, not antagonistic. Merton concurs, but from a different perspective, because for him *eros* is about the contemplative life, "the yearning of the human heart for the vision of beauty," whereas *agape* is about "prophetic ardor" in response to the Word of God in history.[76] In other words, it has to do with the connection between the contemplative and the active life.

Olivier Clément, the Orthodox patristic scholar, agrees. If the Song of Songs is a song of love that is both affectionate and erotic—symbolizing the union of God and the soul—it is because human love is at the same time affectionate and erotic, it has something to do with God. Indeed, for many people love is one of the few mystical experiences that is granted to them in this life. They would understand, in light of a theological exploration of the passion of love, that their lives had all along been dedicated, perhaps by that love itself, to a search for the Absolute. Truly spiritual people are aware of this and respect it.[77] It also contradicts, says Bonhoeffer. "all those who think being Christian is about tempering one's passions."[78]

To illustrate the point, Bonhoeffer takes the musical analogy of polyphony a step further, saying, "where the cantus firmus is clear and distinct, a counterpoint can develop as mightily as it wants. The two are 'undivided and yet distinct,' as the Definition of Chalcedon says, like the divine and human natures in Christ." He then surmises that he and Bethge are so at home with polyphony in music, "because it is the musical image of this christological fact and thus also our *vita christiana*?"[79] In other

---

74. Bonhoeffer, *Letters and Papers from Prison*, 394.
75. See Barth, *Church Dogmatics* III/4, 216–17.
76. Merton, *Contemplation in a World of Action*, 151.
77. See Clément, *Corps de mort et de gloire*, 83–84. A paraphrased translation.
78. Bonhoeffer, *Letters and Papers from Prison*, 394.
79. Bonhoeffer, *Letters and Papers from Prison*, 393–94.

words, Bonhoeffer relates the "polyphony of life" to our understanding of who Jesus Christ is, for us, today. Faith in the one who is "truly God and truly human" makes the affirmation of the polyphony of life an integral part of our lives as Christians. The Christian life is a blending of the bodily and the spiritual without their confusion. "Christianity," he writes, "puts us into many different dimensions of life at the same time; we make room in ourselves, to some extent, for God and the whole world."[80]

Bonhoeffer's understanding of the "polyphony of life" is an affirmation of what Kierkegaard called "aesthetic existence," but he makes this integral to Christian discipleship rather than placing them in opposition to each other.[81] In fact, says Bonhoeffer, going even further, it is "only from the concept of the church that we can regain the understanding of the open space of freedom (art, education, friendship, play)." Instead of being "banished from the church's sphere," aesthetic existence is founded anew within its life.[82] Entry into life through the narrow gate, or the door of the monastery, should not make life one-dimensional; rather, it should open up the possibility of discovering the polyphony of life in a new way that affirms aesthetic existence. Aestheticism, or "art for art's sake," we might say, is an expression of "obsessive desire," but aesthetic desire, with Christ as cantus firmus, is an expression of our love for God.[83]

Monastics renounce much when they make their profession. They leave their homes and families; their friends, careers, and occupations—that is, they leave their nets behind. And yet, some monks receive these back "a hundredfold."[84] "A mature monk" writes Francis Kline, "can often say, 'I am much more of a painter/scholar/carpenter/sculptor/manager now than I ever would have been had I not come to the monastery.'" But there is a difference because these gifts need to be "remade along monastic lines." No longer constrained by current fads and tastes, a monastic is "limited only by the demands of truth, beauty and timeless good taste." So, Kline continues:

> Outside the track of a professional career, his dimensions are wider, his horizons broader. He can now push out at the

---

80. Bonhoeffer, *Letters and Papers from Prison*, 310.
81. See Coates, *The Aesthetics of Discipleship*.
82. Bonhoeffer, *Letters and Papers from Prison*, 291.
83. See de Gruchy, *Christianity, Art, and Transformation*, 82–94.
84. See Matthew 4:18–20; 19:27–30.

boundaries of what is known. He can become a dreamer. Not confined to the approval of a public, he can afford to take chances.[85]

This is all predicated on having renounced previous attachments rather than clinging to them, otherwise this way of being will cease to be monastic. For once someone responds to the call to follow Christ, then everything that he or she is or does is meant to be reconstructed according to a different set of values and practiced with a different intent; indeed, "everything has become new."[86] Creativity thereby becomes sacramental, moving heart and mind in such a way that it transforms our perception of reality and awakens a thirst for justice as well as a hunger for beauty.[87] Such creativity could not be more needed than at *this* monastic moment.

Acedia: Personal & Social

When Pachomius formed the first community of monastics, he did not ban them from living as hermits but ruled that they should always do so as part of a community. Being a hermit in the desert was not for novices; it required maturity and communal support. To think otherwise is, as Merton puts it, "thinking oneself a completely self-sufficient unit and asserting this imaginary 'unity' against all others."[88] But, as Merton also tells us, the more he affirmed others, the more real he became, and he only became "fully real" when his own heart said "*yes to everyone.*"[89] The truth is, being alone and being in community are part of the same journey with Christ into the mystery of God. As Bonhoeffer wrote in *Life Together*:

> only as we stand within the community can we be alone, and only those who are alone can live in the community. Both belong together. Only in the community do we learn to be properly alone; and only in being alone do we learn to live properly in the community. It is not as if the one preceded the other;

---

85. Kline, *Lovers of the Place*, 104–5.
86. 2 Corinthians 5:17.
87. See de Gruchy, *Christianity, Art and Transformation*, 241.
88. Merton, *Conjectures of a Guilty Bystander*, 143 (italics original).
89. Merton, *Conjectures of a Guilty Bystander*, 144 (italics original).

rather both begin at the same time, namely, with the call of Jesus Christ.⁹⁰

But Bonhoeffer also recognized that each of these "by itself has profound pitfalls and perils," for those who seek "community without solitude plunge into the void of words and feelings, and those who seek solitude without community perish in the bottomless pit of vanity, self-infatuation, and despair." His punch line is to the point: "Whoever cannot be alone should beware of community. Whoever cannot stand being in community should beware of being alone."⁹¹

When he was incarcerated in Cell 92 in Tegel Prison, the normally gregarious Bonhoeffer suddenly had to learn how to "be alone" as never before, without any of his normal support structures—whether his family, his fiancée, his friends, or his church community. His prison cell became his hermitage in a very threatening environment. Every day, the silence was broken by the cries of prisoners, the falling of bombs on Berlin, and the intrusion of wardens. But, like every monastic, he also had to learn to live with the daily monotony of time, which became most unbearable at "noonday" when time seemed to stand still.⁹² In documenting the experience of Carthusian monks, Nancy Maguire describes this as experiencing "an infinity of little hours."⁹³ It is then that the "noonday demon" Greek monks called *acedia* and Latin ones *tristitia*, or Shakespeare's melancholy, attacks us.

Acedia can be more debilitating than what we call depression which, serious as it can become, is a psychological ailment that usually can be managed by medication. Acedia is certainly related to depression and shares similar symptoms, but it is a spiritual problem. It is a loss of the desire to live or achieve goals, not least a loss of the desire for God. Or, as Enzo Bianchi puts it, "it is a sort of asphyxiation or suffocation of the spirit" that causes us not only to fall prey to unfounded fears, but also to question whether everything we have tried to live for has been a mistake.⁹⁴ What is the point of carrying on? I feel suffocated in this place, so let me move to fresh pastures! If we lose the desire to live for something that gives life meaning, we have no reason to live. That is why suicide

---

90. Bonhoeffer, *Life Together*, 83.
91. Bonhoeffer, *Life Together*, 83.
92. See his notes in *Letters and Papers from Prison*, 70–73.
93. Maguire, *An Infinity of Little Hours*.
94. Bianchi, *Echoes of the Word*, 31.

statistics rocket in *kairos* times. "What is the point of living?" people say. I have heard it myself and have come close to saying it.

Bonhoeffer's experience of self-doubt and depression in prison was nothing new.[95] From the time Bethge became Bonhoeffer's confessor at Finkenwalde, Bethge tells us, his friend "would be overwhelmed by self-contempt and a sense of inadequacy so strong that it threatened to rob him of his happiest and most successful undertakings of all meaning. His intellect," says Bethge, "had gained an evil ascendency over his faith."[96] But it was in his prison cell that he began to experience acedia in its monastic sense. In a letter written in May 1943 he tells his parents that he had "never understood as clearly" as he now did, what the Bible and Luther mean by "temptation" [*Anfechtung*].[97] A year later, in another letter meant for Bethge alone, he asks him to be his confessor once more; for now, more than ever, after "so many long months without worship, confession, and the Lord's Supper and without *consolation fratrum* [the consolation of the brotherhood]," he needed Bethge to listen to him. For Bethge alone knew that acedia "with its ominous consequences has often haunted" him.[98] Indeed, Bonhoeffer experienced acedia so acutely that he even contemplated suicide, "not out of a sense of guilt," but because, as he told Bethge, "I am practically dead already."[99]

We recall that the first monastics went into the desert to "find God," but in doing so they also began to discover themselves. And, as for them, it is when we are face-to-face with ourselves that acedia forces us to come to terms with who we are. It is not surprising, then, that at the same time as Bonhoeffer struggled with the question of God, he also struggled with his own identity. "Who am I?" he asks himself.

> Am I really what others say of me?
> Or am I only what I know of myself?
> Restless, yearning, sick, like a caged bird,
> struggling for life breath, as if I were being strangled,
> starving for colors, for flowers, for birdsong,
> thirsting for kind words, human closeness,
> shaking with rage at power lust and pettiest insult,
> tossed about, waiting for great things to happen,

---

95. Bethge, *Dietrich Bonhoeffer*, 39.
96. Bethge, *Dietrich Bonhoeffer*, 506.
97. Bonhoeffer, *Letters and Papers from Prison*, 79.
98. Bonhoeffer, *Letters and Papers from Prison*, 180–81.
99. Bonhoeffer, *Letters and Papers from Prison*, 74.

> helplessly fearing for friends so far away,
> too tired and empty to pray, to think, to work,
> weary and ready to take my leave of it all?[100]

Being "too tired to pray, think and work" is precisely the inability to live by Benedict's *Rule*, which requires prayer, study, and manual labor. And "taking leave of it all" happens when life becomes unbearably unbalanced, for it is then that acedia reaches an extreme, irrespective of who we are, where we might be, and what hour of the day it is.

Acedia is, however, more than an affliction that strikes us individually; it is also a social malaise characteristic of the time in which we live. Monastics and prisoners might experience this more acutely because of their isolation, but it is the constant temptation facing Christians, the church, and all who struggle for justice and peace. In the "war of the Spirit" acedia tempts us to lose hope as communities committed to justice, and so resign from the struggle. Social acedia takes hold of us when we begin to think that "injustice, poverty, perpetual conflict . . . are inevitable, the only possible reality, and lose our ability to imagine that there are other ways of being, other courses of action."[101] In *Melancholic Freedom*, David Kim explores this in terms of political agency and notes that the loss of empathy for human suffering, and of passion for changing the world for the better, is connected to the rise of secular individualism and enlightened skepticism, which lead to the loss of wonder and mystery.[102]

The first monastics criticized the church for becoming worldly, not because it existed in the world, but because it had succumbed to the demons of wealth, possessions, food, and promiscuity. This compromised its witness in a world of poverty, corruption, and hunger, where the abuse of women, children, and slaves, was also rife. This loss of care and concern about what matters most we might call ecclesial acedia. For when the church loses its desire to love others, especially those in need, it has, as the Spirit told the church in Ephesus, "abandoned the love it had at first."[103]

The advice given by the desert fathers and mothers to monastics assailed by acedia was down-to-earth. "Control your tongue and your belly," said one, or as Norris translates it, "take a hot bath and sip a glass

---

100. Bonhoeffer, *Letters and Papers from Prison*, 459–60.
101. Norris, *Acedia & Me*, 127.
102. Kim, *Melancholic Freedom*.
103. Revelation 2:4.

of wine," go for a long walk, work in the garden, or have coffee with a "soul friend."[104] On a more serious note, Bianchi counsels us to accept the limitations "that define human existence, namely, the passing of time and mortality . . . by taking responsibility for our past, and by accepting our own limitations and imperfections."[105] Pious counsel, such as "pray more," is not much help, because acedia makes prayer so difficult, as Bonhoeffer discovered. At first, when imprisoned, he could no longer pray, and even reading the Bible was difficult.

But, certainly, monastics cope with acedia only because they have learnt the disciplines of the spiritual life that enable them to persevere when the going gets tough, as it invariably does. This is clearly recognized in the New Testament where discipleship and discipline are inseparable. So, in describing the war of the Spirit, the writer of the Letter to the Ephesians tells Christians to take up the "whole armor of God" in order to "stand firm." This includes "the belt of truth," the "breastplate of righteousness," the "gospel of peace," the "shield of faith," the "helmet of salvation," and the "sword of the Spirit, which is the word of God."[106] These weapons in the Christian armory have always been considered central in struggling against demonic "principalities and powers" by monastics and the likes of John Bunyan's Christian pilgrim. But it has been the "sword of the Spirit" or the "words of the Bible," as Norris says, that have proved the "most effective weapon in this struggle."[107] Benedict's *Rule* as she says, is "an invitation to remain alert to the challenge of the Word of God."[108] After all, that is how Jesus dealt with acedia, the temptation to give up on the messianic task he faced.[109]

Copies of the Scriptures were rare in the desert, so monastics had to learn texts by heart. But our modern-day inability to remember and use Scripture in the way that Jesus, monastics, and others from Augustine to Barth and Bonhoeffer have done over the centuries, is a major problem for the contemporary church. Learning to do so should not replace the necessary critical study of the Bible, but it is essential if we are to use the "sword of the Spirit." That is why, in *this* monastic moment, the *lectio*

---

104. Norris, *Acedia & Me*, 88.
105. Bianchi, *Echoes of the Word*, 32.
106. Ephesians 6:13–17.
107. Norris, *Acedia & Me*, 89.
108. De Waal, *A Life-Giving Way*, xxiii.
109. Matthew 4:1–11.

divina has become so important in helping us engage in the struggle for justice and peace and resist the temptation to lose hope and give up. "In your life of prayer and meditation," says the *Rule of Taizé*, "seek the word which God addresses to you and put it into practice at once. So read little but dwell on it."[110]

In following Jesus, monastics learn to live in daily dialogue with the Psalms. This enables them to enter the prayer of Jesus for the world in a way that connects with their struggles and informs their prayer.[111] Indeed, if anything keeps us connected to the world, it is the Psalms, which, perplexing as they sometimes are, frame reality in all its wonder and tragedy within a worldview shaped by biblical faith. By adding Trinitarian doxologies to the saying or singing of the Psalms, monastics interpret them from the perspective that in Christ, God has redeemed the world in the power of the Spirit. This is a constant reminder that experiences and expressions of joy or pain, of victory or suffering, even of bloodcurdling vengeance (as in the imprecatory psalms)—indeed that all reality, all human emotions, and everything from sunrise to sunset—must be understood from the perspective of a prayerful faith that is hopeful and sustained by love. That is why Bonhoeffer says, "Whenever the Psalter is abandoned, an incomparable treasure is lost to the Christian church. With its recovery will come unexpected power."[112]

Fortunately, by the time Bonhoeffer found himself in prison, and came face to face with acedia, he had immersed himself in and discovered the consolation of the Psalter. He had also developed a disciplined routine, which included daily reading and meditating on the Moravian *Losungen*, or text for the day, to which he often refers.[113] In addition he read voraciously and widely, from novels and history to philosophy and theology, including Thomas á Kempis's *Imitation of Christ* in Latin. And then, of course, he wrote letters, many to his parents as well as "love letters" to his fiancée, Maria von Wedemeyer.[114] But, as time passed and the hours began to stretch into infinity, he also began to write a book on the future of Christianity and the church in a "world come of age." And it is in the outline for that book, which he discussed at length with Bethge in

110. Br. Roger of Taizé and the Community of Taizé, *The Rule of Taizé* (2012 ed.), 43.

111. See Bonhoeffer, *Life Together*, 55–58.

112. Bonhoeffer, *Life Together*, 162.

113. Bonhoeffer, *Letters and Papers from Prison*, 12 et al.

114. Bonhoeffer and von Wedemeyer, *Love Letters from Cell 92*.

letters smuggled out of prison, that we find some definitive clues for what his new kind of monasticism might look like today.[115]

Open to the World: Hidden in God

As we have seen, in his *Life Together*, Bonhoeffer provides us with a guide for developing a monastic-style community based on his experience at Finkenwalde and his reflections on monasticism. But, in his "Outline for a Book," he sketches the key characteristics of a renewed ecumenical church in a post-Christendom world come of age, each of which is influenced by his earlier thinking about a new kind of monasticism. These characteristics are, first, the inclusive and hospitable nature of the church; second, its common life of sharing resources; third, its servant role in the world; fourth, its values; and finally, its liturgical life, which is complementary to the struggle for a just world. These take us to the core of Bonhoeffer's ecclesiology.

First, then, Bonhoeffer says that the church is only the church "when it is there for others," because Jesus exists "only for others."[116] Monasteries may be enclosed, some far more than others, but for Benedict they existed as much for the outsider as they did for those within. Indeed, he told those who followed his *Rule* that they should treat all who came knocking at the door as though they were Christ himself. They had to be given the best accommodation available. So it has been over the centuries that when faithful to the *Rule*, monasteries have embraced the seeker, the wanderer, the pilgrim, people of other faiths or no faith at all, and those who have been cast aside. Indeed, at Ettal, during the Third Reich, they welcomed a Lutheran theologian working underground for the Resistance; and at Taizé, Jewish refugees fleeing the Gestapo, defeated German soldiers facing reprisal and, in more recent times, thousands of young "post-Christians" disillusioned with the church.

Whereas being in solidarity with the victims of society is a primary mark of the church, by contrast, in Christendom the church has often served the national interest rather than those regarded as beyond the pale. Even in its global missionary outreach, which was an attempt to convert and educate the other, the church often found itself trapped in a colonialism that perpetuated Christendom. But in doing so, as in the expulsion

---

115. Bonhoeffer, *Letters and Papers from Prison*, 499–504.
116. Bonhoeffer, *Letters and Papers from Prison*, 501.

of Jews from Spain in the fifteenth century or from the German Church during the Third Reich, the church excludes Christ, says Bonhoeffer.[117] It is no longer "a witness to the miracle of God in Jesus Christ."[118] Christ may stand at the door and knock, but he is not invited in.[119]

If monasticism began in reaction to Christendom, to the values of the empire and an increasingly worldly church, then, Bonhoeffer insisted, a new kind of monasticism was needed as Christendom collapsed. It was needed to ensure that the church remains faithful to its witness to Christ as the one in whom the reality of God and the world are brought together.[120] Even the Free churches, that is, nonestablished churches, had become religious societies and pious enclaves existing for their membership, and so captive to the values of those who supported them. Financial viability and social acceptability determined their life and witness more than the gospel. It is impossible, for example, for a racially homogenous congregation that willfully chooses to remain exclusive, to witness to the gospel of God's reconciling love for the world in Christ.

Second, says Bonhoeffer, the "church for others" must give "away all its property to those in need."[121] The monastic vision of sharing all things in common challenges the way the church understands and uses its resources. It calls on the church to imitate what liberation theologians have called "God's preferential option for the poor."[122] Along the same lines, Bonhoeffer says that "clergy must live solely on the freewill offerings of the congregations and perhaps be engaged in some secular vocation."[123] This speaks most directly to the church, as in Bonhoeffer's context, when it is a state-supported institution. But it also challenges Christians and congregations that are wealthier than others to share their resources, and raises the question of the just distribution of wealth across society more generally.

Third, Bonhoeffer continues, the church must be self-sustaining, and engage in daily work that makes this possible, as well as participating "in the worldly tasks of life in the community—not dominating but

---

117. See Bonhoeffer, *Ethics*, 105.
118. Bonhoeffer, *Ethics*, 132.
119. See Revelation 3:21.
120. Bonhoeffer, *Ethics*, 54.
121. Bonhoeffer, *Letters and Papers from Prison*, 503.
122. Gutiérrez, *A Theology of Liberation*, 162–73.
123. Bonhoeffer, *Letters and Papers from Prison*, 503.

helping and serving." In this way, the church sets an example to "people in every calling," demonstrating "what a life with Christ is," that is, "to be there for others."[124] The fact that monasteries historically became centers of caring for the sick and infirm as well as places of learning and education is an extension of this ministry. This also reflects Benedict's requirement that monastics not only pray and study but also do manual work, taking great care of their tools and implements.

Fourth, Bonhoeffer discusses the monastic struggle against personal vices in terms of the church itself. For life "with Christ" and "for others" requires not only that monastics or individual Christians but also that the church itself confront and overcome "the vices of hubris, the worship of power, envy, and illusionism as the roots of all evil." By the same token, the church must pursue the contrary virtues: "moderation, authenticity, trust, faithfulness, steadfastness, patience, discipline, humility, modesty, contentment." In doing so, the church will discover that its "word gains weight and power not through concepts but by example."[125]

Finally, we come to the way Bonhoeffer relates the liturgical life of the church to its participation in the struggle for justice in the world. As he wrote in his sermon for the baptism of Dietrich Bethge, "we can be Christians today in only two ways, through prayer and in doing justice among human beings. All Christian thinking, talking, and organizing must be born anew, out of that prayer and action."[126] In this regard, Parker Palmer refers to Thomas Merton's journey as a Trappist monk, in which the rigorous disciplines of the contemplative life led him to a new concern for justice and political engagement as well as to the other.[127]

When Martin Luther King Jr. visited Merton at the Abbey of Gethsemani during the civil rights struggle, Merton is said to have told him that some Catholic activists were critical of him and his fellow monks for not participating in protest marches. King replied, "Let us do the marching, and you do the praying, for without your prayers we cannot protest." Merton knew only too well that monasticism can become "overburdened with cultural and ritual usages and with forms and practices ... which have come to stifle the Spirit."[128] He also believed that the future of

---

124. Bonhoeffer, *Letters and Papers from Prison*, 503.
125. Bonhoeffer, *Letters and Papers from Prison*, 503–4.
126. See Bonhoeffer, *Letters and Papers from Prison*, 389.
127. Palmer, *The Company of Strangers*, 28–29.
128. Merton, *Conjectures of a Guilty Bystander*, 10.

monasticism required monastics to become countercultural prophets, as in the beginning, embracing people and monastics of other faiths as fellow pilgrims working for a just peace in the world.[129] Merton discusses this at length in his book *Contemplation in a World of Action,* where he writes about the need for those in the cloister to be open to the needs of the world, not regarding contemplation and action as alternatives but as complementary to each other. But he also says that anyone "who attempts to act and do things for others in the world without deepening his own self-understanding, freedom, integrity and capacity to love, will not have anything to give others."[130] On the contrary, we will only communicate our own obsessions, aggressions and "ego-centered ambitions," prejudices and ideas.[131]

This was also something that we came to understand during the struggle against apartheid, epitomized in the witness of Desmond Tutu. His ability to relate his own prophetic ministry to spirituality and prayer has arguably been his greatest gift to the church in South Africa, and the ecumenical church worldwide. One of his initiatives was the establishment of the Center for Christian Spirituality in 1987 in Cape Town during his tenure as archbishop of Cape Town and the final years of the struggle against apartheid.[132] And nothing inspired him more than the story of the transfiguration of Christ in which the mountaintop mystical experience of God led to the way of the cross in the valley below. In his sermon at his enthronement as archbishop, Tutu told the vast congregation gathered in St George's Cathedral that "the principle of transfiguration is at work when mundane everyday fare, bread and wine, apparently recalcitrant matter . . . becomes the channel for the divine life."[133] In saying this, Tutu emphatically rejected the heresy of Gnosticism by affirming material reality as the vehicle for God's grace, just as in his prophetic ministry he rejected the triumphalist heresy.

Of one thing I am therefore certain. *This* monastic moment is not a time for Christians to flee the world, but rather for us to participate together more actively in its life, in the interest of its common good. This is premised on the conviction that God still loves the world, despite what

---

129. Letter to Jean Leclercq, July 23, 1968, in Hart, ed., *Survival or Prophecy?,* 129.
130. Merton, *Contemplation in a World of Action,* 178.
131. Merton, *Contemplation in a World of Action,* 179.
132. Gaum and Argent, eds., *Silence and Solidarity.*
133. Tutu, *The Rainbow People of God,* 121.

we have done and continue to do to it. In fact, to be truly human, that is, "in the image of God," we must love the world. And, if we love the world, we dare not lose hope for the world. But how is it possible for the church to be an agent of God's redemptive love in a world that is falling apart? How does it become the church for others, engaged in serving the world in its struggles for justice, without losing its identity as an *ecclesia*? Are there no boundaries between the church and the world? As Bonhoeffer asked Bethge:

> How can we be *ecclesia*, those who are called out, without understanding ourselves religiously as privileged (i.e., as part of Christendom), but instead seeing ourselves as belonging wholly to the world? Christ would then no longer be the object of religion, but something else entirely, truly lord of the world.[134]

Just as Bonhoeffer insisted that his "this-worldly" understanding of discipleship was neither banal or superficial, so he is equally insistent that when the church opens itself up to the world, whether through its embracing hospitality, its solidarity with social victims, or in seeking to interpret the gospel, it should neither surrender its identity nor compromise the mysteries of faith. To this end, Bonhoeffer proposes that we recover the monastic *disciplina arcani* or "arcane (hidden) discipline."[135] The term was first coined by Jean Daillé, a French Reformed theologian in the seventeenth century, to describe the practice adopted in the fourth century church to protect the "inner mysteries of the church, particularly the sacraments of baptism and the Eucharist" by keeping them "hidden" from the world. This was then extended to include the Lord's Prayer and the saying of the Apostles' Creed.[136] Only the baptized could be present, for such mysteries could only be grasped by faith.

This practice was still in force in the congregation where I grew up. When the Lord's Supper was celebrated, those who were not members left the congregation, and the doors of the church were shut, a practice still remembered in some Orthodox liturgies where the priest tells a deacon to "shut the doors" at that moment. The message was clear: "Let us not profane the mystery!" But when the church became established within Christendom, and the more being a Christian became conventional rather than exceptional, the practice was abandoned except in the monasteries. They became the custodians of the Christian mysteries. So,

---

134. Bonhoeffer, *Letters and Papers from Prison*, 364–65.
135. Bonhoeffer, *Letters and Papers from Prison*, 373.
136. Kelly, *Early Christian Creeds*, 168.

Bonhoeffer proposes that the monastic *disciplina arcani* must be reestablished, for in this way the mysteries of the Christian faith are "sheltered against profanation," while (and this is the critical point) at the same time the church becomes more involved in the life of the world.[137] For the church, openness to the world and being hidden in the mystery of faith belong inseparably together, for both are inseparably part of its essential identity.

Of course, this raises a problem for the church today in welcoming all to participate in its life and therefore share in the Eucharist at the invitation of Christ, rather than being subject to disciplines of the church, especially when legalistically understood and applied. How to resolve this problem without indulging in "cheap grace" is the challenge. But too often, the church has excluded people who have come seeking and searching, and has not disciplined those whose hypocrisy and attitudes are unworthy of Christ. I would rather err by being inclusive than exclusive, even "going into the highways and byways," as Jesus said, to draw in and welcome those who are outsiders, rather than legalistically shutting them out.[138] To the outsider, as Hans Urs von Balthasar says, "love alone is credible."[139]

Bonhoeffer's proposed "this-worldly interpretation" of the Bible, which was integral to the church becoming open to the other, was intended to make key concepts such as repentance, faith, justification, rebirth, and sanctification, accessible to secular people; he was not suggesting that these concepts be discarded, any more than he was jettisoning Scripture. Even so, they are terms that speak from "faith to faith"—that is they only make sense within the life of the church where the language of faith is understood. By analogy, there is no reason why cricket-lovers should ditch key words like *googly*, *maiden-over*, or *leg-before*, because the uninitiated do not understand them. They are code words essential to every lover of the game. The same would apply to doctrines like the Trinity or virgin birth, which should not be thrust on the world in a take-it-or-leave-it manner but taught and celebrated in the life of the church as mysteries of faith. In this way, prayer, worship, the sacraments, and the creed remain hidden at the heart of the life of the church. That is why Bonhoeffer says that all Christian talk must arise out of prayer and be expressed by doing justice in the world. The church would then be known by its penultimate

---

137. Bonhoeffer, *Letters and Papers from Prison*, 373.
138. Luke 14:15–24.
139. Von Balthasar, *Love Alone Is Credible*.

witness to the reign of God through its service of the world rather than by the disciplines and doctrines that sustain its life of faith, hope, and love. And it is in that service to the world that the church shares in solidarity with people of other faiths and those of no faith at all.

The fact that the inner life of a monastery is hidden, or enclosed, should not be understood, then, as a sign of escape from the world, but as a way of protecting the mysteries that enable the monastery and the church to serve the world. It reflects the words which Paul wrote to the church at Colossae: "you have died, and your life is hidden with Christ in God."[140] To use Bonhoeffer's terms, we are enabled to live and act as the church in the penultimate because we live in the light of the ultimate, that is, by grace alone.

> This means that visible deeds, which must be done to make people ready to receive Jesus Christ, must be deeds of humility before the coming Lord, which means deeds of repentance. Preparation of the way means repentance (Matt. 3:1ff.). But repentance means concrete changing of one's ways. Repentance demands deeds. So preparing the way indeed has quite definite conditions in view that are to be produced.[141]

We prepare the way for others to know the ultimate word of grace, by responding to the penultimate needs of the world.

> The hungry person needs bread, the homeless person needs shelter, the one deprived of rights needs justice, the lonely person needs community, the undisciplined one needs order, and the slave needs freedom.[142]

Bonhoeffer's "nonreligious" interpretation of the Christian faith is thus primarily driven not by apologetics or hermeneutics but by *metanoia*, the "conversion of manners," or a change of life-style which leads to an identification with Christ in his sufferings, and therefore to a different way of being the church in the world.[143]

---

140. Colossians 3:3.
141. Bonhoeffer, *Ethics*, 164–65.
142. Bonhoeffer, *Ethics*, 163.
143. Bonhoeffer, *Letters and Papers from Prison*, 480.

Pilgrims of Hope

Martin Marty once observed that from the time when the Pilgrim Fathers arrived in New England, the United States became "a nation of pilgrims in search of utopia in their own land." He was reflecting on Jacques Maritain's observation that Americans, like many others across the world today, "are always on the move—available for new tasks, prepared for the possible loss of what they have. They are not *settled, installed.*"[144] Change not tradition, invention not consolidation, new voyages into space as if the earth is no longer home—the horizon is always moving. That is why Merton spoke of the monastery as "the center of America . . . holding the country together . . . keeping the universe from falling apart."[145] Maybe that is the key to what *this* monastic moment is all about. Finding and holding fast to the center, the cantus firmus, which enables us to move more surely into an uncertain and threatening future.

Monastics might appear to be living in the past as custodians of tradition, and sometimes that is an apt description, but Benedict calls them, as does the New Testament, to live eschatologically, that is, to live fully today but with the end in sight. Have your feet firmly planted on the earth but live daily as those who are mindful that this is not your eternal home. When Benedict exhorts us in his *Rule* to "wake up," which monks respond to quite literally each day for their morning vigil, he is calling to mind Jesus's parables of the kingdom, which tell us to live fully today as if it were our last. Apocalyptic texts, whether in the Bible or the daily press, should not drive us to fear and despair, or a state of acedia, but wake us up to reality and responsibility. And taking responsibility to live and act in a certain way is the purpose of monastic vows.

Commitment is in short supply in a world shaped by rapid change. Promises made are often broken without too much thought, whether they be marriage vows, baptismal vows, those that bind friendships or enable institutions to flourish. The taking of monastic vows is therefore of great significance, not just for the sake of monasticism, or the life of monastics, but as a symbol and an example of the importance and seriousness with which they should be made. This is evident in the lengthy preparation of novices for the moment when they will take their vows, and then the time given before they make their final profession. Like marriage vows, or the vows made at ordination, monastic vows are not meant to be taken

---

144. Quoted in Marty, *Pilgrims in Their Own Land*, 1 (italics Marty's).

145. From Merton, *Seven Story Mountain*, as quoted in Marty, *Pilgrims in Their Own Land*, 434.

"lightly or thoughtlessly but solemnly" in the presence of both God and the congregation. As Merton told the novices in his care:

> It is by our vows above all that we seek to imitate Christ, that we seek to unite the sacrifice of our lives with His offering of Himself to the Father. It is by our vows above all that we seek to give ourselves entirely to God.[146]

By way of reminder, Benedictine monastic vows are threefold: stability, conversion of manners, and obedience. The "conversion of manners," is, as I have indicated, the ongoing *metanoia* that is essential to Christian growth and the witness of the church. Obedience signifies that everything else depends on following Christ in obedience to God's call,[147] and is therefore given to Christ's representative, which in the monastery means the abbot or abbess. But stability is about being committed to the monastery in which monastics take their vows and not looking for excuses to escape from it. For that reason, Benedict counsels that entry into the monastery should not be made easy; in fact, a potential novice should be left knocking at the door for a long time if necessary.[148]

In times of rapid social change stability takes on a particular significance and relevance for us. It is about being steadfast, patient, faithful—in short, being committed over the long haul. Of course, it is not always possible for us to remain committed to a particular institution, whether that be a monastery, church, college, marriage, or any other relationship that, sadly, may have to come to an end—a decision that should be taken with the same seriousness that led to the previous commitment. It is not a decision that should be taken when struck down by debilitating despair. What we need above all is an inner stability which, as Esther de Waal so perceptively observes, is "stability in terms of some internal space, that we carry around," so that, no matter where we are, we find ourselves "at home," that is, in the space where God is present.[149]

It is the significance of pilgrimage, and the reason why, especially in times of change and uncertainty, it becomes a means of grace. Going on pilgrimage is a reminder that life is a journey, often through a wilderness desert that is as much a condition in which we find ourselves as it is a place through which we travel—a journey inwards, to find our true

---

146. Merton, *The Life of the Vows*, 234.
147. Merton, *The Life of the Vows*, 237.
148. See Benedict, *Rule*, chapter 58, verses 1–8 (*RB 1980*, 267).
149. De Waal, *Seeking God*, 61.

selves, as much as a journey onwards towards the goal that awaits us. What is critical is that we remain committed to the journey, like pilgrims determined to arrive at their destination despite tired bodies and the miles that lie ahead as the sun reaches its noonday strength.

If monastics represent stability in terms of commitment to "this place," pilgrims who pass through monasteries, as they do through Volmoed, enjoying the hospitality they find there, remind us that we are all on this journey whether we are residents or part of their company. But it makes a huge difference whether our journey is in search of an illusion, a running away from something we cannot face, or whether it is a search for meaning, for transcendent reality defined by love, a "running towards the dawn," as the *Rule of Taizé* exhorts us. It does not matter in which coach we travel to reach our destination; what matters is whether we are on the right train. There are many roads that lead pilgrims to Santiago de Compostela and Canterbury, and several to Cape Aghulas at the southern tip of Africa. What is important is to follow the signs that point the way. The monastic vision provides us with such signposts that help us find our way, whether alone or in community, and irrespective of where we are along the way. It provides pointers, clues, and resources that can help us arrive at the destination we most truly desire when we are most truly ourselves, for then our desire is for the love that embraces us and will not let us go. This is the mystery into which we are being led in hope.

In seeking a title for the journal of theology he was launching in 1921, Karl Barth settled on *Zwischen den Zeiten*, "living between the times." This was to convey the mood of the post-First World War era, which had brought Christendom to its calamitous end and ushered in a new age of uncertainty. This was the *kairos* in which Barth launched his attack on the theologies of Christendom that helped create the crisis in which the world found itself. The title also reflected the eschatological milieu of the New Testament and early church within which monasticism was conceived. That is, a sense of living in the "last days," understood as the time between the death and resurrection of Christ, and the arrival of God's reign of justice and peace. Living within that tension came to characterize the Christian life as one of remembrance and anticipation, a tension largely lost as Christendom developed—except in *kairos* times when fears thrive even as utopian desires are rekindled. But when those desires are rekindled, as they were in the Egyptian desert, Christians recognize that "here we have no lasting city" for we are all pilgrims on a journey, "Living in Between":[150]

> I live in a between time:
> between the promise and its fulfilment;
> between the victory and the mopping up operations;
> between the election and the inauguration.
>
> I live in a between space:
> between earth and air and water;
> between earth and heaven;
> between creation groaning in labor pains
> and creation reborn.
>
> I live in a between mode:
> between wretchedness and glory;
> between dark sin and bright goodness;
> between blindness and vision,
> falling and rising,
> wandering aimlessly and pressing ahead.
>
> And as I live in between,
> my yearning is for God,
> my intention is to wait for him,
> for he opens the eye of my understanding.
>
> And when I fail
> and fall again into blindness,
> I will cling to him
> trusting in him to carry me—
> in between.

---

150. A poem written by Isobel de Gruchy based on Julian of Norwich, *Showings*, chapter 52. See de Gruchy, *Making All Things Well*, 98.

EPILOGUE
On Writing a *Rule*

I will make a new covenant.
I will put my law within them,
I will write it on their hearts.
    —JEREMIAH 31:31, 33

Let us love one another because love is from God.
No one has ever seen God; if we love one another, God lives in us, and his love is perfected in us.
God is love, and those who abide in love abide in God, and God abides in them.
We love because God first loved us.
    —1 JOHN 4:7, 12, 16

Let us set out on this way with the gospel for our guide.
    —*RULE OF ST BENEDICT*[1]

What is essential in the monastic life is not embedded in buildings, is not embedded in clothing, is not necessarily even embedded in a rule ... It is concerned with the business of total inner transformation.
    —THOMAS MERTON[2]

---

1. Benedict, prologue, verse 21 (*RB 1980*, 161).
2. Merton, "Marxism and Monastic Perspectives," 340.

AT THE FINAL SESSION of our workshop on "This Monastic Moment" at Volmoed in January 2021, we focused attention on writing a *Rule* that would guide us into the future. Having existed for thirty-five years without a *Rule*, based on shared Christian values and commitments, we were unconvinced that we needed anything more. We were also wary of the word *rule*, for it suggested laws and regulations that needed to be strictly applied and monitored, something that seemed contrary to the gospel and to our ethos. After all, we were a loosely structured group, even though we prayed together daily, shared occasional meals, and were engaged in serving Volmoed in various ways. But now, as Volmoed had entered a new phase in its journey, considerably larger in size and varied in activity, with undefined boundaries as to who was part of the community, we discerned the need to journey more intentionally into the future in partnership with St Benedict's Priory,

The monks of the priory live according to the *Rule of St Benedict*. That defines their identity and guides their way of life. We respect their *Rule*, share together in worship, consider their presence as a gift and an opportunity to build an ecumenical intentional community in association with one that is explicitly monastic. How, then, are we to define our relationship? And what does it mean for our own self-understanding, and our response to the challenges that face the church and the world at this *kairos* time?

What follows are my own reflections and some proposals for consideration in drafting a rule as I ponder these questions in the light of the story of monasticism and informed by conversations within the Volmoed Community as well as with the monks of the priory. They may be helpful for other communities and congregations who, at this monastic moment, are reflecting on the need to become more intentional in their life together.

A Rule

The writing of monastic *Rules* has been integral to the monastic story from the time of Pachomius to the present day. This has been a cumulative process as each generation has learned from those who have gone before, modifying according to circumstances and contexts. *Rules* for those who are the cloistered and celibate in a rural environment do not necessarily fit the circumstances of those who live inclusively together in a city, or who are more engaged in teaching, nursing, or social justice ministries. Volmoed is neither a monastery nor a religious order. It is an ecumenical, gender-inclusive community that services a retreat center, guided by its founding vision to provide a place for God's ministry of transformation. Nevertheless, monastic *Rules* do provide a treasury on which to draw in guiding us, even if they are not designed for that purpose. The question we therefore face is, How should our founding vision be embodied today, and how can it be sustained going into the future? Do we need a *Rule* to help us, and, if so, how should it be written and what should it contain?

Rules are necessary in all spheres of life, from government to sports, just as they are in the life of the church. "Do everything decently and in order," Paul counsels the unruly Corinthian church.[3] Obeying rules is necessary for the common good, just like discipleship requires discipline. But writing and obeying rules runs the danger of legalism and self-righteousness unless we understand their purpose and how to live accordingly.

The word "rule" derives from the Latin *regula*, a feminine noun suggesting wisdom, not law, something to guide and help us to stay on course.[4] Understood in this sense, the word *rule* has been used to describe what is written to guide monastic communities from Pachomius to Taizé. But, as Benedict said of his *Rule*, it was only "written for beginners" as a "tool" for "the cultivation of virtues" as they hastened toward their "heavenly home."[5] That is why Merton insisted that the monastic life is not about obeying a rule, but is "concerned with the business of total inner transformation."[6]

The truth is, simply having a splendid *Rule* does not guarantee that a community will become a community of transformation any more than having a splendid constitution guarantees a healthy democracy. For a *Rule* to be effective it must be "written on the heart"—to use the words of the prophet Jeremiah[7]—a means towards transformation, not simply an aid for organization and to ensure continuity. In the case of Volmoed, if we adopt a *Rule* it must enable us to better fulfill our reason for existence.

During the COVID-19 pandemic we learned that protocols, such as wearing a mask, irksome as they are, are an expression of respect and

---

3. 1 Corinthians 14:40.
4. De Waal, *A Life-Giving Way*, xxii.
5. Benedict, chapter 73, verses 6–8 (*RB 1980*, 297).
6. Merton, "Marxism and Monastic Perspectives."
7. See Jeremiah 31:33.

love for other people. Maintaining physical distance saves lives. In the same way, the "rule of law" is meant to be an instrument of justice which is the exercise of love in the public sphere. Likewise, discipline in the life of the church or any other ecclesial community is not meant to be an instrument of control, but a tool to enable discipleship informed by God's love—a love that is both creative and redemptive, costly yet renewing. Discipleship is a response to the love of God, who loves the world and embraces us in forgiveness and grace. For this reason, Jesus said that we should love not only our neighbors, but also our enemies, and pray for those who persecute us.[8] Unless motivated by love and applied with wisdom, obeying rules results in self-righteousness and hypocrisy, or leads to an unhealthy sense of shame and failure. That is why rules need to be written, interpreted, and implemented wisely through listening to the Spirit that gives them life.[9]

Listening to the Word and Spirit

In the same way as theology begins in the silence necessary to hear "the Word that was in the beginning,"[10] so the writing of a *Rule* is the outcome more of contemplation than it is of group discussion. But it also requires that we listen to the shared wisdom of experience, whether of our ancestors in faith or each other. *Rules* emerge in practice before they are codified. They are not just written with ink on paper but on the heart, and practiced in daily life by those who seek to follow Jesus as members of a community guided by the gospel. Listening to the Word reminds us following Jesus is neither cheap nor burdensome,[11] for God requires that we should "love mercy, do justice, and walk humbly,"[12] and we have received the Spirit to help us. Scripture also teaches us that it is not fulfilling the letter of the law that matters, for it is the Spirit that gives words life.[13]

Listening to what the Spirit is saying to us through the Word always takes place within a specific context. *Rules* are not cast in stone because they guide a community on a journey of openness to the Spirit. They

---

8. Matthew 5:43.
9. See 2 Corinthians 3:6.
10. John 1:1.
11. Matthew 11:30.
12. Micah 6:8.
13. 2 Corinthians 3:6.

therefore need to be interpreted by the community as it "seeks the mind of Christ" together here and now.¹⁴ For it is today that we must listen, and it is in this place that we are called to follow Jesus both singly and together. *Rules* are therefore not handbooks of wise aphorisms or moral principles culled from various sources that may be universally valid, though they may contain such; they are about what it means to follow Jesus here and now. Like Scripture, such *Rules* are, therefore, not only written for the sake of the community, but also mindful of the needs of the world.

A Covenant of Love

To avoid misunderstanding, and not to confuse any prospective Volmoed *Rule* with that of the Benedictine priory, we decided to use the word *covenant* rather than *rule*. We also decided that this Covenant should explicitly reject any hint of legalism by being referred to as a *Covenant of Love*. This is nothing novel, for in the twelfth century a *Charter of Love* was drafted by those Cistercians who were critical of some of the obligations demanded of them at Cluny.¹⁵

Covenant is about God's gracious commitment to the world and to us, as well as our commitment to each other; it is about building community, reaching a common mind, and serving the common good. In this respect, monastic or intentional communities are no different from any family, congregation, or monastery that seeks to be a covenant community. Indeed, the word *covenant* describes the bonds of marriage, of friendship, and of the relationships that should characterize our life together in the church.

We take our cue from the fact that in the biblical narrative the relationship between God and those who become the people of God is described in terms of a covenant. This is initiated by the call of Abraham to begin a pilgrimage of faith towards the land of promise. This covenant was ratified following the liberation of Abraham's descendants from slavery in Egypt and the reception of God's Torah (the "Ten Words" or Commandments) at Mount Sinai. Codified in the Book of the Covenant (or Old Testament), the life-giving Torah became the *Rule of Israel* to which the prophets bore witness.

---

14. 1 Corinthians 1:10.
15. See Knowles, *The Monastic Order in England*, 752.

The early church believed that in and through the death and resurrection of Jesus Christ, the covenant made with Abraham had been renewed and become inclusive of all people who believed in Jesus as the Christ—irrespective of ethnicity, gender, or class. In Christ, we have been set free from the "burden of the law" and discovered, with Paul, that the "only thing that counts is faith working through love."[16] Jesus's "new commandment" that we should "love one another" and, audaciously, also "love [our] enemies," thus became the *Rule of the Church*.[17] This *Covenant of Love* should define every Christian community.

In Covenant with One Another

The Volmoed Community comprises several constituent parts or intersecting circles: those in residence, including the brothers of St Benedict's Priory; those who are employed members of staff; those who regularly participate in its life of worship and other activities; those who are guests; and those friends and partners who, throughout the world, support Volmoed's mission in prayer and through giving. In writing the *Covenant of Love*, we must be cognizant of each constituency, listening to the voices and serving the needs of all, just as we seek to develop and deepen the relationship between each constituent part. For in the body of Christ, though there are many members with varying gifts and responsibilities, we all "drink of the same Spirit."[18] Special attention should be given to dissenting voices that ask disturbing questions and challenge the community. But we must "test the spirits" and learn how "to speak the truth in love."[19] For this is how communities remain faithful to Christ and are built up in love.[20]

In making decisions that affect the Community, we should ensure, then, that all those affected should participate in the process, and we should aim for consensus. This will not only require listening to the other, but also patience with one another. "Love is patient,"[21] just as God is patient with us, and our conversion into the fulness of life in Christ both as

---

16. Galatians 5:6.
17. John 13:34; Matthew 5:44.
18. 1 Corinthians 12:13.
19. 1 John 4:1–6; Ephesians 4:15.
20. 1 Corinthians 13.
21. 1 Corinthians 13:4.

persons and as community takes time. But patience is not prevarication, it is part of the process to reach a goal, and there is sometimes a necessary urgency required if we are to find our way. The time will come when a decision must be made; otherwise the community will become a talk-shop, sharing ideas rather than listening to the Spirit in obedience to Christ. This raises the question of leadership for who decides when consensus is reached, and words must be translated into action?

Every intentional community needs leaders and someone who is elected as the first among them. Monastic *Rules* give clear guidance on the election of abbots and abbesses, and rightly so, for wise, thoughtful, and loving leadership is one of the keys to a healthy community. Of critical importance in choosing leaders (and the leader) is that they have the confidence and trust of the community and the necessary skills for the position. For that reason, there must be a process of selection in which all members can participate, and agreement about the rules that govern the process. Equally important is the need for guidelines that should be followed for changing leaders, to ensure continuity, maintain stability, and allow the Spirit to breathe fresh life and insight into the community. Change is inevitable in communities, as it is more generally in life, but how we manage change is critical.

We have learned from the monastic story that the welfare of the community is dependent as much on how we live alone as on how we live together. For that reason, a community should care for the spiritual and physical well-being of all who belong, ensuring that there is space and opportunity for times of retreat, silence, study, and recreation. Members will vary in terms of skills, capacities, energy, and personality traits, and they are also at different stages in their own personal journey. A healthy community is sensitive to such diversity and need, and the *Covenant of Love* must reflect such awareness and concern.

As Christian community is nourished through prayer, breaking bread together, listening together to the gospel, and sharing, there should be clear guidelines as to how, when, and where the community meets for these purposes. Likewise, if the community is residential, there need to be clear guidelines that govern how life together should be structured. This includes guidelines for consultation, study, work, eating together, and recreation.

On these matters, and on all that goes into developing a *Covenant of Love* at this time and in any place, we have a wealth of material to help us formulate what needs to be included and what omitted. But, whatever is included, we should never forget that it should help us to follow Jesus Christ together as a community committed to serving the world according to the gospel. We freely commit ourselves to it, because we freely commit ourselves to Christ and the world. In doing so, we also commit ourselves to the community of which we are members, always mindful that it is God's love for us in Jesus Christ, who is present through the Spirit, that unites us in faith, keeps hope alive, and enables us to serve the world in love.

In Covenant with Others

A *Covenant of Love* cannot be sectarian in spirit but must express a desire to be in fellowship with, and of service to, the ecumenical church. In writing our *Covenant* we must, therefore, be mindful that the Volmoed Community, while not formally associated with any one denomination, is composed of members from many Christian confessions. We therefore commit ourselves to listen carefully to the voice of the ecumenical church, to respect the traditions of all, and to seek to provide a facility that is of service and value to the church.

The Volmoed Community has a special family relationship with the Order of the Holy Cross and St Benedict's Priory. This, too, is a relationship that must be defined in terms of the *Covenant of Love*. Already within the first year of living together at Volmoed, we have begun to discern ways we can be associated to the advantage of both, as well as to the advantage of the ecumenical church. How this relationship of mutual trust and commitment will or should develop over the coming years is difficult to predict or plan, for it is a work of the Spirit in progress.

Volmoed also has a relationship with other communities, including the Community of the Cross of Nails based in Coventry, England. We treasure such relationships and partnerships with others who share our vision and wish to be in solidarity with us.

Undoubtedly one of the most significant developments in the life and ministry of Volmoed over recent years has been its ecumenical Volmoed Youth Leadership Training Program (VYLTP). This program, which has been inspired in part by the Taizé Community, with which we have developed a strong bond, is important to the future of Volmoed. But it is also a ministry that is mindful of the greater need to provide programs of Christian formation for the next generation of leaders. In doing so, Volmoed seeks to be a sign of hope for the future, and it also acknowledges the contribution that the VYLTP makes to its own life. In writing our *Covenant of Love*, we commit ourselves to the next generation.

Hospitality is at the core of the Volmoed vision. We welcome people of all denominations, people of other faiths, and people who do not profess any faith to enjoy and benefit from the beauty and peace that Volmoed offers. In particular, we welcome those who are in need of God's healing, those seeking to find direction in life, and those who need time for renewal. In being open to all, Volmoed is not denying its Christian convictions; on the contrary, it is the love of Christ that inspires us to welcome all to participate in our worship, programs, and community life.

Volmoed is inescapably part of God's world in all its brokenness and pain, diversity and cultural achievement, struggle and hope. In writing the *Covenant of Love*, we acknowledge that to love God's world requires that we also work to establish God's justice and peace. This is necessary within the Volmoed Community, in Hermanus and the wider Overstrand region, and in South Africa as a whole. Unjust social realities rooted in our colonial and apartheid past are still everywhere apparent. As a community committed to the gospel, the Volmoed Community dares not discriminate in terms of ethnicity, gender, and class, either in providing hospitality or within its own life, for "in Christ there is no longer Jew or Greek, slave or free, male or female, for all are one in Christ."[22]

In Covenant with God's Creation

The fundamental premise of the *Covenant of Love* is that the earth belongs to God, and that God loves the world and seeks to redeem it.[23] As stewards of God's earth, we recall Bonhoeffer's statement that "only those who remain true" to the earth as "our mother are placed by her into the father's arms."[24] Volmoed is a beautiful place in God's creation, internationally known for its indigenous vegetation, and habitat to many different animal species. Volmoed is "God's garden," and we are called to care for it on behalf of all who desire to enjoy what God has provided. This also requires that we care for the environment in its entirety. In writing the *Covenant of Love*, we must be mindful that we remain committed to

---

22. Ephesians 3:28.
23. John 3:16.
24. See p. 11, above.

ensuring that Volmoed is maintained, developed, and used in ways that honor our love for God, whose creative beauty surrounds us.

Renewing Our Covenant

Benedictine monastics read a section from their *Rule* each day. This not only prevents the *Rule* from becoming a document that is shelved alongside others, but is a daily reminder of their vocation. In my own tradition, each congregation is annually invited to renew its covenant on a Sunday set aside for this purpose, for the same reason. As in the biblical narrative, so in the life of the church, covenants are too often forgotten and broken. They become a dead letter; the Spirit has departed. That is why monastic reforms have been so much a part of *This Monastic Moment*. In writing the *Covenant of Love*, we must make provision for times of reflection on our life together, times when we revisit the *Covenant*, and if necessary revise what we have previously written. We live "between the times," so, as much as we cherish where we have come from and the rich traditions we have inherited, our *Covenant of Love* is open to God's future for us. Volmoed is a place set aside by God, but it is not a place where we can settle indefinitely; it is, rather, a place where we discover that we are all pilgrims on a journey.

> Let us not forget:
> we are a pilgrim church,
> subject to misunderstanding,
> to persecution,
> but a church that walks serene,
> because it bears the force of love.[25]

---

25. From Archbishop Oscar Romero's sermon preached on March, 14, 1977, at the funeral of one of his priests and two parishioners murdered by agents of the state in El Salvador. In Romero, *The Violence of Love*, 3.

BIBLIOGRAPHY

Anselm, St. *Basic Writings.* Translated by S. N. Deane. 2nd ed. The Open Court Library of Philosophy. La Salle, IL: Open Court, 1968.
Athanasius, St. *The Life of Antony and the Letter to Marcellinus.* Translated and introduced by Robert C. Gregg. Classics of Western Spirituality. New York: Paulist, 1980.
Augustine, St. *The City of God (Civitate Dei).* Translated by John Healey. Rev. ed. 2 vols. Everyman's Library 983. London: Dent, 1945.
———. *Confessions and Enchiridion.* Newly translated and edited by Albert C. Outler. LCC 7. London: SCM, 1955.
———. *The Trinity (De Trinitate).* Introduction, translation, and notes by Edmund Hill, OP. Edited by John E. Rotelle, OSA. The Works of Saint Augustine: A New Translation for the 21st Century, Part I, 5. New York: New City, 1991.
Bainton, Roland H. *Here I Stand: A Life of Martin Luther.* Nashville: Abingdon, 1950.
Balthasar, Hans Urs von. *Love Alone is Credible.* Translated by D. C. Schindler. San Francisco: Ignatius, 2004.
Barr, James. *The Semantics of Biblical Language.* Oxford: Oxford University Press, 1961.
Barth, Karl. *Anselm: Fides Quarens Intellectum.* Translated from the 2nd German edition by Ian W. Robertson. London: SCM, 1960.
———. *Church Dogmatics.* Vol. I/2, *The Doctrine of the Word of God.* Edited by G. W. Bromiley and T. F. Torrance. Translated by G. T. Thomson and Harold Knight. Edinburgh: T. & T. Clark, 1956.
———. *Church Dogmatics.* Vol. III/4, *The Doctrine of Creation.* Edited by G. W. Bromiley and T. F. Torrance. Translated by A. T. MacKay et al. Edinburgh: T. & T. Clark, 1961.
———. *Church Dogmatics.* Vol. IV/2, *The Doctrine of Reconciliation.* Edited by G. W. Bromiley and T. F. Torrance. Translated by G. W. Bromiley. Edinburgh: T. & T. Clark, 1958.
Battle, Michael. *Desmond Tutu: A Spiritual Biography of South Africa's Confessor.* Louisville, Kentucky: Westminster John Knox, 2021.
———. *Reconciliation: The Ubuntu Theology of Desmond Tutu.* Foreword by Desmond Tutu. Cleveland: Pilgrim, 1997.
Bauer, Walter. *Orthodoxy and Heresy in Earliest Christianity.* Translated by a team from the Philadelphia Seminar on Christian Origins, and edited by Robert A. Kraft and Gerhard Krodel. Philadelphia: Fortress, 1971.
Bede, St. *The Ecclesiastical History of the English People; the Greater Chronicle; Bede's Letter to Egbert.* Translated by Bertram Colgrave. Edited with an introduction

and notes by Judith McClure and Roger Collins. Rev. ed. Oxford World's Classics. Oxford: Oxford University Press, 2000.

Benedict, St. *RB1980: The Rule of St. Benedict in Latin and English with Notes*. Edited by Timothy Fry, OSB et al. Collegeville, MN: Liturgical, 1981.

Bethge, Eberhard. *Dietrich Bonhoeffer: A Biography*. Revised and edited by Victoria J. Barnett. Minneapolis: Fortress, 2000.

Berger, Peter L. *The Heretical Imperative*. Garden City, NY: Anchor/Doubleday, 1980.

Bettenson, Henry, ed. *Documents of the Christian Church*. The World's Classics 495. London: Oxford University Press, 1954.

Bianchi, Enzo. *Echoes of the Word: A New Kind of Monk on the Meaning of Life*. Brewster, MA: Paraclete, 2013.

Boesak, Allan A., and Charles Villa-Vicencio, eds. *When Prayer Makes News*. Philadelphia: Westminster, 1986.

Bonhoeffer, Dietrich. *Act and Being: Transcendental Philosophy and Ontology in Systematic Theology*. Edited by Wayne Whitson Floyd Jr. Translated by H. Martin Rumscheidt. DBWE 2. Minneapolis: Fortress 1996.

———. *Barcelona, Berlin, New York, 1928–1931*. Edited by Clifford J. Green. Translated by Douglas W. Stott. DBWE 10. Minneapolis: Fortress, 2008.

———. *Conspiracy and Imprisonment: 1940–1945*. Edited by Mark S. Brocker. Translated by Lisa E. Cahill. DBWE 16. Minneapolis: Fortress, 2006.

———. *Creation and Fall: A Theological Exposition of Genesis 1–3*. Edited by John W. de Gruchy. Translated by Douglas Stephen Bax. DBWE 3. Minneapolis: Fortress 1997.

———. *Discipleship*. Edited by Geffrey B. Kelly and John D. Godsey. Translated by Barbara Green and Reinhard Krauss. DBWE 4. Minneapolis: Fortress 2001.

———. *Ecumenical, Academic and Pastoral Work, 1931–1932*. Edited by Victoria J. Barnett et al. Translated by Anne Schmidt-Lange et al. DBWE 11. Minneapolis: Fortress, 2012.

———. *Ethics*. Edited by Clifford J. Green. Translated by Reinhard Krauss et al. DBWE 6. Minneapolis: Fortress, 2005.

———. *Letters and Papers from Prison*. Edited by John W. de Gruchy. Translated by Isabel Best et al. DBWE 8. Minneapolis: Fortress, 2010.

———. *Life Together; Prayerbook of the Bible*. Edited by Geoffrey B. Kelly. Translated by Daniel W. Bloesch and James H. Burtness. DBWE 5. Minneapolis: Fortress, 1996.

———. *London, 1933–1935*. Edited by Keith Clements. Translated by Isabel Best. Supplementary material translated by Douglas W. Stott. DBWE 13. Min-neapolis: Fortress, 2007.

———. *Sanctorum Communio: A Theological Study of the Sociology of the Church*. Edited by Clifford J. Green. Translated by Reinhard Krauss and Nancy Lukens. DBWE 1. Minneapolis: Fortress, 1998.

———. *Theological Education at Finkenwalde, 1935–1937*. Edited by H. Gaylon Barker and Mark S. Brocker. Translated by Douglas W. Stott. DBWE 14. Minneapolis: Fortress, 2013.

———. *Theological Education Underground, 1937–1940*. Edited and translated by Victoria J. Barnett. DBWE 15. Minneapolis: Fortress, 2011.

———. *The Young Bonhoeffer, 1918–1927*. Edited by Paul Duane Matheny et al. Translated by Mary C. Nebelsick with the assistance of Douglas W. Stott. DBWE 9. Minneapolis: Fortress, 2003.

Bonhoeffer, Dietrich, and Maria von Wedemeyer. *Love Letters from Cell 92*. London: HarperCollins, 1994.
Bradley, Ian, *Following the Celtic Way: A New Assessment of Celtic Christianity*. London: Darton, Longman & Todd, 2018.
Brico, Rex. *Taizé: Brother Roger and His Community*. London: Collins, 1978.
Brook, Carl I. "Resonance at Rutba: The Relevance of New Monasticism for South Africa." *Missionalia* 42 (2013) 195–210.
Brown, Peter "The Notion of Virginity in the Early Church." In *Christian Spirituality*. Vol. 1, *Origins to the Twelfth Century*, edited by Bernard McGinn et al., 427–43. 3 vols. World Spirituality 16. New York: Crossroad, 1989.
Brown, Raymond E. *The Epistles of John*. Anchor Bible 30. Garden City, NY: Doubleday, 1982.
Brunner, Emil. *Dogmatics*, Vol. 3, *The Christian Doctrine of the Church, Faith, and the Consummation*. Translated by David Cairns in collaboration with T. H. L. Parker. 3 vols. Lutterworth Library 35. London: Lutterworth, 1962.
Busch, Eberhard. *Karl Barth: His Life from Letters and Autobiographical Texts*. Philadelphia: Fortress, 1976.
———. *Karl Barth: His Life from Letters and Autobiographical Texts*. 1976. Reprint, Eugene, OR: Wipf & Stock, 2005.
Byassee, Jason. *An Introduction to The Desert Fathers*. Cascade Companions. Eugene, OR: Cascade Books, 2007.
Calvin, John. *The Institutes of the Christian Religion*. Edited by John T. McNeill. Translated and indexed by Ford Lewis Battles. 2 vols. LCC 21. Philadelphia: Westminster, 1960.
Campenhausen, Hans von. *The Fathers of the Latin Church*. Translated by Manfred Hoffmann. London: Black, 1964.
———. *Tradition and Life in the Church: Essays and Lectures on Church History*. Translated by A. V. Littledale. London: Collins, 1968.
Cassian, John. *The Conferences*. Translation and preface by Colm Luibheid. The Classics of Western Spirituality. New York: Paulist, 1985.
———. *Conference 1 [of Cassian]*. In *Western Asceticism*, edited by Owen Chadwick, 195–289. LCC 12. Philadelphia: Westminster, 1963.
Chadwick, Owen, ed. and trans. *Western Asceticism*. LCC 12. Philadelphia: Westminster, 1958.
Chittister, Joan. "Old Vision for a New Age." In *A Monastic Vision for the 21st Century*, edited by Patrick Hart, 89–104. Kalamazoo, MI: Cistercian Publications, 2006.
Chryssavgis, John. *In the Heart of the Desert: The Spirituality of the Desert Fathers and Mothers*. Treasures of the World's Religions. Bloomington, IN: World Wisdom, 2003.
Clément, Olivier. *Corps de mort et de gloire: Petite introduction à une théopoétique du corps*. Paris: Brouwer, 1995.
Coates, Adrian. *The Aesthetics of Discipleship: Everyday Aesthetic Existence and the Christian Life*. Eugene, OR: Pickwick Publications, forthcoming.
Cochrane, Charles Norris. *Christianity and Classical Culture*. A Galaxy Book. New York: Oxford University Press, 1957.
Cowan, James, *Desert Father: A Journey in the Wilderness with Saint Anthony*. Boston: New Seeds, 2006.

Curtius, Ernst Robert. *European Literature and the Latin Middle Ages*. Translated from the German by Willard R. Trask. Princeton: Princeton University Press, 1953.
Cyril of Jerusalem, St. *Cyril of Jerusalem and Nemesius of Emesa*. Edited by William Telfer. LCC 4. London: SCM, 1955.
Dalrymple, William. *From the Holy Mountain: A Journey in the Shadow of Byzantium*. London: HarperCollins, 1997.
Dante Alighieri. *The Comedy of Dante Alighieri, the Florentine*. Vol. 3, *Paradise*. Translated by Dorothy L. Sayers and Barbara Reynolds. Harmondsworth, UK: Penguin, 1962.
de Gruchy, Isobel. *Making All Things Well: Finding Spiritual Strength with Julian of Norwich*. Norwich, UK: Canterbury, 2012.
———. *Making All Things Well: Finding Spiritual Strength with Julian of Norwich*. New York: Paulist, 2013.
de Gruchy, John W. *Bonhoeffer's Questions: A Life-Changing Conversation*. Lanham, MD: Lexington Books/Fortress Academic, 2019.
———. *Christianity, Art, and Transformation: Theological Aesthetics and the Struggle for Justice*, Cambridge: Cambridge University Press, 2001.
———. *Confessions of a Christian Humanist*. Minneapolis: Fortress, 2006.
———. *Daring, Trusting Spirit: Bonhoeffer's Friend Eberhard Bethge*. London: SCM, 2005.
———. *The End Is not Yet: Standing Firm in Apocalyptic Times*. Minneapolis: Fortress, 2017.
———. *I Have Come a Long Way*. Eugene, OR: Cascade Books, 2016.
———. *Led into Mystery: Faith Seeking Answers in Life and Death*. London: SCM, 2013.
———. "Redefining Sainthood and Martyrdom: The Case of Dietrich Bonhoeffer." In *Theology and Human Flourishing: Essays in Honor of Timothy J. Gorringe*, edited by Mike Higton et al., 157–68. Eugene, OR: Cascade Books, 2011.
de Gruchy, John, and Isobel de Gruchy. *The Volmoed Journey: Thirtieth Anniversary Edition 1986–2016*. Cape Town: Methodist Publishing House, 2016.
de Gruchy, John, and Steve de Gruchy. *The Church Struggle in South Africa*. 25th anniversary ed. London: SCM, 2004.
de Gruchy, John, and Charles Villa-Vicencio, eds. *Apartheid Is a Heresy*. Grand Rapids: Eerdmans, 1983.
de Waal, Esther. *A Life-Giving Way: A Commentary on the Rule of St. Benedict*. Norwich, UK: Canterbury, 2013.
———. *Seeking God: The Way of St Benedict*. London: Collins, 1984.
Dickens, A. G. *The English Reformation*. Rev. ed. Fontana Library. London: Collins, 1967.
———. *The German Nation and Martin Luther*. London: Arnold, 1974.
Draper, John. *Listening to God: Fuel for Ministry?* Winchester, UK: Circle Books, 2016.
Earle, Mary C. *The Desert Mothers: Spiritual Practices from the Women of the Wilderness*. Harrisburg, PA: Morehouse, 2007.
Eberle, Luke, trans. *The Rule of the Master*. Introduced by Adalbert de Vogue. Translated by Charles Philippi. Cistercian Studies Series 6. Kalamazoo, MI: Cistercian Publications, 1977.
Elshtain, Jean Bethke. *Augustine and the Limits of Politics*. Frank M. Covey, Jr. Loyola Lectures in Political Analysis. Notre Dame, IN: University of Notre Dame Press, 1995.

Farmer, D.H., ed. *Benedict's Disciples*. Leominster, UK: Fowler Wright, 1980.
Fernández-Armesto, Felipe, and Derek Wilson. *Reformation: Christianity and the World, 1500–2000*. London: Bantam, 1996.
Flanagan, Sabina. *Hildegard of Bingen, 1098–1179: A Visionary Life*. London: Routledge, 1989.
Fletcher, Richard. *Conversion of Europe: From Paganism to Christianity; 371–1386 AD*. London: HarperCollins, 1997.
Forest, Jim. *Living with Wisdom: A Life of Thomas Merton*. Maryknoll, NY: Orbis, 1991.
Fox, Matthew. *Original Blessing*. Santa Fe, NM: Bear, 1983.
Fox, Robin Lane. *Pagans and Christians*. Penguin History. London: Penguin, 1988.
Freeman, Charles. *The Closing of the Western Mind: The Rise of Faith and the Fall of Reason*. London: Pimlico, 2002.
Frend, W. H. C. *The Rise of Christianity*. Philadelphia: Fortress, 1984.
Frick, Peter. The *Imitatio Christi* of Thomas a' Kempis and Dietrich Bonhoeffer, in Frick, Peter ed. Bonhoeffer's Intellectual Formation, Tübingen, Germany: Mohr Siebeck, 2008, 31–52.
Fukuyama, Francis. *The End of History and the Last Man*. London: Penguin, 1992.
Gaum, Laurie, and Sallie Argent, eds. *Silence and Solidarity: Celebrating 30 Years of the Centre for Christian Spirituality*. Wellington, South Africa: Centre for Christian Spirituality, 2017.
Gardiner, Craig. *Melodies of a New Monasticism: Bonhoeffer's Vision, Iona's Witness*. Eugene, OR: Cascade Books, 2018.
Gelineau, Joseph. *The Psalms: A New Translation*. Fontana Books. London: Collins, 1963.
Gioia, Luigi. "Word of God and Monasticism in Karl Barth." *American Benedictine Review* 68 (2017) 418–32.
Goehring, James E. *Ascetics, Society, and the Desert: Studies in Early Egyptian Monasticism*. Studies in Antiquity and Christianity. Harrisburg, PA: Trinity, 1999.
González-Balado, José Luis. *The Story of Taizé*. Mowbray's Popular Christian Paperbacks. London: Mowbray, 1980.
Gorringe, T. J. *The Education of Desire*. Diocese of British Columbia John Albert Hall Lectures 2000. London: SCM, 2001.
Grant, Robert M. *Greek Apologists of the Second Century*. Philadelphia: Westminster, 1988.
Green, Michael Cawood. *For the Sake of Silence*. Roggebaai, South Africa: Umuzi, 2008.
Greenslade, S. L., ed. *Early Latin Theology*, LCC 5. London: SCM, 1961.
Gregory the Great, Pope. *The Life of St Benedict*. Translated by Hilary Costello and Eoin de Bhaldraithe, Commentary by Adalbert de Vogüé OSB. Petersham, MA: St. Bede's Publications, 1993.
Gutiérrez, Gustavo. *A Theology of Liberation*. Translated and edited by John Eagleson and Sr. Caridad Inda. Rev. ed. with a new introduction. Maryknoll, NY.: Orbis, 1988.
Harnack, Adolf. *Monasticism*. Translated by E. E. Kellett and F. H. Marseille. Crown Theological Library. London: Williams & Norgate, 1901.
Hart, Patrick, ed. *Survival or Prophecy? The Correspondence of Jean Le Clercq & Thomas Merton*. Monastic Wisdom Series 17. Kalamazoo, MI: Cistercian Publications, 2008.
Hoffman, Bengt R. *Luther and the Mystics*. Minneapolis: Augsburg, 1976.

Hofmeyr, Isabel. *The Portable Bunyan: A Transnational History of "The Pilgrim's Progress."* Translation/Transnation. Princeton: Princeton University Press, 2004.
Housden, Roger. *For Lovers of God Everywhere: Poems of the Christian Mystics.* Carlsbad, CA: Hay House, 2009.
Huddleston, Trevor. *Naught for Your Comfort.* London: Collins, 1956.
John Climacus, St. *The Ladder of Divine Ascent.* Translated by Colm Luibheid and Norman Russell. Classics of Western Spirituality. New York: Paulist, 1982.
Johnston, William, ed. *The Cloud of Unknowing; and The Book of Privy Counseling.* Image Books. Garden City, NY: Doubleday, 1973.
———. *The Still Point: Reflections on Zen and Christian Mysticism.* Perennial Library 227. New York: Harper & Row, 1971.
Julian of Norwich, St. *Showings.* Translated from the critical text, with an introduction by Edmund Colledge and James Walsh. Classics of Western Spirituality. New York: Paulist, 1978.
Kairos Theologians. *The Kairos Document.* Johannesburg: Institute for Contextual Theol-ogy, 1986.
Kardong, Terence G. *Benedict's Rule: A Translation and Commentary.* Collegeville, MN: Liturgical, 1996.
Kelly, Geffrey B., ed. *Karl Rahner: Theologian of the Graced Search for Meaning.* The Making of Modern Theology. Minneapolis: Fortress, 1992.
Kelly, J. N. D. *Early Christian Creeds.* London: Longmans, Green, 1950.
Kierkegaard, Søren. *Concluding Unscientific Postscript.* Translated by David F. Swenson and Walter Lowrie. Princeton: Princeton University Press, 1941.
———. *Kierkegaard's "Attack upon "Christendom," 1854–1855.* Translated with an introduction by Walter Lowrie. Princeton: Princeton University Press, 1946.
———. *Purity of Heart Is to Will One Thing.* Translated and with an introduction by Douglas Steere Fontana Books. London: Fontana, 1961.
———. *The Journals of Søren Kierkegaard: A Selection.* Edited and translated by Alexander Dru. Fontana Books. London: Collins, 1958.
Kim, David Kyuman. *Melancholic Freedom: Agency and the Spirit of Politics.* Reflection and Theory in the Study of Religion Series. New York: Oxford University Press, 2007.
King, Margot H. *The Desert Mothers: A Survey of the Feminine Anchoretic Tradition in Western Europe.* Saskatoon, SK: Peregrina, 1984.
Kline, Francis. *Lovers of the Place: Monasticism Loose in the Church.* Collegeville, MN: Liturgical, 1997.
Knowles, David. *The Evolution of Medieval Thought.* 5th imprint. London: Longman, 1973.
———. *The Monastic Order in England.* Cambridge: Cambridge University Press, 1963.
———. *The Religious Orders in England.* Vol. 1. Cambridge: Cambridge University Press, 1948.
Küng, Hans. *On Being a Christian.* Translated by Edward Quinn. London: Collins, 1976.
LaCugna, Catherine Mowry, *God for Us: The Trinity and Christian Life.* San Francisco: HarperSanFrancisco, 1991.
Latourette, Kenneth Scott. *A History of the Expansion of Christianity.* Vol. 2, *The Thousand Years of Uncertainty: AD 500—AD 1500.* 7 vols. Contemporary Evangelical Perspectives. London: Eyre & Spottiswood, 1938.

Leclercq, Jean. *The Love of Learning and the Desire for God: A Study of Monastic Culture.* Translated by Catharine Misrahi. New York: Fordham University Press, 1982.

Leclercq, Jean, et al. *The Spirituality of the Middle Ages.* Translated by the Benedictines of Holme Eden Abbey, Carlisle. A History of Christian Spirituality 2. London: Burns & Oates, 1968.

Loewenich, Walther von. *Luther's Theology of the Cross.* Translated by Herbert J. A. Bouman. Belfast: Christian Journals, 1976.

Lossky, Vladimir. *The Mystical Theology of the Eastern Church.* Translated from the French by members of the Fellowship of St. Alban and St. Sergius. Crestwood, NY: St. Vladimir's Seminary Press, 1976.

Louth, Andrew. *The Origins of the Christian Mystical Tradition: From Plato to Denys.* Oxford: Clarendon, 1983.

Lowrie, Walter, ed. *Kierkegaard.* Vol. 2. 2 vols. New York: Harper & Brothers, 1962.

Luther, Martin. *Judgment on Monastic Vows.* In LW 44:251–400. Edited by James Atkinson. Philadelphia: Fortress, 1966.

———. *Lectures on Romans.* Translated and edited by Wilhelm Pauck. LCC 15. Philadelphia: Westminster, 1961.

———. *Martin Luther's Basic Theological Writings.* Edited by Timothy F. Lull. Minneapolis: Fortress, 1989.

———. *The Sermon on the Mount and the Magnificat.* In LW, 21:1–194, edited by Jaroslav Pelikan. St Louis: Concordia, 1956.

MacIntyre, Alasdair. *After Virtue.* Notre Dame, IN: University of Notre Dame Press, 1981.

Maguire, Nancy Klein. *An Infinity of Little Hours.* New York: Public Affairs, 2006.

Maitland, Sara. *A Book of Silence.* Wellbeing Collection. London: Granta, 2009.

Mann, Thomas. *Doctor Faustus.* Translated by John E. Woods. New York: Vintage, 1999.

Marty, Martin E. "Hope and Courage in Volmoed." *Christian Century*, September 10–17, 1986.

———. *Pilgrims in Their Own Land: 500 Years of Religion in America.* Boston: Little, Brown, 1984.

Matarasso, Pauline, ed. and trans. *The Cistercian World: Monastic Writings of the Twelfth Century.* Penguin Classics. London: Penguin, 1993.

Matheson, Peter, ed. *Argula von Grumbach: A Woman's Voice in the Reformation.* Edinburgh: T. & T. Clark, 1995.

McLoughlin, William, OSM, and Jill Pinnock, eds. *Mary Is for Everyone.* Leominster, UK: Gracewing, 1997.

Meinardus, Otto F. A. *Monks and Monasteries of the Egyptian Deserts.* Second printing of rev. ed. with additional material. Cairo: American University in Cairo Press, 1992.

Merton, Thomas, *The Asian Journal of Thomas Merton.* Edited by Naomi Burton et al. London: Sheldon, 1974.

———. *Cassian and the Fathers: Initiation into the Monastic Tradition 1.* Edited with an introduction by Patrick F. O'Connell. Monastic Wisdom Series 1. Kalamazoo, MI: Cistercian Publications, 2005.

———. *Conjectures of a Guilty Bystander.* Image Books. Garden City, NY: Doubleday, 1968.

———. *Contemplation in a World of Action.* Image Books. Garden City, NY: Doubleday, 1973.

———. *The Hidden Ground of Love: Letters on Religious Experience and Social Concerns.* London: Collins/Flame, 1990.

———. *The Life of the Vows: Initiation into the Monastic Tradition 6.* Edited with an introduction by Patrick F. O'Connell. Monastic Wisdom Series 30. Trappist, KY: Cistercian Publications, 2012.

———. "Marxism and Monastic Perspectives." In *The Asian Journal of Thomas Merton*, edited by Naomi Burton et al., 326–43. London: Sheldon, 1974.

———. *Seeking Paradise: The Spirit of the Shakers.* Maryknoll, NY: Orbis, 2003.

———. *The Seven Story Mountain*, New York: Image, 1970.

———. *The Silent Life.* London: Sheldon, 1975.

———, trans. *The Wisdom of the Desert: Sayings from the Desert Fathers of the Fourth Century.* London: Sheldon, 1974.

Metz, Johann Baptist. *Theology of the World.* Translated by William Glen-Doepel. London: Burns & Oates, 1968.

Milbank, John. *Theology and Social Theory: Beyond Secular Reason.* Signposts in Theology. 1990. Reprint, Oxford: Blackwell, 1993.

Mitton, Michael. *Restoring the Woven Cord: Strands of Celtic Christianity for the Church Today.* London: Darton, Longman & Todd, 1995.

Moltmann, Jürgen. *The Church in the Power of the Spirit.* Translated by Margaret Kohl. London: SCM, 1977.

———. *Experiences in Theology: Ways and Forms of Christian Theology.* Translated by Margaret Kohl. London: SCM, 2000.

Niebuhr, H. Richard. *Christ and Culture.* New York: Harper & Row, 1951.

Norris, Kathleen. *Acedia & Me: A Marriage, Monks, and a Writer's Life.* New York: Riverhead, 2008.

———. *The Cloister Walk.* New York: Riverhead, 1996.

Northumbria Community. "Story of the Community." www.northumbriacommunity.org/who-we-are/story-of-the-community/.

Nuttall, Geoffrey F. *Visible Saints: The Congregational Way.* Oxford: Blackwell, 1957.

Oberman, Heiko A. *Luther: Man between God and the Devil.* Translated by Eileen Walliser-Schwarzbart. New Haven: Yale University Press, 1989.

———. *The Forerunners of the Reformation: The Shape of Late Medieval Thought.* Translated by Paul L. Nyhus. London: Lutterworth, 1967.

Oden, Thomas C. *How Africa Shaped the Christian Mind.* Downers Grove, IL: InterVarsity Press, 2007.

Oulton, John E. L., and Henry Chadwick, eds. *Alexandrian Christianity.* LCC 2. Philadelphia: Westminster, 1954.

Ovenden, Richard. *Burning the Books: A History of Knowledge under Attack.* London: Murray, 2020.

Ozment, Steven. *The Age of Reform: 1250–1550 An Intellectual and Religious History of Late Medieval and Reformation Europe*, New Haven: Yale University Press, 1980.

Pagels, Elaine. *The Gnostic Gospels* New York: Vintage, 1981.

Palmer, G. E. H., et al., eds. and trans. *The Philokalia.* Compiled by St. Nikodimos of the Holy Mountain and St. Makarios of Corinth. 3 vols. London: Faber & Faber, 1986.

Palmer, Parker J. *The Company of Strangers: Christians and the Renewal of America's Public Life.* New York: Crossroad, 1981.

Palmisano, Stephania. *Exploring New Monastic Communities: The (Re)invention of Tradition*. Ashgate AHRC/ESRC Religion and Society Series. London: Routledge, 2019.

Pangritz, Andreas. *The Polyphony of Life: Bonhoeffer's Theology of Music*. Edited by John W. de Gruchy and John Morris. Eugene, OR: Cascade Books, 2019.

Parpert, Friedrich, *Das Mönchtum und die evangelische Kirche: Ein Beitrag zur Ausscheidung des Monchtums aus der evangelischen Soziologie*. Aus der Welt christlicher Frömmigkeit 10. Munich: Reinhardt, 1930.

Pearson, Birger A. *Ancient Gnosticism: Traditions and Literature*. Minneapolis: Fortress, 2007.

Pelikan, Jaroslav. *The Christian Tradition: A History of the Development of Doctrine*. Vol. 2, *The Spirit of Eastern Christendom 600-1700*. 5 vols. Chicago: University of Chicago Press, 1974.

———. *Spirit versus Structure: Luther and the Institutions of the Church*. London: Collins, 1968.

Pennington, Basil. "The Cistercians." In *Christian Spirituality*. Vol. 1, *Origins to the Twelfth Century*, edited by Bernard McGinn et al., 205-17. 3 vols. World Spirituality 16. New York: Crossroad, 1989.

Pfeifer, Claude. "Monastic Formation and Profession." In *RB 1980: The Rule of St. Benedict in Latin and English with Notes*, edited by Timothy Fry, OSB, et al., 437-66.Collegeville, MN: Liturgical, 1981.

———. "The Rule in History." In *RB 1980: The Rule of St. Benedict in Latin and English with Notes*, edited by Timothy Fry, OSB, et al. 113-51. Collegeville, MN: Liturgical, 1981.

———. "The Rule of St. Benedict." In *RB 1980: The Rule of St. Benedict in Latin and English with Notes*, edited by Timothy Fry, OSB, et al., 65-112. Collegeville, MN: Liturgical, 1981.

Pribbenow, Brad. *Prayerbook of Christ: Dietrich Bonhoeffer's Christological Interpretation of the Psalms*. Lanham, MD: Lexington Books/Fortress Academic, 2018.

Price, Neil. *The Children of Ash and Elm: A History of the Vikings*. London: Lane, 2020.

Raine, Andy, and John T. Skinner, comps. *Celtic Daily Prayer: A Northumbrian Office*. London: Pickering, 1994.

Rees, Daniel, et al. *Consider Your Call: A Theology of the Monastic Life Today*. London: SPCK, 1978.

Rolf, Veronica Mary. *Julian's Gospel: Illuminating the Life and Revelations of Julian of Norwich*. Maryknoll, NY: Orbis, 2013.

Roger, Br., of Taizé. *This Day Belongs to God*. Translated by J. C. Dickinson. London: Faith Press, 1961.

Roger, Br., of Taizé, and the Community of Taizé. *The Rule of Taizé in French and English*. Taizé: Les Preses de Taizé, 1961.

———. *The Rule of Taizé in French and English*. London: SPCK, 2012.

Romero, Oscar. *The Violence of Love*. Translated by James R. Brockman. London: Collins, 1988.

Santos, Jason Brian. *A Community Called Taizé*. Downers Grove, IL: InterVarsity Press, 2008.

Sheridan, Mark. "The Origins of Monasticism in the Eastern Church." In *RB 1980: The Rule of St. Benedict in Latin and English with Notes*, edited by Timothy Fry, OSB et al., 3-41. Collegeville, MN: Liturgical, 1981.

Slane, Craig J. *Bonhoeffer as Martyr: Social Responsibility and Modern Christian Commitment*. Grand Rapids: Brazos, 2004.

Sölle, Dorothee. *The Silent Cry: Mysticism and Resistance*. Translated by Barbara and Martin Rumscheidt. Minneapolis: Fortress, 2001.

Spencer, Bonnell. *Dietrich Bonhoeffer: Prophet for Our Time*. West Park, NY: Holy Cross, 1966.

Spink, Kathryn. *A Universal Heart: The Life and Vision of Brother Roger of Taizé*. London: SPCK, 1986.

Spinka, Matthew, ed. *Advocates of Reform: From Wyclif to Erasmus*. LCC 14, London: SCM, 1963.

Stephens, W. P. *The Theology of Huldrych Zwingli*. Oxford: Clarendon, 1986.

Stjerna, Kirsi. *Women and the Reformation*. Oxford: Blackwell, 2009.

Tellenbach, Gerd. *The Church in Western Europe from the Tenth to the Early Twelfth Century*. Translated by Timothy Reuter. Cambridge Medieval Textbooks. Cambridge: Cambridge University Press, 1993.

Tillich, Paul *A History of Christian Thought*. Edited by Carl E. Braaten. 3rd ed., revised. London: SCM, 1968.

Tutu, Desmond. *The Rainbow People of God: The Making of a Peaceful Revolution*. Edited by John Allen. New York: Doubleday, 1994.

———. Review of *Taizé: Brother Roger and His Community*, by Rex Brico. *Journal of Theology for Southern Africa* (36 September 1981) 80-81.

Vatican Council. *The Documents of Vatican II*. Edited by Walter M. Abbott, SJ, et al. London: Chapman, 1966.

Villain, Maurice. *Unity: A History and Some Reflections*. London: Harvill, 1961.

Waddell, Helen, trans. *The Desert Fathers: Translations from the Latin, with an Introduction*. London: Constable, 1936.

———. *Peter Abelard: A Novel*. London: Fontana, 1958.

Ward, Benedicta, trans. *The Sayings of the Desert Fathers: The Alphabetical Collection*. Rev. ed. Kalamazoo, MI: Cistercian Publications, 1984.

Williams, George H. *The Radical Reformation*. Philadelphia: Westminster, 1962.

———, ed. *Spiritual and Anabaptist Writers*. LCC 25. London: SCM, 1962.

Williams, Rowan, *Arius: Heresy and Tradition*. 2nd ed. London: SCM, 2001.

Winter, Ernst F, ed. *Erasmus-Luther. Discourse on Free Will*. New York, NY: Frederick Ungar, 1967.

Wulf, Friedrich. "Decree on the Appropriate Renewal of the Religious Life." In *Commentary on the Documents of Vatican II*, edited by Herbert Vorgrimler et al., 2:301–370. Translated by Ronald Walls. 5 vols. London: Burns & Oates, 1968.

Wüstenberg, Ralf K. *A Theology of Life: Dietrich Bonhoeffer's Religionless Christianity*. Translated by Douglas W. Stott. Grand Rapids: Eerdmans, 1998.

Zimmermann, Jens. *Incarnational Humanism: A Philosophy of Culture for the Church in the World*. Strategic Initiatives in Evangelical Theology. Downers Grove, IL: IVP Academic, 2012.

INDEX OF NAMES

Abelard, Peter, 96
Aelred of Riveaulx, 90, 95
Alaric, 61
Alcuin, 86
Alois, Bro., 2, 135
Ambrose, St., 63, 64, 65, 68–69
Anselm, St., 91–92, 94, 96, 105, 107, 144
Anthony, St., 26–27, 40, 44–49, 52, 62–64, 67–68, 102, 109, 112, 115, 116, 118, 148
Argula von Grumbach, 111
Arnold, Eberhard, 128
Arnold, Hardy, 127
Arius, 46
Athanasius, St., 27, 29, 44–46, 62, 67, 103
Augustine, St., 20, 41, 45, 53–54, 61–73, 77–79, 84, 91–92, 96, 103–5, 107, 109, 112, 132, 144–45, 162,
Aurelius, Marcus, 39
Balthasar, Hans Urs von, 169
Bainton, Roland H., 103
Barth, Karl, 16, 19, 21, 22, 92, 98, 110, 120, 122–26, 147, 149, 156, 162, 173,
Barr, James, 7
Basil of Caesarea, St, 32, 35, 47, 65, 77–78, 82, 112
Battle, Michael, 6, 129
Bauer, Walter, 10
Bede, the Venerable, 83–84
Benedict, St, 6, 7, 15, 20, 26, 54, 74–82, 86, 88, 110, 115, 117, 132, 138, 140, 164, 166, 171–72, 177
Benedict of Aniane, St, 86,
Berger, Peter, 9
Bernard of Clairvaux, St, 20, 32, 76, 90, 94–97, 104–5, 108–10, 112
Bethge, Eberhard, 122, 146, 151–52, 155–56, 160, 163, 168
Bianchi, Enzo, 126, 158, 162,
Bonhoeffer, Dietrich, 5, 11, 14, 16–19, 21–26, 28, 37–38, 102, 110, 112, 118, 122, 125–31, 140–47, 149–52, 154–60, 162–66, 168–69
Bonhoeffer, Karl-Friedrich, 128
Boniface, St., 85
Bradley, Ian, 84
Bramante, Donato, 63
Brasó, Gabriel, 125
Bridget of Sweden, 90
Brook, Carl, I., 19
Brown, Peter, 42, 62
Brown, Raymond, 55
Brunner, Emil, 121–22
Bruno, St., 88
Bunyan, John, 115–16, 118, 120
Busch, Eberhard, 125, 149
Byassee, Jason, 50–51
Calvin, John, 112, 114–15, 120–21
Campenhausen, Hans von, 42–43, 66, 71, 73, 82
Cassian, John St., 20, 53, 65, 73–78, 80, 88, 116–17, 132
Catherine of Siena St., 95

INDEX OF NAMES

Chaucer, Geoffrey, 117
Chittister, Joan, 142
Clebsch, William, 62
Clement of Alexandria, St., 29–31, 34, 40, 42–43, 48, 95, 144
Clément, Olivier, 156
Climacus, John, St., 76
Chadwick, Owen, 34, 42, 44, 48
Charlemagne, emperor, 69, 85,
Charles V, emperor, 105
Chittister, Joan, 142
Chryssavgis, John, 48
Coates, Adrian, 118
Cochrane, Charles Norris, 13
Coello, Claudio, 71
Columba, St., 83
Columbanus, St., 83
Constantine, emperor, 8, 12, 14, 46, 61, 65, 87
Corman, 83
Couturier, Paul, 16
Cowan, James, 50
Curtius, Ernst Robert, 1
Cyril of Jerusalem, St., 56–57
Dalrymple, William, 20, 60
Dante, Alighieri, 97
de Gruchy, Isobel, 2, 4–5, 23–24, 85, 117, 132
de Gruchy, Steve, 132, 134, 148
de Waal, Esther, 5, 81, 172
Dickens, A.G., 107
Dionysius the Areopagite, 30, 32, 77
Draper, John, 79
Dunstan, St., 84, 90
Earle, Mary C., 48, 50, 62, 78
Eberle, Luke, 53–54
Eckhart, Meister, 33, 72, 102
Elshtain, Jean Bethke, 67
Erasmus, Desiderus, 71, 103, 106–7
Eugenius, pope, 94
Eusebius, bishop, 8, 61, 103
Evagrius, Pontus, 32, 34, 40, 48, 62, 65, 73, 116, 142
Farmer, D.H., 84
Fernández-Armesto, Felipe, 111
Flanagan, Sabina, 61, 93,
Fletcher, Richard, 68
Forkbeard. Sven, 86

Forest,, Jim, 19
Fox, Matthew, 72
Fox, George, 33
Fox, Robin Lane, 8, 40, 45
Francis, St., 102
Freeman, Charles, 14, 39
Frick, Peter, 102
Frend, W.H.C., 62
Fukuyama, Francis, 130, 139
Gaum, Laurie, 167
Gandhi, Mahatma, 127
Gardiner, Craig, 25
Gelineau, Joseph, 27
Gibbon, Edward, 65
Gioia, Luigi, 125
Goehring, James E, 45
González-Balado, José Luis, 132
Gorringe, Timothy J., 142, 153
Grant, Robert M., 29, 30
Green, Michael Cawood, 24, 90
Gregory of Nanzianus, St., 32, 112
Gregory of Nyssa, St., 32
Gregory the Great, St., 69, 77, 81, 84
Gregory VII, pope, 70
Gregory of Rimini, 103, 108
Groote, Gerhard, 102
Grünewald, Matthias, 45
Guido II, 142
Gutiérrez, Gustavo, 165
Hadewijch of Antwerp, 102
Harnack, Adolf von, 88
Harris, John, 77
Hegel, G.W.F., 141
Heloise d'Argenteuil, 96
Henry VIII, king, 113, 132
Henry, Matthew, 116
Hildegard of Bingen, St., 61, 72, 90, 93–94
Hilarion St., 45–46
Hoffman, Bengt, R., 102
Hofmeyr, Isabel, 116
Housden, Roger, 33
Huddleston, Trevor, 128
Hus, John, 102
Irenaeus, St., 11
Jerome, St., 45, 71, 148
Joachim of Fiore, 104
John XXIII, pope, 133

INDEX OF NAMES

Julian, emperor, 8, 28
Julian of Norwich, 5, 33, 50, 72, 95, 142
Justin Martyr, St., 29
Kardong, Terence G., 74
Kelly, Geffrey, 33
Kelly, J.N.D., 168
Kierkegaard, Søren, 21, 110, 118–20, 157
Kim, David Kyuman, 161
King, Jnr., Martin Luther, 166
King, Margo, 48
Kline, Francis, 137, 157,
Knowles, David, 86, 94, 96–97, 115, 179
Küng, Hans, 57
LaCugna, Catherine M., 145
Lanfranc, abbot, 91, 132
Lasserre, Jean, 127, 151
Latourette, Kenneth, 86
Leclercq, Jean, 23, 45, 73, 87, 93, 100, 154, 167
Leo III, pope, 69, 85
Leo X, pope, 105
Loewenich, Walter von, 101
Lossky, Vladimir, 33, 72
Louth, Andrew, 31
Luther, Martin, 16, 20–21, 25, 33, 53, 67, 71, 91, 94, 98, 100–114, 117–20, 123, 126, 129–30, 147, 160
Luthuli, John Bunyan, 116,
Macarius, St., 47
MacIntyre, Alasdair, 140
Maguire, Nancy Klein, 30, 89, 159
Maitland, Sara, 93
Mandela, Nelson R., 3, 5
Mann, Thomas, 30
Marcion, 10
Maritain, Jacques, 19
Mark St., 28
Martin of Tours, St., 82
Martin E, Marty, 4, 5, 171
Matarasso, Pauline, 89, 95–96
Mechthild of Magdeburg, St., 90, 102
Meinardus, Otto F.A., 44, 46

Merton, Thomas, 1, 4, 7, 18–19, 21, 31–32, 48, 50–52, 58, 70, 77, 79–80, 88, 106, 110, 123, 140, 152–53, 156, 158, 166–67, 171–72, 175, 177
Metz, Johann Baptist, 152
Milbank, John, 67
Mitton, Michael, 83
Moltmann, Jürgen, 58, 93
Monica St., 62
Murray, Jr. Andrew, 17, 72
Newman, John Henry, 23
Niebuhr, H. Richard, 13
Norris, Kathleen, 137–38, 161–62
Nuttall, Geoffrey, 115
O'Connell, Patrick, 18
Oberman, Heiko, A., 105
Odo, St., 87
Origen, 29, 30–32, 34, 40–41, 45, 48, 63, 144
Ovenden, Richard, 113
Ozment, Steve, 87, 96, 99
Pachomius, St., 46–47, 53, 78, 148, 158, 176–177
Palmer, Parker J., 140, 150, 166
Palmisano, Stefania, 126
Pangritz, Andreas, 155
Parpert, Friedrich, 112–3
Patrick, St., 83
Paul, St., 30, 33, 40–42, 53–54, 63, 71, 79, 105, 142, 148, 151, 170, 177, 192
Paul VI, pope, 133
Pearson, Birger A., 11
Pelagius, 70–72
Pelikan, Jaroslav, 113–14
Pennington, Basil, 87–88
Pfeifer,, Claude, 78–81, 87–88
Philo, 29–30
Pius XII, pope, 101
Price, Neil, 86
Rahner, Karl, 33
Raine, Andy, 85
Rees,, Daniel, 58, 81
Robert of Molesmes, 89
Roger, Br. (see Shutz), 26, 132–35
Rolf, Veronica Mary, 72, 95
Romero, Oscar, 184

INDEX OF NAMES

Romuald St., 90
Ruether, Rosemary Radford 19
Santos, Jason Brian, 134
Sayers, Dorothy, 97
Schlink, Basilea, 5
Scholastica, St., 78
Scotus, Duns, 99
Schütz, Katherine, 111
Shutz, Roger (see Roger)
Seneca, 39
Shakespeare, William, 41
Sigismund, emperor, 100
Shenouda III, pope, 25, 28
Sölle, Dorothee, 108
Spencer, Bonnell, 6
Spink, Kathryn, 132
Spinka, Matthew, 100
Staupitz, Johannes von, 105
Stjerna, Kirsi, 111
Stephens, W.P., 112
Sutz, Erwin, 122, 128
Syncletica, St., 48, 50, 94
Tauler. John, 33, 102
Tellenbach, Gerd, 85–86
Tertullian, 34
Theodosius, emperor, 8, 68
Theophan the Recluse, 51

Thomas a' Kempis, 102, 163
Thomas Aquinas, 91, 99
Tillich, Paul, 29
Timothy, Bro., 5
Turkstra, Bernhard, 4
Turkstra, Jane, 4
Tutu, Desmond, 3, 128–29, 134, 167
Valdes, Peter, 102
Villain, Maurice, 16
Villa-Vicencio, 9
Waddell, Helen, 52, 96
Ward, Benedicta, 68
Wedemeyer, Maria von, 163
Wilhelm, II, Kaiser, 120
William of St-Thierry, 90
William of Ockham, 100
William the Conqueror, 91
Williams, George, 114
Williams, Rowan, archbishop, 45–46, 57
Williams, Vaughn, 117
Woods, Barry, 4
Wulf, Friedrich, 124
Zimmermann, Jens, 23, 91
Zwingli, Ulrich, 111–12, 114, 120

INDEX OF SUBJECTS

abbot/s, 47
   election of, 68, 80
   obedience to, 79, 172
   political role, 88
acedia, 171
   ecclesial, 161
   personal, 158–61
   social, 161–64
Act of Uniformity, 115
action, 78, 161, 181
   and contemplation, 104, 147, 167
   and prayer, 166
   and will power, 67
aesthetic existence, 157
Africa/n
   Christianity in, 3
   refugees, 4
   Stone Age, 3
   North, 20, 47, 62, 70, 73, 86
African-American Church, 127
Alexandria, 3, 28, 29, 35, 46–47, 62, 144
   Academy of, 28, 30
   Catechetical School of, 29, 34, 40, 45
   Christians in, 35, 44, 53–54, 135
   St Mark's Cathedral, 28
alone (see silence, solitude), 44, 53, 116, 118, 139, 158–59, 173, 181
   being lonely, 58, 117–18, 170
American/s, North 18, 171
   Church, 127

Native, 117
   triumphalism, 117
Anabaptists (see Reformation), 21, 114–15, 118
Andrew Murray Center, Wellington, xi, 17
Anglican (see Church of England), 2, 4, 17, 23, 90, 121, 128
   monasticism, 22–3, 90, 121
Antioch, 144
Anti-Apartheid Movement, 128
Anglo-Saxons, 83
Apartheid (see racism, South Africa), 4–5, 7, 9, 12–14, 61, 117, 183
   heresy of, 9
   defence of, 145
   government/regime, 134, 139
   struggle against 167
apocalyptic, 7–8, 15, 34, 41, 104, 171
Apollonian, 39
Apologists, 11
Arcane discipline (see *disciplina arcani*)
Arezzo, 90
Arianism, 46
Art, 2, 157
   Renaissance, 45
Asceticism, 39–42, 48, 51, 57–8, 60, 74, 83, 123, 128, 152–53
   austere, 30, 39–40, 42, 51, 57, 70, 74, 83, 105, 117
Asia Minor, 11, 15, 20, 43, 47, 61, 63
Athens 28, 30, 32, 34, 53,

INDEX OF SUBJECTS

Attack on Christendom
  (Kierkegaard) 98, 119,
atonement
  satisfaction theory of 91, 96,
    107
Babylon, 65, 66
balance, 48, 74–76, 88–89,
Balkans, 62
baptism, 109, 118, 168
  politics of 14, 87, 118
  of Jesus, 35
  second baptism (see martyrdom,
    monastic vows, anabaptists)
  sermon on baptism
    (Bonhoeffer), 166
Baptists, 17, 115
Barcelona, 143
Barmen Declaration 122
Battle of Schleswig, 118
Beatific Vision, 31, 38, 135
  St Bernard's, 97
Benedictine monasticism (see *Rule of Benedict*)
  ecumenical influence, 16–18
  Camaldolese, 90
  Cistercian, 18, 20, 25, 89, 90, 94,
    115, 153
  Trappist, 89, 139, 166
Berlin, 126, 159
  Fall of the Wall 139
Bethlehem, 45,71, 73, 147–48
beauty, 3, 23, 72, 142, 144, 156–58,
  183–84
Bible, (see Scripture Index, Old and
  New Testaments, tradition),
  30, 39, 64, 79, 87, 93, 171
  Augustine and, 64, 70, 73
  Barth and, 122
  Benedict and, 79,
  Bonhoeffer and, 127, 146, 162
  Cassian and, 75
  Gregory and, 77
  Hildegard and, 93
  interpretation of, 32, 70, 160
  Kierkegaard and, 119
  lectio divina, 79,
  Luther and, 103–4
  meditation on, 75

Origen and 46
  study of, 64, 87
  sword of the Spirit, 162
  this-worldly interpretation, 169
bishops, 90, 111, 120
  African, 71
  appointment of, 68–69
  Arian, 46
  authority of, 57
  Coptic, 28
  English, 84
  responsibility of 68
  Orthodox 46
Black Death, 113
Blombos Cave, 3
body, the 10, 12, 41, 65, 153
  resurrection of 30
  mortifying, 39
  locus of freedom, 42
  of Christ, 54, 148–49, 180
  temple of Holy Spirit 41
Bonn, 122
Book of Common Prayer 115
Bonhoeffer the Prophet (Spencer), 6
Bose monastery, 126
Brethren of the Common Life,
  102–3
Bruderhof Community, 127
Byzantium, 8
Cairo, 3, 28
Calvinists, 71
Camino d'Santiago (see Santiago de
  Compostela)
Canterbury, 82, 84, 117
Canterbury Tales (Chaucer), 117,
  173
cantus firmus, 155–57, 171,
Cape Aghulas, 3, 173
Cape Town, 3, 135, 167
  University of, 2, 4
Cappadocian Fathers, 32, 144
Carthage, 34, 62, 64, 70
Carolingian reforms, 20, 32, 85, 87
Carthusian monasticism, 30, 88–9,
  117, 142, 159
Catholic (see church, councils,
  Rome, saints), 19, 23–24,
  28, 56, 62, 71–72, 75, 84–85,

INDEX OF SUBJECTS

91, 95, 107, 114, 120–21, 125–26, 129
   faith, 86
celibacy (see vows), 42, 70, 79, 109, 155
cell, 34, 58, 88, 104, 148
   hermitage, 58, 82
   prison, 34, 159–60
   Celtic Christianity, 25, 84–85,
   Missionaries, 83–85,
   monasticism, 81, 82–85
   monks, 20, 78, 85, 116
   pilgrims, 82–85
   spirituality, 84
cenobitic, 47, 53
Center for Christian Spirituality, 167
Chartres, Battle of, 86
Chastity (see monastic vows, sexuality, virginity), 40–43, 109, 153–54
Chicago 132
   Theological Seminary, 24
Christendom 8, 14, 69, 79, 85, 88, 100, 106–7, 114, 117–20, 130, 141, 164–65, 168, 173
   post-Christendom, 21, 141, 164
Christ and Culture, (Niebuhr) 13
Christian humanism, 23, 80, 91, 152
Christ (see body of, cantus firmus, church, conversion, discipleship, Jesus)
   and culture, 13, 34
   and heresy, 10–13, 31
   commitment to, 4, 79, 109, 115, 120, 127–30, 158, 163, 181–83
   covenant relationship with, 180
   death of, 35, 105, 108, 110, 148, 178, 180
   devotion to, 31, 52, 95, 106
   existing as community, 121, 127, 148–49
   eroticism, 95
   faith in, 18, 105, 109
   in the other, 75, 164–66, 169
   hidden in, 170
   mind of, 179
   obedience to, 79, 116, 119, 172
   our sanctification, 151
   Spirit of, 79, 110, 148–51, 181
   taking form, 148–151
   witness to, 12, 14, 125, 146, 165
   world and, 18, 95, 123, 130, 136, 148–51, 168
christology, 38–46, 66, 143
   atonement, 91, 96, 107
   Chalcedonian, 145, 156–57
   incarnation, 29, 55
   cross, 35, 51, 56, 71, 91, 101, 146, 149–51, 180
   resurrection, 35, 101, 146, 149–51, 180
   suffering, 101, 146, 152, 170
   second coming, 41, 173
church, (see community, *ecclesia*)
   and state, 69–70
   boundaries of, 168, 176
   ecumenical, 10, 12, 15–18, 24, 53, 56, 121–22, 126, 164, 167, 176–77, 182
   inclusive, 18, 24, 54, 63, 125, 164, 169, 176–77, 180,
   mission, 12, 85, 180
   open to the world, 54, 58, 157, 164–69
   servant of, 14, 56, 58, 164,
Church of England (see Anglican), 113, 115
Church Dogmatics (Barth), 98, 123–25, 147, 149, 156
Church Fathers, (see Patristics)
Church of the Savior, 24
Citeaux, 89
City of God (Augustine), 65–68, 104–5
Civil Rights Struggle, 166
Clairvaux, 20, 89, 97
Cluny, 20, 25, 87, 133 179
   reforms of, 87
common good, 68, 140, 143, 167, 177, 179
community, see (cenobitic, church, *ecclesia, koinonia*), 23, 53, 57–58, 62, 118, 121, 128, 141, 148–51, 159, 180

community (*continued*)
  beloved, 54–56, 148
  Christ existing as, 127, 148–49
  covenant, 53, 179, 182
  decline of, 140
  of disciples, 54, 57, 120, 129, 178
  of faith, 120
  of love, 127, 145, 180
  inclusive, 157
  intentional, 2, 24, 47, 127, 132–33, 176–77, 181–82
  parable of, 135
  of saints, 121, 149
  of the Spirit, 178–79
Community of the Resurrection, 128
Conciliar Movement, 101
Concluding Unscientific Postscript (Kierkegaard), 120
Confessions (Augustine), 41, 63–65, 70, 73, 92
Conferences (Cassian), 53, 73–77
Congregational/ism, 17, 115–116
  church, 22
  covenant, 18
  membership vows, 18
Conjectures of a Guilty Bystander (Merton), 19, 99, 110, 152, 158, 166,
consolation
  of brothers 160
  , of the Psalter, 163
Constantinople, 14, 62, 73, 86, 144
contemplation, 31, 33, 102, 104, 150, 154, 178
  and action, 15, 104, 147, 167
  and reflection, 92
Contemplation in a World of Action (Merton) 156, 167
conversion
  as *metanoia*, 80, 103
  as process, 33, 35, 180
  evangelical, 79
  of Ambrose, 68
  of Augustine, 62–64, 79
  of Constantine, 14
  of Hilarion, 46
  of the will, 68, 76
  of manners (see vows), 43, 76, 79–80, 110, 170, 172
  mass conversion 119
Coptic/Copts, 11, 28, 35–38
  cathedrals, 28
  church, 3, 15, 28, 44
  martyrs, 28
  monasticism, 20, 24, 44, 47,
  monastics/hermits, 58, 62, 73, 116
Corinth, 54
Council of
  Carthage, 71
  Chalcedon, 15
  Constance, 100
  Ephesus, 95
  Orange, 71
  Trent, 109
  Vatican II, 124–25, 133
covenant (see community) 18, 175, 179
  renewing of 184
Covenant of Love, 21, 110, 179–84
Covid-19, 2, 6–7, 90, 139–40, 148, 154, 177
Creativity, 3, 39, 140, 158
Cross (see Christ, christology)
  scandal of, 9
crusade
  Second, 94
culture (see Christ) 54
  contemporary, 155
  dominant 12
  decadent, 14, 140
  global, 6
  Greco-Roman, 39, 62
  modern, 139
Cur Deus Homo (Anselm), 91, 107
Dark Ages, 20, 61, 81, 99
Darmstadt Sisters, 5, 26
death (see Black Death, Christ, martyrdom), 118, 147–50
  and rebirth/resurrection, 44, 152
  darkness of, 15, 99
  life and, 138, 144
  love and, 143, 148
  of self, 129, 147–48
  pain of, 148

democracy, 70, 141, 177
　globalization of, 139, 141
Denmark, 118, 120
　Church of, 120
desert, 8, 25–26, 29, 36, 38, 40, 42, 53, 56, 162, 172,
　as city, 29, 58
　Egyptian (Western), 20, 24, 29, 43–44, 73, 173
　fathers and mothers 40, 44–45, 48–52, 59–60, 74, 76–77, 88, 112, 116, 118, 120, 161
　retreat to, 43, 50, 57, 92, 94, 123, 129, 135, 148,
　spirituality of, 48–49, 58, 65, 67, 74–76, 88–89, 94, 158, 160
　wisdom of, 49–51, 76, 142
demons, 12, 44, 46, 104, 116, 139, 143–44, 161
desire (see Beatific Vision), 42, 92, 173
　aesthetic, 157
　conflicting, 142
　demonic, 30, 66, 154
　educating, 151–53
　false, 30, 38–39, 66, 142, 154
　for community, 182
　for God, 16, 21, 23, 29–35, 38, 44, 50, 52, 73, 75, 92, 97, 104, 142, 154
　loss of, 159–61
　obsessive, 154–57
　of the heart, 142
　for justice, 141
　for love, 144
　for martyrdom, 40
　for unity & reform, 107, 114
　sensual, 39, 41–42, 153–55, 183
despair (see *acedia*), 105–6, 110, 138–39, 143, 152, 159, 171–72
Devotio Moderna, 102
Diet of Worms, 105
Dionysian, 33, 39
Discipleship (see martyrdom), 8, 37–38, 41–43, 79–81, 87, 92, 124
　aesthetics and, 118, 157

and love, 178
　call to, 38–39
　costly (see asceticism), 14, 43, 58, 79, 114, 118, 120, 127–29, 167–68, 177
　this-worldly, 168
Discipleship (Bonhoeffer), 151
disciplina arcani, 168–69
discipline, 37, 162, 177
Dissolution of Monasteries (see monasteries) 113
Divine Comedy (Dante) 97
divinization, 33
docetism, 55
Dominicans, 104
doubt, 64, 144, 171
　and faith, 9
　self-doubt, 160
Dr Faustus (Mann), 30
earth, 3, 38, 51–52, 141, 174, 183
　as mother, 11
Eastern, Orthodoxy, 32, 46, 62, 65, 72–73
ecclesia (see church, saints), 53–58, 67, 114–15, 118, 120–22, 127, 145, 148–49, 155, 168
ecclesia reformata semper reformanda, 121
Ecclesiastical History of the English People (Bede), 83
ecstasy, (see desire, mysticism, Song of Songs), 33, 39
ecumenical church (see church, monasticism)
Edifying Addresses (Kierkegaard), 120
Edinburgh, 117
Education of Desire (Gorringe), 142, 153
Egypt (see also Coptic, desert), 3, 11, 28–29, 43, 82, 179
Empire, (see church/state)
　Holy Roman, 69, 85–86, 88, 144
　Roman, 7–8, 28, 37, 46, 54, 56, 65–66, 69, 85
　Western, 8, 69
　values of, 12–14, 165

environment (see earth), 7, 140, 159, 183
Ephesus, 161
Epicurean, 39
Erfurt, 103-4
eschatology, 171
Ethics (Bonhoeffer), 19, 75, 143, 150-51, 165, 170
Ethiopian Orthodoxy, 15
eucharist, 53, 135, 168-69
Europe,
  destiny of, 61
  evangelization of, 16, 20, 82-85
  Post-Christendom, 141
  Post-Reformation, 106, 113-14
  Post-World War II, 5, 133
  Western, 20, 61, 62, 73, 85-86, 133
faith (see justification), 18, 145, 151-52, 157, 182
  alone, 102, 105, 108, 130
  and doubt, 23
  and guidance, 82
  and hope, 170
  and knowledge, 31, 92, 105
  and love, 96, 108, 163, 180
  and obedience, 44, 129
  and reason, 23, 75, 92, 99, 108
  and works, 76-77, 108
  biblical, 29-30, 163
  childlike, 19
  Catholic, 86
  Christian, 11, 23, 29, 31, 35, 46, 81, 87, 92, 120, 146, 170
  community of, 120
  death of, 50
  household of, 15, 67
  journey of, 31
  language of, 169
  monasticism and, 108-9, 124
  moralizing, 63
  mystery of, 143, 147, 163, 169
  seeking understanding, 105
  shield of, 162
Fall, the,
  of Adam, 65-66, 153
  of Babylon, 65-66
  of Rome, 46, 61, 63, 65-66, 69, 71
Finkenwalde Seminary, 122, 129-31
House of Brethren, 26, 127, 131-32, 164
First World War, 16, 120, 173
Flossenberg Concentration Camp, 25
Franciscan Spirituals, 102
Franks, 86,
freedom,
  church as sphere of, 157
  evangelical, 81
  from oppression, 48, 170
  of the will, 42, 70, 72, 77
  of women, 111
  to love, 167
French Revolution, 141
Friendship
  covenant, 179
  in the church, 155, 157
  Platonic, 155
From the Holy Mountain (Dalrymple), 20, 60, 83
Gaul, 11, 61-62, 67, 73, 78, 82-83, 86
Gaza, 45
Genadendal, 3
gender, 54, 180, 183
  based violence, 153, 155
  inclusivity, 48, 125, 177
Geneva, 112, 114, 135
Germany, 5, 83, 85, 93, 106, 114, 120, 127-28, 130-31
  Nazi, 14, 61, 130
Ghost Ranch, 5
Gnosticism (see Manicheanism), 10-12, 167
God (see Christ, ecclesia, faith, grace, Holy Spirit, idolatry, kingdom, predestination)
  and empire, 8, 13, 18, 65-66, 144
  and human freedom, 70-71
  and sexuality, 155-58
  and world, 10-11, 33, 38, 41, 55, 138, 165, 167, 183
  armor of, 116, 162

INDEX OF SUBJECTS   205

as personal, 30
creator, 30
covenant with, 179
desire for, 16, 21, 23, 29–35, 52,
    75, 92, 104, 141–42, 159
experience of, 3, 32–33, 50
fear of, 124
glory of, 97
guidance of, 78, 82
hidden in, 150, 164–70
holiness, 91, 105–6
image, 146, 168
justice, (see justice)
knowledge of, 11, 39, 43–44,
    73, 77, 92, 97, 153–55
love of, 13, 36, 48, 56, 96, 108,
    138, 142, 144–51, 167
love for, 39, 148, 154–55, 157,
    179, 184
mercy, 125
mother of, 95, 111, 147
mystery of, 22, 32, 44, 82, 144,
    147–48,151, 158
Old Testament, 10
or Caesar, 8, 14
patience of, 180
power of, 146
promises of, 152
proof of, 91, 101
providence, 65, 72, 82, 117
reality of, 130, 165
redeemer, 30, 71, 144, 163
righteousness of, 107
suffering of, 146–48, 152
triune, 33, 73, 144–45, 148
triumphalist, 145–46
union with, 31, 158
vision of, 97
will of, 75
wisdom of, 101
word of (see Bible), 131, 156,
    162–63
work of God (*opus dei*), 52, 58
wrath of, 105
gospel, 4, 15, 34–35, 56, 59, 70, 80,
    106, 107, 165, 168, 176 181
as guide, 78, 81, 178
faithful to, 107, 182–83

of grace, 101
of peace, 162
proclaiming, 56
Gospels (see Index of Scriptures),
    35–7, 57, 135
Gospel of St. Thomas, 29
Gospel of Truth, 29
grace, 77–79, 116
    alone, 102, 170
    and freedom, 77
    amazing, 101
    asceticism and, 39
    cheap, 1, 28, 38–39, 129–30, 169
    costly, 1, 14, 28, 129
    free, 125
    material reality and, 167
    mystery of, 72
    pilgrimage and, 172
    prevenient, 71, 76
    triumph of, 70, 72
Grande Chartreuse, 88
Great Schism, 15
greed, 67, 109, 113
Greek (see Hellenistic), 10, 29, 38,
    87, 47, 54, 56, 81
    Fathers, 87, 102–3
    monks, 159
    philosophers 42
happiness, 36, 141
Heidelberg Disputation (Luther) 101
Hellenistic (see Greek,
    Neoplatonism)
    Christians, 10
Here I Stand (Bainton), 103
heresy (see Gnosticism), 8, 9–15, 69,
    101, 144
    apartheid as, 9
    Arian, 46
    denominationalism as, 121
    Origenism, 32
    orthodoxy versus, 28
    Pelagian, 63, 70–71
    triumphalist, 9, 12, 15, 130, 167
Hermanus, 3
Hermits, 4, 38, 44, 48, 50, 53, 56–58,
    74, 85, 88, 90, 104, 116–18,
    120, 142, 158
    women (anchoresses), 48

history (see *kairos*), 65
  apocalyptic, 104–5
  church, 7, 9, 12, 34, 56
  end of, 22–23, 139–141
  English, 83
  European, 14
  French feminism, 96
  of Christianity of monasticism, 17, 20, 29, 34, 37, 42, 54, 88, 96
  of religions, 31
  of Roman empire, 65
  of Reformation, 121
  of Spirit, 149
  of theology, 96
  Protestant, 115
  Western, 99
Holden Village, 5, 34
Holy Spirit
  community of, 151
  joy in, 136
  led by, 110, 135
  life in, 92
  of the risen Christ, 79–80, 148–149, 163
  openness to, 178
  power of, 146, 148, 163
  presence of, 37, 53, 148–49, 181–82,
  stifling the, 166
  sword of, 162
  temple of, 41, 136–37
  war of, 138–48, 152, 161–62
  wisdom of, 50
  Word and, 17, 125, 131, 136, 138, 144, 178–79
hope, 3–6, 136, 138, 140–41, 152, 170, 182–83
  and despair, 105, 161, 163
  journey of (see Pilgrimage of), 31, 138, 143, 171–73
  for the world, 168
hospitality (see pilgrimage), 2, 4, 25, 37, 47, 50–51, 55, 68, 74. 80, 117, 124, 168, 173, 183
  monasticism as synonym, 133
humility, 9, 50–51, 54, 75, 80, 166, 170

idolatry, 66, 145–146
incarnation, (see christology)
Independents, (see Congregationalism)
indulgences, 100–101, 103, 105–6, 108
Inquisition, 102
Investiture, 69
Isenheim altarpiece, 45
ISIS, 113
Iona, 83
Iona Community, 5, 25, 83, 121
Ireland, 20, 25, 82–83, 86
Jerusalem (see new Jerusalem), 12, 34–35, 53, 56, 65, 117
Jesus of Nazareth (see Christ, christology),
  and church, 57
  and monasticism, 57–58
  as mother, 95
  entry into Jerusalem, 12,
  following, 8, 34–5, 39–45, 53–4, 129–30, 151, 163, 178–79, 182
  for others, 164
  God of, 66, 92, 107, 144–46, 149
  ministry of, 39–45
  parables of, 36, 135
  prayer, 51, 163
  teaching of, 8, 17, 39–45, 142, 169, 178
  temptation of, 45, 162
  transfiguration, of, 167
Johannesburg, 18, 132
Journal (Kierkegaard), 118
Justice, (see peace, prayer), 11–13, 21, 23, 66, 95
  basis of life, 66
  communities of, 135–36, 161, 177
  desire for, 141, 158
  disregard for, 66–67
  of God, 35–7, 91, 105, 107, 142–45, 173, 178, 183
  redemptive, 144
  struggle for, 23, 75–76, 129, 140, 142, 161–63, 166, 168
justification, 169

by faith, 120, 129–130
of sin, 130
of heresy, 9, 12–13
kairos (see history, time), 6–7, 23, 26, 63, 86, 99, 143, 160, 173
and *chronos*, 6–7
First World War as, 173
grasping the, 6–7, 18, 26, 35, 131
the Middle Ages as, 99, 103
the present, 16, 19, 138, 176
the gospel, 35, 41, 147
Second World War as, 131, 143
Kairos Document, 7
kingdom/reign of God, (see eschatology), 17, 35, 42, 52
Klu Klux Klan, 24
knowledge (see God)
and wisdom, 52, 79, 92
experience and, 49, 92, 130
faith and, 31
love of, 92
sight and, 32–33
of self, 43, 142, 154
of good and evil, 154
worldly, 53
Koinonia Farm, 24
ladder of ascent, 31
leadership, 54, 56, 69, 94, 100, 140, 181
lectio divina (see Bible, scripture), 79, 87, 89, 122
legalism, 57, 80, 179
Lectures on Romans (Luther), 105, 108, 177
Letters and Papers from Prison (Bonhoeffer), 19, 130, 146, 151–152, 155–170
Life of Antony (Athanasius), 27, 44–45, 62, 67, 116
Life Together (Bonhoeffer), 24, 126, 132, 158, 164
Ligugé, 82
Lindisfarne, 25, 83–84, 86
liturgy, 58, 86, 88
listening
to the other, 180

to Word and Spirit, 1, 7, 15–16, 21, 26, 81, 122, 136, 138, 178–81
Living in between (I de Gruchy), 174
Lollards, 102
London, 86, 127, 132, 145–47
loneliness (see alone, solitude), 139
Lord's Prayer, 168
Losungen, 163
Love (see God), 9–10, 23,
and faith, 18
as *agape*, 144, 156
as life-principle, 150
costly, 39
desire for, 30
earthly, 155
eros, 122, 156
for world (see world), 37
mysticism of, 33
of beauty, 32
of learning/wisdom, 16, 23
of other, 36, 38, 43
of self, 43
the rule of, 36, 138, 154
works of, 31
Lutheran, 5, 24, 118, 120, 164
lust, 40–41, 64, 142, 160
for power, 141
Manicheanism, 62
Marianhill monastery, 24, 89–90
marriage, 14, 40–43
covenant 179,
sanctity of, 109
vows, 155, 171–72
martyrdom, 8, 14, 25, 31, 40, 148
Bonhoeffer's, 127
monasticism as, 34, 108, 114
Martyrs' Mirror, 114
Mary St. (see "mother of God"), 41, 95–96, 103, 111–12, 146–48
as prophet, 145
Bonhoeffer on, 147
Calvin on, 112
cult of, 41, 95
ecumenical significance, 147
humility of, 111, 147
Luther on, 111
Song of, 145

Mary St. *(continued)*
  theotokos, 111, 147
  virgin birth, 169
Melancholic Freedom (Kim), 161
melancholy (see *acedia*), 54, 159
Mennonite/s, 24, 114
Methodist, 17, 79
Middle Ages, 20, 45, 74, 62, 69, 86, 90–91, 95, 99, 101–3, 105
Middle East, 20, 61, 113
Milan, 62–63, 68
Mirfield Community, 128–29
Monasteries (see Cluny, Coptic, Dissolution of, Taizé)
  Bec, 90
  Christ in the Desert, 25
  Clonmacnoise, 25
  Debra Dano, 47
  Ettal, 25, 130, 151, 164
  Gethsemani, 89, 166
  Glastonbury, 25, 90, 113, 117
  Maria Laach, 25, 122,
  Marianhill, 24, 89, 90
  Melk, 25
  Montserrat, 125, 134, 149
  Jasna Góra, 25
  Ripon, 25
  Riveaulx, 25
  Tintern Abbey, 25
  Waldsassen Abbey, 25
monastic (see cenobitic, community)
  community, 58, 62, 64–65, 77, 79–80, 90, 108, 131–33, 136, 158–59, 164–65, 173
  vows, 18, 37, 43, 79, 89, 108–12, 114, 123, 171–72
monastics (see cenobitic, hermits), 8, 11, 15, 17–18, 20, 23–25, 29, 43, 53, 59
  and Augustine's *Confessions*, 63, 73
  and emperor, 46
  and perfection, 73
  as humanists, 23, 32, 48, 73, 87
  as lay, 34
  as puritans, 115
  discipline of (see *Rule of St Benedict*), 79–81, 88
  power of, 83, 88
  the first, 15, 29, 34, 36, 39–40, 44, 58, 112, 119, 129, 138, 143, 148, 160–161
  victims of Vikings, 86,
  women, 42
monasticism (see Anglican, Benedictine, Coptic, Orthodox)
  ecumenical gift, 15–18, 126, 133, 182
  invisible , 16, 58
  movement of the Spirit, 133
  new, 17, 25, 84, 102, 122
  reformation of, 86–89
monastery (see monastic, monasticism)
  as empire, 88
Monophysitism, 15
Monte Cassino, 78
Montserrat, 134
moralism (see Pelagianism), 71, 118
Moravian
  Brotherhood, 102, 163
  Losungen, 163
  missionaries, 3
Mother of God *(theotokos)* (see Mary)
mystery (see God, mysticism)
  journey into, 30, 33, 82, 143, 147–48, 173
  loss of, 161
mysteries of faith, 143–44, 149, 151, 169
mysticism, 30–33, 73
  apophatic, 32
  Bernard's, 95
  Christian, 29–30, 33
  intellectual, 31
  of love, 33
Nag Hammadi manuscripts, 11, 29
nationalism, 129, 145
  Christian, 12
Nazism, 9, 16, 122
New England, 115–17, 171

New Monasticism (see monasticism)
New Testament (see Bible, Scripture Index), 12, 15, 20, 31, 53–55, 80 103, 114–15, 121, 142, 162
  canon, 36, 47
  eschatological milieu 171
New Jerusalem, 29, 67
New York, 5, 122, 127, 129
Neoplatonism (see philosophy),
Nicene Creed, 144
Ninety-Five Theses (Luther), 100, 105
Nonconformists, English, 115
Norcia, 20, 77
Normans (see Vikings), 78, 87
Northumbrian Community, 84
obedience, 115, 130
  blind, 81
  childlike, 92
  faith and, 44, 129
  labor of, 78–80
  to Christ, 129–30, 172, 181
  to abbot, 79
  vow of, 43, 109, 172
offices, daily (see *lectio* divina, prayer), 112, 134
Old Testament (see Bible)
On the Bondage of the Will (Luther), 67, 107
On the Work of Monks (Luther), 65
opus Dei, 58, 87, 124
Order of the Holy Cross, 5, 90, 18272,
Oriental Orthodoxy, 15
Original Blessing (Fox), 72
original sin, 70, 107
orthodoxy, 10, 28, 46
other faiths, 2, 164, 167, 170, 183
Outline for a Book (Bonhoeffer), 164
Oxford, 99
Palestine, 7, 20, 29, 45, 70,
Papacy, 69–70, 77
  and empire, 88
  and monasteries, 69, 86
  authority of, 69–70, 100–101
  Avignon exile, 90, 100
  corruption of, 101
Patristic, 16, 32, 87, 102, 144
  theology, 48, 91, 106
  manuscripts, 87
peace, 51, 78
  God's, 73
  justice and, 21, 35–37
  in Mozambique, 24
  in Normandy, 87, 100
  of Christendom, 107
Pelagianism, 39, 63, 71
  Semi-, 71, 75
penance (see *metanoia*) 103, 108
Pentecostal, 18
penultimate/ultimate, 148, 169–170
persecution, 8–9, 38, 44, 55
  of Anabaptists, 114–115
  of Congregationalists, 115
  of homosexuals, 155
perfection
  and justice, 76, 104
  Christian, 16–17, 40, 73–74, 76, 80, 121, 145
  Jesus and, 57
  monastic, 80, 104–105, 109–110
Philokalia (St Basil), 32
philosophy, 34, 92, 120, 163
  Christian, 45, 92
  Neoplatonist, 28–31, 62–63, 65, 73
  seduction of, 34
pilgrimage/s (see hospitality), 22, 31, 82, 113, 117, 123, 133–34
  as means of grace, 172
  of faith, 179
  shrines, 113
pilgrims, 6, 25, 56, 117–18, 135, 164, 173–174, 184
  Celtic, 82–83
  Puritan, 116, 162
  Pilgrim Fathers, 116, 171
Pilgrim's Progress (Bunyan) 115–117, 162
Pilgrimage of Hope, 6, 134–135
place (see stability)
plague, 47
  Black Death 99
Poitiers, 82

210 INDEX OF SUBJECTS

Poland, 25, 131
polyphony, 156
   of life, 153, 155–57
Polyphony of Life (Pangritz), 155
poverty, 16, 134, 161
   monastic vow of, 88, 109
prayer (see contemplation, offices), 15, 18, 33, 40, 51–52, 88, 133, 163
   and justice, 15, 129, 136, 140, 166–167, 169–170
   and theology, 92
   and work, 75, 126, 161
   common prayer, 47, 53, 79, 87, 89, 104, 134, 181
   difficulty in, 162
   high priestly, 55
   personal, 88
predestination, 71–72, 107
Presbyterians, 115
pride (*superbia*), 40, 66–67, 109, 152
prophetic, 1
   and *agape*, 156
   and contemplative, 153
   monasticism as, 57, 70
   theology, 7
   witness, 9, 12, 14, 56, 58, 70
Protestant/ism (see Reformation)
   and monasticism, 16, 21, 108, 112, 118–19, 123–25, 127
   church (see *ecclesia*), 17, 112, 127, 150
   radical (see Anabaptists), 114
   Reformation, 15–16, 20, 70
   theology, 118, 120
psalms (see Scripture index), 20, 58, 87
   christological interpretation of, 163
   Luther's lectures on, 105
   monastic use of, 163
purgatory, 101
Puritans, 41, 115, 117
purity of heart, 38, 50, 74, 80
Purity of Heart (Kierkegaard), 120
racism, 9, 12, 22, 142
radicalism, 75
rationalism, 71

Ravenna, 14
Reba Place, 24
reason (see faith)
Reformation (see monasticism, Protestant)
   churches of the, 17, 21, 121, 129
   consequences, of, 106–107
   magisterial, 114
   forerunners, 102–103
   patriarchal, 111
   radical (see Anabaptist)
   and women, 111
Reformed
   Dutch Reformed (South Africa), 17
   French, 127, 168
   Swiss, 16, 24, 122, 133
   theology (see *ecclesia*), 92, 102, 121–22, 147
Religious orders, 102, 121
repentance (see "conversion of manners", *metanoia*) 80. 101, 103, 169–70
resurrection (see body, christology)
   of Christ, 148, 152, 180
   via the cross, 118
Robben Island, 3
Roman Catholic Church (see catholic, papacy) 15, 126
Roman Empire (see Empire)
Rome (see papacy), 12, 28–29, 61–62, 82, 85, 101, 105, 113, 144
   Bonhoeffer in, 126
   Fall of, 20, 46, 61, 63, 65–67, 69–71
   Luther in, 101, 105
   pagan, 62
   site of pilgrimage, 82, 117, 134
Rule
   as *regula*, 177
   1 John as, 56
   love as premise (see *Covenant of Love*) 36, 110, 112, 138, 150, 178–79
   of the church, 180
   of law, 141, 178
   Torah as, 179
   writing a, 21, 175–84

INDEX OF SUBJECTS 211

Rules (see *Covenant of Love,
  kingdom/reign of God, Life
  Together, Rule of St Benedict*)
 Augustinian, 63, 65, 78, 103
 Basil, 32, 78
 Cassian, 74, 78
 Columbanus, 78
 Master, 53–54, 78, 80
 Pachomius, 47, 148
 Taizé, 132–33, 135–36, 163, 173
 Trappist, 89
Rule of St Benedict, 2, 7, 15, 20, 26,
  48, 60, 77–82, 86, 89–90,
  138, 154, 161, 164, 171,
  176–84
 and Bible, 80, 162
 Barth on, 124
 Gospel as guide, 78–81
 living the, 81
Russia, 4, 51, 69, 86
St Alban's Abbey, 132
St Benedict's Priory, Volmoed, 6, 90,
  176, 179–80, 182
St Peter's Basilica, Rome, 101
San Vitale, 14
Salisbury, 69
Sant' Egidio Community, 24
saints, 28, 75, 96, 109, 138
 Bonhoeffer on, 151
 communities of (see *ecclesia*),
  116–17, 121, 149
 models of imitation, 52
 relics, 117
sanctification, 124–25, 151, 169
Sanctorum Communio (Bonhoeffer),
  124, 126–27, 148–50
Santiago de Compostela, 6, 82, 90,
  117, 173
scholasticism, 144
School for disciples (*Rule of St
  Benedict*)
Scetis, 43, 46–47
Scripture (see Bible, *lectio divina*,
  Old and New Testaments),
  51, 58, 76, 79, 92, 100, 108,
  134, 142, 154, 169, 178–79
 alone, 102
 memorizing, 162

science, 23, 29, 34, 139
 as knowing (epistemology),
  91–92
Scotland, 5, 20, 25, 83, 121
Second Advent (see christology,
  eschatology), 41
Second World War (see *kairos*)
secularism, 21, 140–41
Seeking God (de Waal), 82, 172
Semi-Augustinianism, 71
Sermon on the Mount, 106, 109,
  127–28
Separatists, 114
sexuality (see chastity, desire,
  virginity), 41, 96, 153–55
Shakers, 153
Showings (Julian), 50, 72, 95, 142,
  174
silence (see alone, solitude), 49–50,
  58, 79–80, 130, 139, 178, 181
 Bonhoeffer and 130
 Trappist rules of, 89
 sound of, 31
Sinai, 43–44, 76, 179
sin, 51, 59, 150,
 as alienation, 142
 consequences of, 142
 deadly, 142
 justification of, 130
 original, 65, 70–71, 107
 redemption from, 30, 91
Sisterhood of Darmstadt, 5, 26
Sisterhood of Gelterkinden, 121
Sisterhood of Grandchamp, 121
Smalcald Articles (Luther), 112
Solesmes Abbey, 16
solitude (see alone, silence), 58, 77,
  83, 106, 116–18, 148, 159
 Benedict and, 77
 Bonhoeffer and 158–59
 Celts and, 83
 and community, 159
 Erasmus and, 106
 in the desert, 58, 148
Spain, 67, 100, 125, 165
Song of Songs, 11, 95, 143, 154, 156

South Africa (see apartheid, Covid, church struggle, *kairos*, Volmoed), 24, 145
State of Emergency, 4, 7
post-apartheid, 5, 61
Taizé connection, 134
stability (see conversion of manners, vows), 6, 43, 50, 79, 131, 172–73, 181
social change and, 91, 99
state (see Christendom, church, democracy, empire), 12–14, 68–69, 85, 100
Ambrose on, 65, 68–69
Augustine on, 65–68
theology (see *Kairos Document*), 7–8
Stoic/ism, 29, 34, 39–40
Suffering (see Christ, God)
of world, 135, 148, 152, 161
redemptive, 56
suicide, 159–60
Syria, 20, 29
Syrian Church 15
Tabennisi, 47
Taizé Community, 2, 18, 24, 26, 121, 132–36
Council of Youth, 134
Pilgrimage of Hope, 134
Rule of, 133, 135
Tutu and, 134
songs, 134,
temptation (see *acedia*, demons, Jesus), 50, 104, 116, 161–63
Bonhoeffer and, 160
of flesh, 116
of pride, 67
Ten Commandments, 44
The Company of Strangers (Palmer), 140
The Decline and Fall of the Roman Empire (Gibbon), 65
The Idea of the monastic life (Shutz), 133
The Imitation of Christ (Thomas a' Kempis), 102, 163
The Judgment on Monastic Vows (Luther), 108, 110–11

The Ladder of Paradise (Climacus), 119
The Misunderstanding of the Church (Brunner), 121
The Seven Story Mountain (Merton), 19
Third use of the Law, 121
This Day Belongs to God (Schutz), 132, 136
Theologia Germanica, 102
theology (see Catholic, christology, God, *Kairos Document*, Lutheran, mystery, Orthodox, Protestant, Reformed, faith)
begins in silence, 178
biblical (see Bible), 16, 55, 63
feminist, 93
monastic, 23, 34, 92, 108
mystical, 32–33, 48, 92
of the cross, 101–2, 120
of glory, 101
patristic, 48, 91
philosophical, 28
prophetic, 7
scholastic, 34, 91, 101
state, 7–9
Third Reich, 14, 164–65
time (see history, *kairos*)
canonical hours, 47, 87–88, 104, 126, 159
Tours, 82,
tradition, 23, 123, 171, 182
Augustinian, 72
biblical, 31, 65
Benedictine, 17–18, 171
Christian, 16, 31
Congregational, 17, 184
Coptic, 3, 28
monastic, 5, 73, 124–26, 137
mystical, 32–33
Orthodox, 33, 72–73
Reformed, 112, 120
transcendence (see God, mystery), 30, 33
transformation (see conversion), 80, 177
inner, 51, 97, 175, 177

of desire, 153
of world, 11, 177
Trier, 169
tristitia (see *acedia*)
trinity (see God)
triumphalism (see heresy), 10, 12, 15, 143, 145
truth (see knowledge, wisdom), 10, 22–23, 92, 138, 157, 162
  defending the, 110
  love of, 104, 142, 144–45
  speaking the, 180
  truth to power, 70
Union Theological Seminary, 127, 151
United States of America (see America)
utopia, 141, 171, 173
Vatican II, 124–25, 133
Via Moderna, 100, 104–5
Vikings (see Normans), 25, 61, 86
Virgins/ity (see sexuality), 40–42, 64
Volmoed (see St Benedict's Priory), 3–6, 90
  Community, 2, 4–7, 21, 84, 132, 134–35, 173, 176–77
  Covenant of love, 21, 179–84
  Youth Leadership Programme, 182
vows (see monastic, conversion of manners, stability, chastity, wealth, work, balance)

Vulgate, 103
Waldensian Brotherhood, 102
War of the Spirit, 138–41, 143–45, 148, 152, 161–62
Wealth, 14, 16, 37–38, 102, 161, 165
Week of Prayer for Christian Unity, 16
West Park monastery, 5
Whitby, synod of, 83
Who am I? (Bonhoeffer), 160
wisdom (see desert, God, Holy Spirit, knowledge), 75, 79, 81, 92, 141–42, 177–78
  of the cross, 54, 101
  of experience, 4, 49–51, 76, 92, 178
  love of, 23, 48
Wittenberg, 100, 104–5, 111
Word and Spirit (see Bible, Holy Spirit, christology), 17, 144, 178–79
work, manual, 37, 75, 79, 88–89, 130, 161, 165–66, 181
world come of age (see secularism, worldliness), 163–64
worldliness
  mature, 151–52
  of church, 14, 57, 102
youth, 2, 134, 182
Zurich, 112, 114, 121
Zwischen den Zeiten (Barth), 173

INDEX OF SCRIPTURE

OLD TESTAMENT

Genesis
1:31	41
3	153
3:1–7	66
4:1	154
28:17	137

Exodus
3	31
34:6	138

I Kings
19:9–13	31

Psalms
34:8	142
46	98
51	71
51:5	71
54:7–8	27
95:8	7

Song of Songs
7:6	156
8:6b	143

Isaiah
6	31

Jeremiah
31:31, 33	175

Micah
6:8	178

NEW TESTAMENT

Matthew
4:1–11	162
4:17	103
4:18–20	157
5:6	142
5:8	38, 53, 135
5:14	67
5:43	178
5:44	180
5:48	43
11:29	78
11:30	37, 178
13:46	38
13:52	17
16:24	56
18:20	37
19:12	41
19:21	43, 45
19:16–22	42
19:27–30	157
21:1–2	12

25:35	75	3:1–23	54
23:29	119	6:19	41
28:19	56	7:9	41
		12:13	180
		13	180
Mark		13:4	138, 180
1:14–15	35	3:8	77
4:15–20	38	14:34	111
8:34	36	14:40	177
		15:31	40

Luke

1:46–55	146	**2 Corinthians**	
3:7	116	3:6	178
10:39–41	96	4:7	54
14:26	37	5:17	158
14:15–24	169	6:17	114
		12:2	31

John

1:1	178	**Galatians**	
1:14	11, 41, 53	4:4	147
3:16	55, 183	5:6	180
3:16–21	55		
13:34	180	**Ephesians**	
17	55	2:11–22	149
17:15–16	55	3:28	183
		4:15	180
Acts		6:11	116
1:1	53	6:12	143
2:42–45	54	6:13	116
4:32–35	54	6:13–17	162
17:22–31	30, 33		

Romans

Colossians

1:18–31	142	1:15	145
7	71	3:3	170
7:14–25	67		
13:13	64	**Hebrews**	
14:1–13	108	13:13–14	27
		13:14	29

1 Corinthians

1:10	179	**1 Peter**	
1:10–17	54	4:17	15
1:18–25	101		
1:23	9		
1:30	151		

1 John

	55, 56
1:1	12
2:27–28	55
4:1–6	180
4:2	53
4:7	175
4:12	175
4:16	56, 144, 175

2 John

7, 9	55

Revelation

2:4	15, 161
2:7	1
3:21	165
21:2	67
21:10	60
21:24	60

You may also be interested in:

Community of the Transfiguration

The Journey of a New Monastic Community

by Paul R. Dekar

In the 1930s, German theologian Dietrich Bonhoeffer anticipated the restoration of the Church after the coming Second World War through a new kind of monasticism, a way of life of uncompromising adherence to the Sermon on the Mount in imitation of Christ.

Since then, the renewal of Christian monasticism has become a great spiritual movement. Imbued with a love for God and neighbor, and with a healthy self-love, people are going to monasteries to deepen their relationship with God, to pray, and to find peace. While some monastic institutions are suffering a decline in traditional vocations, many Christians are exploring monastic lifestyles.

This book introduces The Community of the Transfiguration in Australia, the story of a new monastic community and an inspiring source of hope for the world at another time of spiritual, social, and ecological crisis.

> *'Intentional Christianity provides all Christians, and indeed all persons, with a window into the possibilities of the gospel of Jesus Christ, and the prospect of a world remade.'* – **Br Jeffrey Gros,**
> Memphis Theological Seminary

Paul R. Dekar is Niswonger Professor of Evangelism and Missions at Memphis Theological Seminary. He is author of *Creating the Beloved Community: A History of the Fellowship of Reconciliation in the United States* (Herald, 2005) and *Holy Boldness: Practices of an Evangelistic Lifestyle* (Smyth and Helwys, 2004). He and his wife Nancy are North American members of the Holy Transfiguration Monastery in Australia.

Published 2008

Paperback ISBN: 978 0 7188 9182 4
PDF ISBN: 978 0 7188 4282 6